JAPAN

AN ATTEMPT AT INTERPRETATION

JAPAN

AN ATTEMPT AT INTERPRETATION

BY

LAFCADIO HEARN

Soft-Cover Edition

CHARLES E. TUTTLE COMPANY
Rutland, Vermont & Tokyo, Japan

Representatives
Continental Europe: BOXERBOOKS, INC., *Zurich*
British Isles: PRENTICE-HALL INTERNATIONAL, INC., *London*
Australasia: PAUL FLESH & CO., PTY. LTD., *Melbourne*

Printed in Japan

Contents

CHAPTER   PAGE

I. DIFFICULTIES 1

II. STRANGENESS AND CHARM 5

III. THE ANCIENT CULT 21

IV. THE RELIGION OF THE HOME . . . 33

V. THE JAPANESE FAMILY 55

VI. THE COMMUNAL CULT 81

VII. DEVELOPMENTS OF SHINTŌ 107

VIII. WORSHIP AND PURIFICATION . . . 133

IX. THE RULE OF THE DEAD 157

X. THE INTRODUCTION OF BUDDHISM . . 183

XI. THE HIGHER BUDDHISM 207

XII. THE SOCIAL ORGANIZATION . . . 229

XIII. THE RISE OF THE MILITARY POWER . . 259

XIV. THE RELIGION OF LOYALTY . . . 283

XV. THE JESUIT PERIL 303

XVI. FEUDAL INTEGRATION 343

XVII. THE SHINTŌ REVIVAL 367

XVIII. SURVIVALS 381

XIX. MODERN RESTRAINTS 395

XX. OFFICIAL EDUCATION 419

XXI. INDUSTRIAL DANGER 443

XXII. REFLECTIONS 457

APPENDIX 481

BIBLIOGRAPHICAL NOTES 487

INDEX 489

" Perhaps all very marked national characters can be traced back to a time of rigid and pervading discipline." — WALTER BAGEHOT.

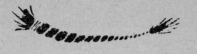

Difficulties

A THOUSAND books have been written about Japan; but among these, — setting aside artistic publications and works of a purely special character, — the really precious volumes will be found to number scarcely a score. This fact is due to the immense difficulty of perceiving and comprehending what underlies the surface of Japanese life. No work fully interpreting that life, — no work picturing Japan within and without, historically and socially, psychologically and ethically, — can be written for at least another fifty years. So vast and intricate the subject that the united labour of a generation of scholars could not exhaust it, and so difficult that the number of scholars willing to devote their time to it must always be small. Even among the Japanese themselves, no scientific knowledge of their own history is yet possible; because the means of obtaining that knowledge have not yet been prepared, — though mountains of material have been collected. The want of any good history upon a modern plan is but one of many discouraging wants. Data for the study of sociol-

ogy are still inaccessible to the Western investi-
gator. The early state of the family and the
clan; the history of the differentiation of classes;
the history of the differentiation of political from
religious law; the history of restraints, and of
their influence upon custom; the history of regulative and coöperative conditions in the development of industry; the history of ethics and
æsthetics, — all these and many other matters
remain obscure.

This essay of mine can serve in one direction
only as a contribution to the Western knowledge
of Japan. But this direction is not one of the least
important. Hitherto the subject of Japanese religion has been written of chiefly by the sworn
enemies of that religion: by others it has been
almost entirely ignored. Yet while it continues to
be ignored and misrepresented, no real knowledge
of Japan is possible. Any true comprehension of
social conditions requires more than a superficial
acquaintance with religious conditions. Even the
industrial history of a people cannot be understood
without some knowledge of those religious traditions and customs which regulate industrial life
during the earlier stages of its development. . . .
Or take the subject of art. Art in Japan is so
intimately associated with religion that any attempt
to study it without extensive knowledge of the

beliefs which it reflects, were mere waste of time. By art I do not mean only painting and sculpture, but every kind of decoration, and most kinds of pictorial representation, — the image on a boy's kite or a girl's battledore, not less than the design upon a lacquered casket or enamelled vase, — the figures upon a workman's towel not less than the pattern of the girdle of a princess, — the shape of the paper-dog or the wooden rattle bought for a baby, not less than the forms of those colossal Ni-Ō who guard the gateways of Buddhist temples. . . . And surely there can never be any just estimate made of Japanese literature, until a study of that literature shall have been made by some scholar, not only able to understand Japanese beliefs, but able also to sympathize with them to at least the same extent that our great humanists can sympathize with the religion of Euripides, of Pindar, and of Theocritus. Let us ask ourselves how much of English or French or German or Italian literature could be fully understood without the slightest knowledge of the ancient and modern religions of the Occident. I do not refer to distinctly religious creators, — to poets like Milton or Dante, — but only to the fact that even one of Shakespeare's plays must remain incomprehensible to a person knowing nothing either of Christian beliefs or of the beliefs which preceded them. The real mastery of any European tongue is impossible without a knowledge of European religion. The language of even the unlettered is full of religious meaning : the proverbs and household-phrases of the poor, the songs of the street, the speech of the workshop, — all are infused with significations unimaginable by any one ignorant of the faith of the people. Nobody knows this better than a man who has passed many years in trying to teach English in Japan, to pupils whose faith is utterly unlike our own, and whose ethics have been shaped by a totally different social experience.

Strangeness and Charm

THE majority of the first impressions of Japan recorded by travellers are pleasurable impressions. Indeed, there must be something lacking, or something very harsh, in the nature to which Japan can make no emotional appeal. The appeal itself is the clue to a problem; and that problem is the character of a race and of its civilization.

My own first impressions of Japan,— Japan as seen in the white sunshine of a perfect spring day, — had doubtless much in common with the average of such experiences. I remember especially the wonder and the delight of the vision. The wonder and the delight have never passed away: they are often revived for me even now, by some chance happening, after fourteen years of sojourn. But the reason of these feelings was difficult to learn,— or at least to guess; for I cannot yet claim to know much about Japan. . . . Long ago the best and dearest Japanese friend I ever had said to me, a little before his death: "When you find, in four or five years more, that you cannot understand the Japanese at all, then you will begin to know something about them." After having realized the truth of my friend's prediction, — after having discovered that I cannot understand the Japanese at all, — I feel better qualified to attempt this essay.

As first perceived, the outward strangeness of things in Japan produces (in certain minds, at least) a queer thrill impossible to describe, — a feeling of weirdness which comes to us only with the perception of the totally unfamiliar. You find yourself moving through queer small streets full of odd small people, wearing robes and sandals of extraordinary shapes; and you can scarcely distinguish the sexes at sight. The houses are constructed and furnished in ways alien to all your experience; and you are astonished to find that you cannot conceive the use or meaning of numberless things on display in the shops. Food-stuffs of unimaginable derivation; utensils of enigmatic forms; emblems incomprehensible of some mysterious belief; strange masks and toys that commemorate legends of gods or demons; odd figures, too, of the gods themselves, with monstrous ears and smiling faces, — all these you may perceive as you wander about; though you must also notice telegraph-poles and type-writers, electric lamps and sewing machines. Everywhere on signs and hangings, and on the backs of people passing by, you will observe wonderful Chinese characters; and the wizardry of all these texts makes the dominant tone of the spectacle.

Further acquaintance with this fantastic world will in nowise diminish the sense of strangeness evoked by the first vision of it. You will soon observe that even the physical actions of the people are unfamiliar, — that their work is done in ways the opposite of Western ways. Tools are of surprising shapes, and are handled after surprising methods: the blacksmith squats at his anvil, wielding a hammer such as no Western smith could use without long practice; the carpenter pulls, instead of pushing, his extraordinary plane and saw. Always the left is the right side, and the right side the wrong; and keys must be turned, to open or close a lock, in what we are accustomed to think the wrong direction. Mr. Percival Lowell has truthfully observed that the Japanese speak backwards, read backwards, write backwards, — and that this is " only the *abc* of their contrariety." For the habit of writing backwards there are obvious evolutional reasons; and the requirements of Japanese calligraphy sufficiently explain why the artist pushes his brush or pencil instead of pulling it. But why, instead of putting the thread through the eye of the needle, should the Japanese maiden slip the eye of the needle over the point of the thread? Perhaps the most remarkable, out of a hundred possible examples of antipodal action, is furnished by the Japanese art of fencing. The swordsman, delivering his blow with both hands, does not pull the blade towards him in the moment of striking, but pushes it from him. He uses it, indeed, as other Asiatics do, not on the principle of the wedge, but of the saw ; yet there is a pushing motion where we should expect a pulling motion in the stroke. . . . These and other forms of unfamiliar action are strange enough to suggest the notion of a humanity even physically as little related to us as might be the population of another planet, — the notion of some anatomical unlikeness. No such unlikeness, however, appears to exist; and all this oppositeness probably implies, not so much the outcome of a human experience entirely independent of Aryan experience, as the outcome of an experience evolutionally younger than our own.

Yet that experience has been one of no mean order. Its manifestations do not merely startle : they also delight. The delicate perfection of workmanship, the light strength and grace of objects, the power manifest to obtain the best results with the least material, the achieving of mechanical ends by the simplest possible means, the comprehension of irregularity as æsthetic value, the shapeliness and perfect taste of everything, the sense displayed of harmony in tints or colours, — all this must convince you at once that our Occident has much to learn from this remote civilization, not only in matters of art and taste, but in matters likewise of economy and utility. It is no barbarian fancy that appeals to you in those amazing porcelains, those astonishing embroideries, those wonders of lacquer and ivory and bronze, which educate imagination in unfamiliar ways. No: these are the products of a civilization which became within its own limits, so exquisite that none but an artist is capable of judging its manufactures,—a civilization that can be termed imperfect only by those who would also term imperfect the Greek civilization of three thousand years ago.

But the underlying strangeness of this world,— the psychological strangeness,— is much more startling than the visible and superficial. You begin to suspect the range of it after having discovered that no adult Occidental can perfectly master the language. East and West the fundamental parts of human nature—the emotional bases of it—are much the same : the mental difference between a Japanese and a European child is mainly potential. But with growth the difference rapidly develops and widens, till it becomes, in adult life, inexpressible. The whole of the Japanese mental superstructure evolves into forms having nothing in common with Western psychological development: the expression of thought becomes regulated, and the expression of emotion inhibited in ways that bewilder and astound. The ideas of this people are not our ideas; their sentiments are not our sentiments; their ethical life represents for us regions of thought and emotion yet unexplored, or perhaps long forgotten. Any one of their ordinary phrases, translated into Western speech, makes hopeless nonsense; and the literal rendering into Japanese of the simplest English sentence would scarcely be comprehended by any Japanese who had never studied a European tongue. Could you learn all the words in a Japanese dictionary, your acquisition would not help you in the least to make yourself understood in speaking, unless you had learned also to think like a Japanese, — that is to say, to think backwards, to think upside-down and inside-out, to think in directions totally foreign to Aryan habit. Experience in the acquisition of European languages can help you to learn Japanese about as much as it could help you to acquire the language spoken by the inhabitants of Mars. To be able to use the Japanese tongue as a Japanese uses it, one would need to be born again, and to have one's mind completely reconstructed, from the foundation upwards It is possible that a person of European parentage, born in Japan, and accustomed from infancy to use the vernacular, might retain in after-life that *instinctive* knowledge which could alone enable him to adapt his mental relations to the relations of any Japanese environment. There is actually an Englishman named Black, born in Japan, whose profi-

ciency in the language is proved by the fact that he
is able to earn a fair income as a professional story-
teller (*hanashika*).   But this is an extraordinary case.
. . .   As for the literary language, I need only observe that to make acquaintance with it requires very
much more than a knowledge of several thousand
Chinese characters.   It is safe to say that no Occidental can undertake to render at sight any literary
text laid before him — indeed the number of native
scholars able to do so is very small ; — and although
the learning displayed in this direction by various
Europeans may justly compel our admiration, the
work of none could have been given to the world
without Japanese help.

But as the outward strangeness of Japan proves
to be full of beauty, so the inward strangeness appears to have its charm, — an ethical charm reflected
in the common life of the people.   The attractive
aspects of that life do not indeed imply, to the
ordinary observer, a psychological differentiation
measurable by scores of centuries : only a scientific
mind, like that of Mr. Percival Lowell, immediately
perceives the problem presented.   The less gifted
stranger, if naturally sympathetic, is merely pleased
and puzzled, and tries to explain, by his own experience of happy life on the other side of the world,
the social conditions that charm him.   Let us suppose that he has the good fortune of being able to

live for six months or a year in some old-fashioned
town of the interior. From the beginning of this
sojourn he can scarcely fail to be impressed by the
apparent kindliness and joyousness of the existence
about him. In the relations of the people to each
other, as well as in all their relations to himself,
he will find a constant amenity, a tact, a good-nature
such as he will elsewhere have met with only in the
friendship of exclusive circles. Everybody greets
everybody with happy looks and pleasant words ;
faces are always smiling ; the commonest incidents
of everyday life are transfigured by a courtesy at
once so artless and so faultless that it appears to
spring directly from the heart, without any teaching.
Under all circumstances a certain outward cheerfulness never fails : no matter what troubles may come,
— storm or fire, flood or earthquake, — the laughter
of greeting voices, the bright smile and graceful
bow, the kindly inquiry and the wish to please, continue to make existence beautiful. Religion brings
no gloom into this sunshine : before the Buddhas
and the gods folk smile as they pray ; the temple-
courts are playgrounds for the children ; and within
the enclosure of the great public shrines — which
are places of festivity rather than of solemnity —
dancing-platforms are erected. Family existence
would seem to be everywhere characterized by
gentleness : there is no visible quarrelling, no loud
harshness, no tears and reproaches. Cruelty, even

to animals, appears to be unknown: one sees farmers, coming to town, trudging patiently beside their horses or oxen, aiding their dumb companions to bear the burden, and using no whips or goads. Drivers or pullers of carts will turn out of their way, under the most provoking circumstances, rather than overrun a lazy dog or a stupid chicken. . . . For no inconsiderable time one may live in the midst of appearances like these, and perceive nothing to spoil the pleasure of the experience.

Of course the conditions of which I speak are now passing away; but they are still to be found in the remoter districts. I have lived in districts where no case of theft had occurred for hundreds of years, — where the newly-built prisons of Meiji remained empty and useless, — where the people left their doors unfastened by night as well as by day. These facts are familiar to every Japanese. In such a district, you might recognize that the kindness shown to you, as a stranger, is the consequence of official command; but how explain the goodness of the people to each other? When you discover no harshness, no rudeness, no dishonesty, no breaking of laws, and learn that this social condition has been the same for centuries, you are tempted to believe that you have entered into the domain of a morally superior humanity. All this soft urbanity, impeccable honesty, ingenuous kindliness of speech and act, you might naturally interpret as conduct directed by perfect goodness of heart. And the simplicity that delights you is no simplicity of barbarism. Here every one has been taught; every one knows how to write and speak beautifully, how to compose poetry, how to behave politely; there is everywhere cleanliness and good taste; interiors are bright and pure; the daily use of the hot bath is universal. How refuse to be charmed by a civilization in which every relation appears to be governed by altruism, every action directed by duty, and every object shaped by art? You cannot help being delighted by such conditions, or feeling indignant at hearing them denounced as "heathen." And according to the degree of altruism within yourself, these good folk will be able, without any apparent effort, to make you happy. The mere sensation of the *milieu* is a placid happiness: it is like the sensation of a dream in which people greet us exactly as we like to be greeted, and say to us all that we like to hear, and do for us all that we wish to have done, — people moving soundlessly through spaces of perfect repose, all bathed in vapoury light. Yes — for no little time these fairy-folk can give you all the soft bliss of sleep. But sooner or later, if you dwell long with them, your contentment will prove to have much in common with the happiness of dreams. You will never forget the dream, — never; but it will lift at last, like those vapours of spring which lend preternatural loveliness to a Japanese landscape in the forenoon of radiant days. Really you are happy because you have entered bodily into Fairyland, — into a world that is not, and never could be your own. You have been transported out of your own century — over spaces enormous of perished time — into an era forgotten, into a vanished age, — back to something ancient as Egypt or Nineveh. That is the secret of the strangeness and beauty of things, — the secret of the thrill they give, — the secret of the elfish charm of the people and their ways. Fortunate mortal! the tide of Time has turned for you! But remember that here all is enchantment, — that you have fallen under the spell of the dead, — that the lights and the colours and the voices must fade away at last into emptiness and silence.

     *   *   *   *   *

Some of us, at least, have often wished that it were possible to live for a season in the beautiful vanished world of Greek culture. Inspired by our first acquaintance with the charm of Greek art and thought, this wish comes to us even before we are capable of imagining the true conditions of the antique civilization. If the wish could be realized, we should certainly find it impossible to accommodate ourselves to those conditions, — not so much because of the difficulty of learning the environment, as because of the much greater difficulty of feeling just as people used to feel some thirty centuries

ago. In spite of all that has been done for Greek
studies since the Renaissance, we are still unable to
understand many aspects of the old Greek life: no
modern mind can really feel, for example, those
sentiments and emotions to which the great tragedy
of Œdipus made appeal. Nevertheless we are much
in advance of our forefathers of the eighteenth century, as regards the knowledge of Greek civilization.
In the time of the French revolution, it was thought
possible to reëstablish in France the conditions of a
Greek republic, and to educate children according
to the system of Sparta. To-day we are well aware
that no mind developed by modern civilization
could find happiness under any of those socialistic
despotisms which existed in all the cities of the ancient world before the Roman conquest. We could
no more mingle with the old Greek life, if it were
resurrected for us, — no more become a part of it,
— than we could change our mental identities. But
how much would we not give for the delight of
beholding it, — for the joy of attending one festival in Corinth, or of witnessing the Pan-Hellenic
games? . . .

And yet, to witness the revival of some perished Greek civilization, — to walk about the very
Crotona of Pythagoras, — to wander through the
Syracuse of Theocritus, — were not any more of
a privilege than is the opportunity actually afforded
us to study Japanese life. Indeed, from the evolu-

tional point of view, it were less of a privilege, —
since Japan offers us the living spectacle of conditions older, and psychologically much farther away
from us, than those of any Greek period with which
art and literature have made us closely acquainted.

The reader scarcely needs to be reminded that a
civilization less evolved than our own, and intel-
lectually remote from us, is not on that account to
be regarded as necessarily inferior in all respects.
Hellenic civilization at its best represented an early
stage of sociological evolution ; yet the arts which it
developed still furnish our supreme and unapproach-
able ideals of beauty.   So, too, this much more archaic civilization of Old Japan attained an average
of æsthetic and moral culture well worthy of our
wonder and praise.   Only a shallow mind — a very
shallow mind — will pronounce the best of that culture inferior.   But Japanese civilization is peculiar
to a degree for which there is perhaps no Western
parallel, since it offers us the spectacle of many successive layers of alien culture superimposed above
the simple indigenous basis, and forming a very
bewilderment of complexity.   Most of this alien
culture is Chinese, and bears but an indirect relation
to the real subject of these studies.   The peculiar
and surprising fact is that, in spite of all superim-
position, the original character of the people and
of their society should still remain recognizable.

The wonder of Japan is not to be sought in the countless borrowings with which she has clothed herself, — much as a princess of the olden time would don twelve ceremonial robes, of divers colours and qualities, folded one upon the other so as to show their many-tinted edges at throat and sleeves and skirt; — no, the real wonder is the Wearer. For the interest of the costume is much less in its beauty of form and tint than in its significance as idea, — as representing something of the mind that devised or adopted it. And the supreme interest of the old Japanese civilization lies in what it expresses of the race-character, — that character which yet remains essentially unchanged by all the changes of Meiji.

"Suggests" were perhaps a better word than "expresses," for this race-character is rather to be divined than recognized. Our comprehension of it might be helped by some definite knowledge of origins; but such knowledge we do not yet possess. Ethnologists are agreed that the Japanese race has been formed by a mingling of peoples, and that the dominant element is Mongolian; but this dominant element is represented in two very different types, — one slender and almost feminine of aspect; the other, squat and powerful. Chinese and Korean elements are known to exist in the populations of certain districts; and there appears to have been a large infusion of Aino blood. Whether there be any Malay or Polynesian element also has not been decided. Thus much only can be safely affirmed, — that the race, like all good races, is a mixed one; and that the peoples who originally united to form it have been so blended together as to develop, under long social discipline, a tolerably uniform type of character. This character, though immediately recognizable in some of its aspects, presents us with many enigmas that are very difficult to explain.

Nevertheless, to understand it better has become a matter of importance. Japan has entered into the world's competitive struggle; and the worth of any people in that struggle depends upon character quite as much as upon force. We can learn something about Japanese character if we are able to ascertain the nature of the conditions which shaped it, — the great general facts of the moral experience of the race. And these facts we should find expressed or suggested in the history of the national beliefs, and in the history of those social institutions derived from and developed by religion.

The Ancient Cult

THE real religion of Japan, the religion still
professed in one form or other, by the entire
nation, is that cult which has been the foundation of all civilized religion, and of all civilized
society,—Ancestor-worship. In the course of thousands of years this original cult has undergone modifications, and has assumed various shapes; but
everywhere in Japan its fundamental character remains unchanged. Without including the different
Buddhist forms of ancestor-worship, we find three
distinct rites of purely Japanese origin, subsequently
modified to some degree by Chinese influence and
ceremonial. These Japanese forms of the cult are
all classed together under the name of "Shintō,"
which signifies, "The Way of the Gods." It is
not an ancient term; and it was first adopted only
to distinguish the native religion, or "Way" from
the foreign religion of Buddhism called "Butsudō,"
or "The Way of the Buddha. The three forms of
the Shintō worship of ancestors are the Domestic
Cult, the Communal Cult, and the State Cult;—
or, in other words, the worship of family ancestors, the worship of clan or tribal ancestors,

and the worship of imperial ancestors. The first is the religion of the home; the second is the religion of the local divinity, or tutelar god; the third is the national religion. There are various other forms of Shintō worship; but they need not be considered for the present.

Of the three forms of ancestor-worship above mentioned, the family-cult is the first in evolutional order, — the others being later developments. But, in speaking of the family-cult as the oldest, I do not mean the home-religion as it exists to-day; — neither do I mean by "family" anything corresponding to the term "household." The Japanese family in early times meant very much more than "household": it might include a hundred or a thousand households: it was something like the Greek γένος or the Roman gens, — the patriarchal family in the largest sense of the term. In prehistoric Japan the domestic cult of the house-ancestor probably did not exist; — the family-rites would appear to have been performed only at the burial-place. But the later domestic cult, having been developed out of the primal family-rite, indirectly represents the most ancient form of the religion, and should therefore be considered first in any study of Japanese social evolution.

The evolutional history of ancestor-worship has been very much the same in all countries; and that of the Japanese cult offers remarkable evidence in support of Herbert Spencer's exposition of the law of religious development. To comprehend this general law, we must, however, go back to the origin of religious beliefs. One should bear in mind that, from a sociological point of view, it is no more correct to speak of the existing ancestor-cult in Japan as "primitive," than it would be to speak of the domestic cult of the Athenians in the time of Pericles as "primitive." No persistent form of ancestor-worship is primitive; and every established domestic cult has been developed out of some irregular and non-domestic family-cult, which, again, must have grown out of still more ancient funeral-rites.

Our knowledge of ancestor-worship, as regards the early European civilizations, cannot be said to extend to the primitive form of the cult. In the case of the Greeks and the Romans, our knowledge of the subject dates from a period at which a domestic religion had long been established; and we have documentary evidence as to the character of that religion. But of the earlier cult that must have preceded the home-worship, we have little testimony; and we can surmise its nature only by study of the natural history of ancestor-worship among peoples not yet arrived at a state of civilization. The true domestic cult begins with a settled civilization. Now when the Japanese race first established itself in Japan, it does not appear to have brought with it any civilization of the kind which we would call settled, nor any well-developed ancestor-cult. The cult certainly existed; but its ceremonies would seem to have been irregularly performed at graves only. The domestic cult proper may not have been established until about the eighth century, when the spirit-tablet is supposed to have been introduced from China. The earliest ancestor-cult, as we shall presently see, *was* developed out of the primitive funeral-rites and propitiatory ceremonies.

The existing family religion is therefore a comparatively modern development; but it is at least as old as the true civilization of the country, and it conserves beliefs and ideas which are indubitably primitive, as well as ideas and beliefs derived from these. Before treating further of the cult itself, it will be necessary to consider some of these older beliefs.

The earliest ancestor-worship, — " the root of all religions," as Herbert Spencer calls it, — was probably coeval with the earliest definite belief in ghosts. As soon as men were able to conceive the idea of a shadowy inner self, or double, so soon, doubtless, the propitiatory cult of spirits began. But this earliest ghost-worship must have long preceded that period of mental development in which men first became capable of forming abstract ideas. The

primitive ancestor-worshippers could not have formed
the notion of a supreme deity; and all evidence existing as to the first forms of their worship tends to
show that there primarily existed no difference whatever between the conception of ghosts and the conception of gods. There were, consequently, no
definite beliefs in any future state of reward or of
punishment, — no ideas of any heaven or hell. Even
the notion of a shadowy underworld, or Hades, was
of much later evolution. At first the dead were
thought of only as dwelling in the tombs provided
for them, — whence they could issue, from time to
time, to visit their former habitations, or to make
apparition in the dreams of the living. Their real
world was the place of burial, — the grave, the tumu-
lus. Afterwards there slowly developed the idea of
an underworld, connected in some mysterious way
with the place of sepulture. Only at a much later
time did this dim underworld of imagination expand
and divide into regions of ghostly bliss and woe. . . .
It is a noteworthy fact that Japanese mythology
never evolved the ideas of an Elysium or a Tartarus,
— never developed the notion of a heaven or a
hell. Even to this day Shintō belief represents the
pre-Homeric stage of imagination as regards the
supernatural.

Among the Indo-European races likewise there
appeared to have been at first no difference between
gods and ghosts, nor any ranking of gods as greater

and lesser. These distinctions were gradually developed. " The spirits of the dead," says Mr. Spencer, " forming, in a primitive tribe, an ideal group the members of which are but little distinguished from one another, will grow more and more distinguished ; — and as societies advance, and as traditions, local and general, accumulate and complicate, these once similar human souls, acquiring in the popular mind differences of character and importance, will diverge — until their original community of nature becomes scarcely recognizable." So in antique Europe, and so in the Far East, were the greater gods of nations evolved from ghost-cults ; but those ethics of ancestor-worship which shaped alike the earliest societies of West and East, date from a period before the time of the greater gods, — from the period when all the dead were supposed to become gods, with no distinction of rank.

No more than the primitive ancestor-worshippers of Aryan race did the early Japanese think of their dead as ascending to some extra-mundane region of light and bliss, or as descending into some realm of torment. They thought of their dead as still inhabiting this world, or at least as maintaining with it a constant communication. Their earliest sacred records do, indeed, make mention of an underworld, where mysterious Thunder-gods and evil goblins dwelt in corruption ; but this vague world of the dead communicated with the world of the living ;

and the spirit there, though in some sort attached to its decaying envelope, could still receive upon earth the homage and the offerings of men. Before the advent of Buddhism, there was no idea of a heaven or a hell. The ghosts of the departed were thought of as constant presences, needing propitiation, and able in some way to share the pleasures and the pains of the living. They required food and drink and light; and in return for these, they could confer benefits. Their bodies had melted into earth; but their spirit-power still lingered in the upper world, thrilled its substance, moved in its winds and waters. By death they had acquired mysterious force; — they had become "superior ones," *Kami*, gods.

That is to say, gods in the oldest Greek and Roman sense. Be it observed that there were no moral distinctions, East or West, in this deification. "All the dead become gods," wrote the great Shintō commentator, Hirata. So likewise, in the thought of the early Greeks and even of the later Romans, all the dead became gods. M. de Coulanges observes, in *La Cité Antique:* — " This kind of apotheosis was not the privilege of the great alone: no distinction was made. . . . It was not even necessary to have been a virtuous man : the wicked man became a god as well as the good man, — only that in this after-existence, he retained the evil inclinations of his former life." Such also

was the case in Shintō belief: the good man became a beneficent divinity, the bad man an evil
deity,— but all alike became *Kami*. "And since
there are bad as well as good gods," wrote Motowori,
"it is necessary to propitiate them with offerings
of agreeable food, playing the harp, blowing the
flute, singing and dancing and whatever is likely
to put them in a good humour." The Latins
called the maleficent ghosts of the dead, *Larvae*,
and called the beneficent or harmless ghosts, *Lares*,
or *Manes*, or *Genii*, according to Apuleius. But
all alike were gods, — *dii-manes*; and Cicero admonished his readers to render to all *dii-manes* the
rightful worship: "They are men," he declared,
"who have departed from this life; — consider
them divine beings. . . ."

In Shintō, as in old Greek belief, to die was to
enter into the possession of superhuman power, —
to become capable of conferring benefit or of inflict-
ing misfortune by supernatural means. . . . But
yesterday, such or such a man was a common toiler,
a person of no importance; — to-day, being dead,
he becomes a divine power, and his children pray
to him for the prosperity of their undertakings.
Thus also we find the personages of Greek tragedy,
such as Alcestis, suddenly transformed into divinities by death, and addressed in the language of worship or prayer. But, in despite of their supernatural

power, the dead are still dependent upon the living for happiness. Though viewless, save in dreams, they need earthly nourishment and homage, — food and drink, and the reverence of their descendants. Each ghost must rely for such comfort upon its living kindred; — only through the devotion of that kindred can it ever find repose. Each ghost must have shelter, — a fitting tomb; — each must have offerings. While honourably sheltered and properly nourished the spirit is pleased, and will aid in maintaining the good-fortune of its propitiators. But if refused the sepulchral home, the funeral rites, the offerings of food and fire and drink, the spirit will suffer from hunger and cold and thirst, and, becoming angered, will act malevolently and contrive misfortune for those by whom it has been neglected. . . . Such were the ideas of the old Greeks regarding the dead; and such were the ideas of the old Japanese.

Although the religion of ghosts was once the religion of our own forefathers — whether of Northern or Southern Europe, — and although practices derived from it, such as the custom of decorating graves with flowers, persist to-day among our most advanced communities, — our modes of thought have so changed under the influences of modern civilization that it is difficult for us to imagine how people could ever have supposed that the happiness of the dead depended upon material food. But it is probable that the real belief in ancient European societies was much like the belief as it exists in modern Japan. The dead are not supposed to consume the substance of the food, but only to absorb the invisible essence of it. In the early period of ancestor-worship the food-offerings were large; later on they were made smaller and smaller as the idea grew up that the spirits required but little sustenance of even the most vapoury kind. But, however small the offerings, it was essential that they should be made regularly. Upon these shadowy repasts depended the well-being of the dead; and upon the well-being of the dead depended the fortunes of the living. Neither could dispense with the help of the other: the visible and the invisible worlds were forever united by bonds innumerable of mutual necessity; and no single relation of that union could be broken without the direst consequences.

The history of all religious sacrifices can be traced back to this ancient custom of offerings made to ghosts; and the whole Indo-Aryan race had at one time no other religion than this religion of spirits. In fact, every advanced human society has, at some period of its history, passed through the stage of ancestor-worship; but it is to the Far East that we must look to-day in order to find the cult coexisting with an elaborate civilization. Now the Japanese ancestor-cult — though representing the beliefs of a non-Aryan people, and offering in the history of its development various interesting peculiarities — still embodies much that is characteristic of ancestor-worship in general. There survive in it especially these three beliefs, which underlie all forms of persistent ancestor-worship in all climes and countries: —

I. — The dead remain in this world, — haunting their tombs, and also their former homes, and sharing invisibly in the life of their living descendants ; —

II. — All the dead become gods, in the sense of acquiring supernatural power; but they retain the characters which distinguished them during life ; —

III. — The happiness of the dead depends upon the respectful service rendered them by the living; and the happiness of the living depends upon the fulfilment of pious duty to the dead.

To these very early beliefs may be added the following, probably of later development, which at one time must have exercised immense influence : —

IV. — Every event in the world, good or evil, — fair seasons or plentiful harvests, — flood and famine, — tempest and tidal-wave and earthquake, — is the work of the dead.

V. — All human actions, good or bad, are controlled by the dead.

The first three beliefs survive from the dawn of civilization, or before it, — from the time in which the dead were the only gods, without distinctions of power.   The latter two would seem rather of the period in which a true mythology — an enormous polytheism — had been developed out of the primitive ghost-worship.   There is nothing simple in these beliefs : they are awful, tremendous beliefs ; and before Buddhism helped to dissipate them, their pressure upon the mind of a people dwelling in a land of cataclysms, must have been like an endless weight of nightmare.   But the elder beliefs, in softened form, are yet a fundamental part of the existing cult.   Though Japanese ancestor-worship has undergone many modifications in the past two thousand years, these modifications have not transformed its essential character in relation to conduct ; and the whole framework of society rests upon it, as on a moral foundation.   The history of Japan is really the history of her religion.   No single fact in this connection is more significant than the fact that the ancient Japanese term for government — *matsuri-goto* — signifies liberally " matters of worship."   Later on we shall find that not only government, but almost everything in Japanese society, derives directly or indirectly from this ancestor-cult ; and that in all matters the dead, rather than the living, have been the rulers of the nation and the shapers of its destinies.

The Religion of the Home

THREE stages of ancestor-worship are to be distinguished in the general course of religious and social evolution; and each of these finds illustration in the history of Japanese society. The first stage is that which exists before the establishment of a settled civilization, when there is yet no national ruler, and when the unit of society is the great patriarchal family, with its elders or war-chiefs for lords. Under these conditions, the spirits of the family-ancestors only are worshipped; — each family propitiating its own dead, and recognizing no other form of worship. As the patriarchal families, later on, become grouped into tribal clans, there grows up the custom of tribal sacrifice to the spirits of the clan-rulers; — this cult being superadded to the family-cult, and marking the second stage of ancestor-worship. Finally, with the union of all the clans or tribes under one supreme head, there is developed the custom of propitiating the spirits of national rulers. This third form of the cult becomes the obligatory reli-

gion of the country ; but it does not replace either
of the preceding cults : the three continue to exist
together.

Though, in the present state of our knowledge,
the evolution in Japan of these three stages of
ancestor-worship is but faintly traceable, we can
divine tolerably well, from various records, how
the permanent forms of the cult were first developed
out of the earlier funeral-rites.   Between the ancient
Japanese funeral customs and those of antique
Europe, there was a vast difference, — a difference
indicating, as regards Japan, a far more primitive
social condition.   In Greece and in Italy it was
an early custom to bury the family dead within the
limits of the family estate ; and the Greek and
Roman laws of property grew out of this practice.
Sometimes the dead were buried close to the house.
The author of *La Cité Antique* cites, among other
ancient texts bearing upon the subject, an interesting
invocation from the tragedy of *Helen*, by Euripides : — " All hail ! my father's tomb !   I buried
thee, Proteus, at the place where men pass out, that
I might often greet thee ; and so, even as I go out
and in, I, thy son Theoclymenus, call upon thee,
father ! . . ."   But in ancient Japan, men fled
from the neighbourhood of death.   It was long
the custom to abandon, either temporarily, or permanently, the house in which a death occurred ;

and we can scarcely suppose that, at any time, it was thought desirable to bury the dead close to the habitation of the surviving members of the household. Some Japanese authorities declare that in the very earliest ages there was no burial, and that corpses were merely conveyed to desolate places, and there abandoned to wild creatures. Be this as it may, we have documentary evidence, of an unmistakable sort, concerning the early funeral-rites as they existed when the custom of burying had become established, — rites weird and strange, and having nothing in common with the practices of settled civilization. There is reason to believe that the family-dwelling was at first permanently, not temporarily, abandoned to the dead; and in view of the fact that the dwelling was a wooden hut of very simple structure, there is nothing improbable in the supposition. At all events the corpse was left for a certain period, called the period of mourning, either in the abandoned house where the death occurred, or in a shelter especially built for the purpose; and, during the mourning period, offerings of food and drink were set before the dead, and ceremonies performed without the house. One of these ceremonies consisted in the recital of poems in praise of the dead, — which poems were called *shinobigoto*. There was music also of flutes and drums, and dancing; and at night a fire was kept burning before the house. After all this had been done for the fixed period of mourning — eight days, according to some authorities, fourteen according to others — the corpse was interred. It is probable that the deserted house may thereafter have become an ancestral temple, or ghost-house, — prototype of the Shintō *miya*.

At an early time, — though when we do not know, — it certainly became the custom to erect a *moya*, or "mourning-house" in the event of a death; and the rites were performed at the mourning-house prior to the interment. The manner of burial was very simple: there were yet no tombs in the literal meaning of the term, and no tombstones. Only a mound was thrown up over the grave; and the size of the mound varied according to the rank of the dead.

The custom of deserting the house in which a death took place would accord with the theory of a nomadic ancestry for the Japanese people: it was a practice totally incompatible with a settled civilization like that of the early Greeks and Romans, whose customs in regard to burial presuppose small landholdings in permanent occupation. But there may have been, even in early times, some exceptions to general custom — exceptions made by necessity. To-day, in various parts of the country, and perhaps more particularly in districts remote from temples, it is the custom for farmers to bury their dead upon their own lands.

— At regular intervals after burial, ceremonies were performed at the graves; and food and drink were then served to the spirits. When the spirit-tablet had been introduced from China, and a true domestic cult established, the practice of making offerings at the place of burial was not discontinued. It survives to the present time, — both in the Shintō and the Buddhist rite; and every spring an Imperial messenger presents at the tomb of the Emperor Jimmu, the same offerings of birds and fish and seaweed, rice and rice-wine, which were made to the spirit of the Founder of the Empire twenty-five hundred years ago. But before the period of Chinese influence the family would seem to have worshipped its dead only before the mortuary house, or at the grave; and the spirits were yet supposed to dwell especially in their tombs, with access to some mysterious subterranean world. They were supposed to need other things besides nourishment; and it was customary to place in the grave various articles for their ghostly use, — a sword, for example, in the case of a warrior; a mirror in the case of a woman, — together with certain objects, especially prized during life, — such as objects of precious metal, and polished stones or gems. . . . At this stage of ancestor-worship, when the spirits are supposed to require shadowy service of a sort corresponding to that exacted during their life-time in the body, we should expect to hear of

human sacrifices as well as of animal sacrifices. At
the funerals of great personages such sacrifices were
common.   Owing to beliefs of which all knowledge
has been lost, these sacrifices assumed a character
much more cruel than that of the immolations of the
Greek Homeric epoch.   The human victims [1] were
buried up to the neck in a circle about the grave,
and thus left to perish under the beaks of birds and
the teeth of wild beasts.   The term applied to this
form of immolation, — *hitogaki*, or " human hedge,"
— implies a considerable number of victims in each
case.   This custom was abolished, by the Emperor
Suinin, about nineteen hundred years ago; and the
Nihongi declares that it was then an ancient custom.
Being grieved by the crying of the victims interred
in the funeral mound erected over the grave of his
brother, Yamato-hiko-no-mikoto, the Emperor is
recorded to have said: " It is a very painful thing
to force those whom one has loved in life to follow
one in death.   Though it be an ancient custom,
why follow it, if it is bad?   From this time forward
take counsel to put a stop to the following of the
dead."   Nomi-no-Sukuné, a   court-noble — now
apotheosized as the patron of wrestlers — then suggested the substitution of earthen images of men and
horses for the living victims; and his suggestion was
approved.   The *hitogaki* was thus abolished; but
compulsory as well as voluntary following of the

---

[1] How the horses and other animals were sacrificed, does not clearly appear.

dead certainly continued for many hundred years
after, since we find the Emperor Kōtoku issuing an
edict on the subject in the year 646 A.D. :—

"When a man dies, there have been cases of people
sacrificing themselves by strangulation, or of strangling
others by way of sacrifice, or of compelling the dead man's
horse to be sacrificed, or of burying valuables in the grave
in honour of the dead, or of cutting off the hair and stab-
bing the thighs and [in that condition] pronouncing a eulogy
on the dead.   Let all such old customs be entirely discontinued." — *Nihongi* ; Aston's translation.

As regarded compulsory sacrifice and popular custom, this edict may have had the immediate effect
desired ; but voluntary human sacrifices were not
definitively suppressed.   With the rise of the military power there gradually came into existence another custom of *junshi*, or following one's lord in
death, — suicide by the sword.   It is said to have
begun about 1333, when the last of the Hōjō regents, Takatoki, performed suicide, and a number
of his retainers took their own lives by *harakiri*, in
order to follow their master.   It may be doubted
whether this incident really established the practice.
But by the sixteenth century *junshi* had certainly
become an honoured custom among the samurai.
Loyal retainers esteemed it a duty to kill themselves
after the death of their lord, in order to attend upon
him during his ghostly journey.   A thousand years

of Buddhist teaching had not therefore sufficed to eradicate all primitive notions of sacrificial duty. The practice continued into the time of the Tokugawa shōgunate, when Iyeyasu made laws to check it. These laws were rigidly applied, — the entire family of the suicide being held responsible for a case of *junshi:* yet the custom cannot be said to have become extinct until considerably after the beginning of the era of Meiji. Even during my own time there have been survivals, — some of a very touching kind : suicides performed in hope of being able to serve or aid the spirit of master or husband or parent in the invisible world. Perhaps the strangest case was that of a boy fourteen years old, who killed himself in order to wait upon the spirit of a child, his master's little son.

The peculiar character of the early human sacrifices at graves, the character of the funeral-rites, the abandonment of the house in which death had occurred, — all prove that the early ancestor-worship was of a decidedly primitive kind. This is suggested also by the peculiar Shintō horror of death as pollution : even at this day to attend a funeral, — unless the funeral be conducted after the Shintō rite, — is religious defilement. The ancient legend of Izanagi's descent to the nether world, in search of his lost spouse, illustrates the terrible beliefs that once existed as to goblin-powers presiding over decay.

Between the horror of death as corruption, and the apotheosis of the ghost, there is nothing incongruous: we must understand the apotheosis itself as a propitiation. This earliest Way of the Gods was a religion of perpetual fear. Not ordinary homes only were deserted after a death: even the Emperors, during many centuries, were wont to change their capital after the death of a predecessor. But, gradually, out of the primal funeral-rites, a higher cult was evolved. The mourning-house, or *moya*, became transformed into the Shintō temple, which still retains the shape of the primitive hut. Then under Chinese influence, the ancestral cult became established in the home; and Buddhism at a later day maintained this domestic cult. By degrees the household religion became a religion of tenderness as well as of duty, and changed and softened the thoughts of men about their dead. As early as the eighth century, ancestor-worship appears to have developed the three principal forms under which it still exists; and thereafter the family-cult began to assume a character which offers many resemblances to the domestic religion of the old European civilizations.

Let us now glance at the existing forms of this domestic cult, — the universal religion of Japan. In every home there is a shrine devoted to it. If the family profess only the Shintō belief, this shrine,

or *mitamaya* [1] (" august-spirit-dwelling "), — tiny
model of a Shintō temple, — is placed upon a shelf
fixed against the wall of some inner chamber, at a
height of about six feet from the floor. Such a shelf
is called *Mitama-San-no-tana*, or " Shelf of the
august spirits." In the shrine are placed thin
tablets of white wood, inscribed with the names of
the household dead. Such tablets are called by
a name signifying " spirit-substitutes " (*mitama-
shiro*), or by a probably older name signifying
" spirit-sticks." . . . If the family worships its ancestors according to the Buddhist rite, the mortuary
tablets are placed in the Buddhist household-shrine,
or *Butsudan*, which usually occupies the upper shelf
of an alcove in one of the inner apartments. Buddhist mortuary-tablets (with some exceptions) are
called *ihai*, — a term signifying " soul-commemoration." They are lacquered and gilded, usually
having a carved lotos-flower as pedestal ; and they
do not, as a rule, bear the real, but only the religious
and posthumous name of the dead.

Now it is important to observe that, in either
cult, the mortuary tablet actually suggests a minia-
ture tombstone — which is a fact of some evolutional
interest, though the evolution itself should be Chinese rather than Japanese. The plain gravestones
in Shintō cemeteries resemble in form the simple

---

[1] It is more popularly termed *miya*, " august house," — a name given also to the
ordinary Shinto temples.

wooden ghost-sticks, or spirit-sticks; while the Buddhist monuments in the old-fashioned Buddhist graveyards are shaped like the *ihai*, of which the form is slightly varied to indicate sex and age, which is also the case with the tombstone.

The number of mortuary tablets in a household shrine does not generally exceed five or six, — only grandparents and parents and the recently dead being thus represented; but the name of remoter ancestors are inscribed upon scrolls, which are kept in the *Butsudan* or the *mitamaya*.

Whatever be the family rite, prayers are repeated and offerings are placed before the ancestral tablets every day. The nature of the offerings and the character of the prayers depend upon the religion of the household; but the essential duties of the cult are everywhere the same. These duties are not to be neglected under any circumstances: their performance in these times is usually intrusted to the elders, or to the women of the household.[1]

[1] Not, however, upon any public occasion, — such as a gathering of relatives at the home for a religious anniversary : at such times the rites are performed by the head of the household.

Speaking of the ancient custom (once prevalent in every Japanese household, and still observed in Shintō homes) of making offerings to the deities of the cooking range and of food, Sir Ernest Satow observes : " The rites in honour of these gods were at first performed by the head of the household ; but in after-times the duty came to be delegated to the women of the family " (*Ancient Japanese Rituals*). We may infer that in regard to the ancestral rites likewise, the same transfer of duties occurred at an early time, for obvious reasons of convenience. When the duty devolves upon the elders of the family — grandfather and grandmother — it is usually the grandmother who attends to the offerings. In the Greek and Roman

There is no long ceremony, no imperative rule
about prayers, nothing solemn : the food-offerings
are selected out of the family cooking; the murmured or whispered invocations are short and few.
But, trifling as the rites may seem, their performance must never be overlooked. Not to make the
offerings is a possibility undreamed of: so long as
the family exists they must be made.

To describe the details of the domestic rite would
require much space, — not because they are complicated in themselves, but because they are of a sort
unfamiliar to Western experience, and vary according to the sect of the family. But to consider the
details will not be necessary : the important matter
is to consider the religion and its beliefs in relation
to conduct and character. It should be recognized
that no religion is more sincere, no faith more touching than this domestic worship, which regards the
dead as continuing to form a part of the household
life, and needing still the affection and the respect
of their children and kindred. Originating in those
dim ages when fear was stronger than love, — when
the wish to please the ghosts of the departed must
have been chiefly inspired by dread of their anger, —
the cult at last developed into a religion of affection ;
and this it yet remains. The belief that the dead

household the performance of the domestic rites appears to have been obligatory
upon the head of the household ; but we know that the women took part in
them.

need affection, that to neglect them is a cruelty, that
their happiness depends upon duty, is a belief that
has almost cast out the primitive fear of their displeasure. They are not thought of as dead: they
are believed to remain among those who loved them.
Unseen they guard the home, and watch over the
welfare of its inmates: they hover nightly in the
glow of the shrine-lamp; and the stirring of its
flame is the motion of them. They dwell mostly
within their lettered tablets; — sometimes they can
animate a tablet, — change it into the substance of a
human body, and return in that body to active life,
in order to succour and console. From their shrine
they observe and hear what happens in the house;
they share the family joys and sorrows; they delight
in the voices and the warmth of the life about them.
They want affection; but the morning and the evening greetings of the family are enough to make them
happy. They require nourishment; but the vapour
of food contents them. They are exacting only as
regards the daily fulfilment of duty. They were
the givers of life, the givers of wealth, the makers
and teachers of the present: they represent the past
of the race, and all its sacrifices; — whatever the living possess is from them. Yet how little do they
require in return! Scarcely more than to be thanked,
as the founders and guardians of the home, in simple words like these: " *For aid received, by day and
by night, accept, August Ones, our reverential grati-*

tude." . . . To forget or neglect them, to treat them
with rude indifference, is the proof of an evil heart;
to cause them shame by ill-conduct, to disgrace their
name by bad actions, is the supreme crime. They
represent the moral experience of the race: whosoever denies that experience denies them also, and
falls to the level of the beast, or below it. They
represent the unwritten law, the traditions of the
commune, the duties of all to all: whosoever offends
against these, sins against the dead. And, finally,
they represent the mystery of the invisible: to
Shintō belief, at least, they are gods.

It is to be remembered, of course, that the Japanese word for gods, *Kami*, does not imply, any more
than did the old Latin term, *dii-manes*, ideas like
those which have become associated with the modern
notion of divinity. The Japanese term might be
more closely rendered by some such expression as
" the Superiors," " the Higher Ones "; and it was
formerly applied to living rulers as well as to deities
and ghosts. But it implies considerably more than
the idea of a disembodied spirit; for, according to
old Shintō teaching the dead became world-rulers.
They were the cause of all natural events, — of
winds, rains, and tides, of buddings and ripenings,
of growth and decay, of everything desirable or
dreadful. They formed a kind of subtler element,
— an ancestral æther, — universally extending and

unceasingly operating.   Their powers, when united
for any purpose, were resistless; and in time of
national peril they were invoked *en masse* for aid
against the foe. . . .   Thus, to the eyes of faith,
behind each family ghost there extended the measureless shadowy power of countless Kami; and the
sense of duty to the ancestor was deepened by dim
awe of the forces controlling the world, — the whole
invisible Vast.   To primitive Shintō conception the
universe was filled with ghosts; — to later Shintō
conception the ghostly condition was not limited by
place or time, even in the case of individual spirits.
"Although," wrote Hirata, "the home of the spirits
is in the Spirit-house, they are equally present
wherever they are worshipped, — being gods, and
therefore ubiquitous."

The Buddhist dead are not called gods, but Buddhas (*Hotoké*), — which term, of course, expresses a
pious hope, rather than a faith.   The belief is that
they are only on their way to some higher state of
existence; and they should not be invoked or worshipped after the manner of the Shintō gods: prayers
should be said *for* them, not, as a rule, *to* them.[1]
But the vast majority of Japanese Buddhists are
also followers of Shintō; and the two faiths, though
seemingly incongruous, have long been reconciled
in the popular mind.   The Buddhist doctrine has

[1] Certain Buddhist rituals prove exceptions to this teaching.

therefore modified the ideas attaching to the cult much less deeply than might be supposed.

In all patriarchal societies with a settled civilization, there is evolved, out of the worship of ancestors, a Religion of Filial Piety. Filial piety still remains the supreme virtue among civilized peoples possessing an ancestor-cult. . . . By filial piety must not be understood, however, what is commonly signified by the English term, — the devotion of children to parents. We must understand the word "piety" rather in its classic meaning, as the *pietas* of the early Romans, — that is to say, as the religious sense of household duty. Reverence for the dead, as well as the sentiment of duty towards the living; the affection of children to parents, and the affection of parents to children; the mutual duties of husband and wife; the duties likewise of sons-in-law and daughters-in-law to the family as a body; the duties of servant to master, and of master to dependent, — all these were included under the term. The family itself was a religion; the ancestral home a temple. And so we find the family and the home to be in Japan, even at the present day. Filial piety in Japan does not mean only the duty of children to parents and grandparents: it means still more, the cult of the ancestors, reverential service to the dead, the gratitude of the present to the past, and the conduct of the individual in relation

to the entire household.   Hirata therefore declared
that all virtues derived from the worship of ancestors; and his words, as translated by Sir Ernest
Satow, deserve particular attention : —

"It is the duty of a subject to be diligent in worshipping his ancestors, whose minister he should consider
himself to be.   The custom of adoption arose from the
natural desire of having some one to perform sacrifices;
and this desire ought not to be rendered of no avail by neglect.   Devotion to the memory of ancestors is the main-
spring of all virtues.   No one who discharges his duty to
them will ever be disrespectful to the gods or to his living
parents.   Such a man also will be faithful to his prince,
loyal to his friends, and kind and gentle to his wife and
children.   For the essence of this devotion is indeed filial
piety."

From the sociologist's point of view, Hirata is
right: it is unquestionably true that the whole system of Far-Eastern ethics derives from the religion
of the household.   By aid of that cult have been
evolved all ideas of duty to the living as well as to
the dead,—the sentiment of reverence, the sentiment
of loyalty, the spirit of self-sacrifice, and the spirit
of patriotism.   What filial piety signifies as a religious force can best be imagined from the fact that
you can buy life in the East — that it has its price
in the market.   This religion is the religion of China,
and of countries adjacent; and life is for sale in
China.   It was the filial piety of China that rendered

possible the completion of the Panama railroad, where to strike the soil was to liberate death, — where the land devoured labourers by the thousand, until white and black labour could no more be procured in quantity sufficient for the work.   But labour could be obtained from China — any amount of labour — at the cost of life; and the cost was paid; and multitudes of men came from the East to toil and die, in order that the price of their lives might be sent to their families. . . .   I have no doubt that, were the sacrifice imperatively demanded, life could be as readily bought in Japan, — though not, perhaps, so cheaply.   Where this religion prevails, the individual is ready to give his life, in a majority of cases, for the family, the home, the ancestors. And the filial piety impelling such sacrifice becomes, by extension, the loyalty that will sacrifice even the family itself for the sake of the lord, — or, by yet further extension, the loyalty that prays, like Kusunoki Masashige, for seven successive lives to lay down on behalf of the sovereign.   Out of filial piety indeed has been developed the whole moral power that protects the state, — the power also that has seldom failed to impose the rightful restraints upon official despotism whenever that despotism grew dangerous to the common weal.

Probably the filial piety that centred about the domestic altars of the ancient West differed in little from that which yet rules the most eastern East. But we miss in Japan the Aryan hearth, the family altar with its perpetual fire. The Japanese home-religion represents, apparently, a much earlier stage of the cult than that which existed within historic time among the Greeks and Romans. The homestead in Old Japan was not a stable institution like the Greek or the Roman home; the custom of burying the family dead upon the family estate never became general; the dwelling itself never assumed a substantial and lasting character. It could not be literally said of the Japanese warrior, as of the Roman, that he fought *pro aris et focis*. There was neither altar nor sacred fire: the place of these was taken by the spirit-shelf or shrine, with its tiny lamp, kindled afresh each evening; and, in early times, there were no Japanese images of divinities. For Lares and Penates there were only the mortuary-tablets of the ancestors, and certain little tablets bearing names of other gods — tutelar gods. . . . The presence of these frail wooden objects still makes the home; and they may be, of course, transported anywhere.

To apprehend the full meaning of ancestor-worship as a family religion, a living faith, is now difficult for the Western mind. We are able to imagine only in the vaguest way how our Aryan forefathers felt and thought about their dead.   But in the

living beliefs of Japan we find much to suggest
the nature of the old Greek piety. Each member of the family supposes himself, or herself,
under perpetual ghostly surveillance. Spirit-eyes
are watching every act ; spirit-ears are listening
to every word. Thoughts too, not less than
deeds, are visible to the gaze of the dead : the
heart must be pure, the mind must be under
control, within the presence of the spirits. Probably the influence of such beliefs, uninterruptedly
exerted upon conduct during thousands of years,
did much to form the charming side of Japanese
character. Yet there is nothing stern or solemn
in this home-religion to-day,— nothing of that rigid
and unvarying discipline supposed by Fustel de
Coulanges to have especially characterized the
Roman cult. It is a religion rather of gratitude
and tenderness ; the dead being served by the
household as if they were actually present in the
body. . . . I fancy that if we were able to enter
for a moment into the vanished life of some old
Greek city, we should find the domestic religion
there not less cheerful than the Japanese home-cult
remains to-day. I imagine that Greek children,
three thousand years ago, must have watched, like
the Japanese children of to-day, for a chance to steal
some of the good things offered to the ghosts of the
ancestors ; and I fancy that Greek parents must
have chidden quite as gently as Japanese parents

chide in this era of Meiji, — mingling reproof with instruction, and hinting of weird possibilities.[1]

[1] Food presented to the dead may afterwards be eaten by the elders of the household, or given to pilgrims ; but it is said that if children eat of it, they will grow up with feeble memories, and incapable of becoming scholars.

The Japanese Family

THE great general idea, the fundamental idea, underlying every persistent ancestor-worship, is that the welfare of the living depends upon the welfare of the dead. Under the influence of this idea, and of the cult based upon it, were developed the early organization of the family, the laws regarding property and succession, the whole structure, in short, of ancient society, — whether in the Western or the Eastern world.

But before considering how the social structure in old Japan was shaped by the ancestral cult, let me again remind the reader that there were at first no other gods than the dead. Even when Japanese ancestor-worship evolved a mythology, its gods were only transfigured ghosts, — and this is the history of all mythology. The ideas of heaven and hell did not exist among the primitive Japanese, nor any notion of metempsychosis. The Buddhist doctrine of rebirth — a late borrowing — was totally inconsistent with the archaic Japanese beliefs, and required an elaborate metaphysical system to support it. But we may suppose the early ideas of the Japanese about the dead to have been much like those of the Greeks of the pre-Homeric era. There was an underground world to which spirits descended; but they were supposed to haunt by preference their own graves, or their "ghost-houses." Only by slow degrees did the notion of their power of ubiquity become evolved. But even then they were thought to be particularly attached to their tombs, shrines, and homesteads. Hirata wrote, in the early part of the nineteenth century: "The spirits of the dead continue to exist in the unseen world which is everywhere about us; and they all become gods of varying character and degrees of influence. Some reside in temples built in their honour; others hover near their tombs; and they continue to render service to their prince, parents, wives, and children, as when in the body." Evidently "the unseen world" was thought to be in some sort a duplicate of the visible world, and dependent upon the help of the living for its prosperity. The dead and the living were mutually dependent. The all-important necessity for the ghost was sacrificial worship; the all-important necessity for the man was to provide for the future cult of his own spirit; and to die without assurance of a cult was the supreme calamity. . . . Remembering these facts we can understand better the organization of the patriarchal family,—shaped to maintain and to provide for the cult of its dead, any neglect of which cult was believed to involve misfortune.

The reader is doubtless aware that in the old Aryan family the bond of union was not the bond of affection, but a bond of religion, to which natural affection was altogether subordinate. This condition characterizes the patriarchal family wherever ancestor-worship exists. Now the Japanese family, like the ancient Greek or Roman family, was a religious society in the strictest sense of the term; and a religious society it yet remains. Its organization was primarily shaped in accordance with the requirements of ancestor-worship; its later imported doctrines of filial piety had been already developed in China to meet the needs of an older and similar religion. We might expect to find in the structure, the laws, and the customs of the Japanese family many points of likeness to the structure and the traditional laws of the old Aryan household,— because the law of sociological evolution admits of only minor exceptions. And many such points of likeness are obvious. The materials for a serious comparative study have not yet been collected : very much remains to be learned regarding the past history of the Japanese family. But, along certain general lines, the resemblances between domestic institutions in ancient Europe and domestic institutions in the Far East can be clearly established.

Alike in the early European and in the old Japanese civilization it was believed that the prosperity

of the family depended upon the exact fulfilment
of the duties of the ancestral cult; and, to a considerable degree, this belief rules the life of the Japanese family to-day.   It is still thought that the good
fortune of the household depends on the observance
of its cult, and that the greatest possible calamity is
to die without leaving a male heir to perform the
rites and to make the offerings.   The paramount
duty of filial piety among the early Greeks and
Romans was to provide for the perpetuation of the
family cult; and celibacy was therefore generally forbidden, — the obligation to marry being enforced by
opinion where not enforced by legislation.   Among
the free classes of Old Japan, marriage was also, as
a general rule, obligatory in the case of a male heir:
otherwise, where celibacy was not condemned by
law, it was condemned by custom.   To die without
offspring was, in the case of a younger son, chiefly
a personal misfortune; to die without leaving a male
heir, in the case of an elder son and successor, was
a crime against the ancestors,—the cult being thereby
threatened with extinction.   No excuse existed for
remaining childless: the family law in Japan, precisely as in ancient Europe, having amply provided
against such a contingency.   In case that a wife
proved barren, she might be divorced.   In case that
there were reasons for not divorcing her, a concubine
might be taken for the purpose of obtaining an heir.
Furthermore, every family representative was privi-

leged to adopt an heir. An unworthy son, again, might be disinherited, and another young man adopted in his place. Finally, in case that a man had daughters but no son, the succession and the continuance of the cult could be assured by adopting a husband for the eldest daughter.

But, as in the antique European family, daughters could not inherit: descent being in the male line, it was necessary to have a male heir. In old Japanese belief, as in old Greek and Roman belief, the father, not the mother, was the life-giver; the creative principle was masculine; the duty of maintaining the cult rested with the man, not with the woman.[1]

The woman shared the cult; but she could not maintain it. Besides, the daughters of the family, being destined, as a general rule, to marry into other households, could bear only a temporary relation to the home-cult. It was necessary that the religion of the wife should be the religion of the husband; and the Japanese, like the Greek woman, on marrying into another household, necessarily became attached to the cult of her husband's family. For this reason especially the females in the patriarchal

---

[1] Wherever, among ancestor-worshipping races, descent is in the male line, the cult follows the male line. But the reader is doubtless aware that a still more primitive form of society than the patriarchal — the matriarchal — is supposed to have had its ancestor-worship. Mr. Spencer observes : "What has happened when descent in the female line obtains, is not clear. I have met with no statement showing that, in societies characterized by this usage, the duty of administering to the double of the dead man devolved on one of his children rather than on others." — *Principles of Sociology*, Vol. III, § 601.

family are not equal to the males; the sister cannot
rank with the brother. It is true that the Japanese
daughter, like the Greek daughter, could remain
attached to her own family even after marriage, providing that a husband were adopted for her, — that
is to say, taken into the family as a son. But even
in this case, she could only share in the cult, which it
then became the duty of the adopted husband to
maintain.

The constitution of the patriarchal family everywhere derives from its ancestral cult; and before
considering the subjects of marriage and adoption
in Japan, it will be necessary to say something about
the ancient family-organization. The ancient family
was called *uji*, — a word said to have originally
signified the same thing as the modern term *uchi*,
"interior," or "household," but certainly used from
very early times in the sense of "name" — clan-
name especially. There were two kinds of *uji*: the
ō-uji, or great families, and the *ko-uji*, or lesser
families, — either term signifying a large body of
persons united by kinship, and by the cult of a
common ancestor. The *ō-uji* corresponded in some
degree to the Greek γένος or the Roman *gens*: the
ko-uji were its branches, and subordinate to it. The
unit of society was the *uji*. Each *ō-uji*, with its
dependent *ko-uji*, represented something like a
phratry or *curia*; and all the larger groups mak-

ing up the primitive Japanese society were but multiplications of the *uji*, — whether we call them clans, tribes, or hordes. With the advent of a settled civilization, the greater groups necessarily divided and subdivided; but the smallest subdivision still retained its primal organization. Even the modern Japanese family partly retains that organization. It does not mean only a household: it means rather what the Greek or Roman family became after the dissolution of the *gens*. With ourselves the family has been disintegrated: when we talk of a man's family, we mean his wife and children. But the Japanese family is still a large group. As marriages take place early, it may consist, even as a household, of great-grandparents, grandparents, parents, and children — sons and daughters of several generations; but it commonly extends much beyond the limits of one household. In early times it might constitute the entire population of a village or town; and there are still in Japan large communities of persons all bearing the same family name. In some districts it was formerly the custom to keep all the children, as far as possible, within the original family group — husbands being adopted for all the daughters. The group might thus consist of sixty or more persons, dwelling under the same roof; and the houses were of course constructed, by successive extension, so as to meet the requirement. (I am mentioning these curious facts

only by way of illustration.) But the greater *uji*,
after the race had settled down, rapidly multiplied;
and although there are said to be house-com-
munities still in some remote districts of the
country, the primal patriarchal groups must have
been broken up almost everywhere at some very
early period. Thereafter the main cult of the *uji*
did not cease to be the cult also of its sub-divi-
sions: all members of the original gens continued
to worship the common ancestor, or *uji-no-kami*,
"the god of the *uji*." By degrees the ghost-house
of the *uji-no-kami* became transformed into the
modern Shintō parish-temple; and the ancestral
spirit became the local tutelar god, whose modern
appellation, *ujigami*, is but a shortened form of his
ancient title, *uji-no-kami*. Meanwhile, after the general establishment of the domestic cult, each separate
household maintained the special cult of its own
dead, in addition to the communal cult. This
religious condition still continues. The family
may include several households; but each household maintains the cult of its dead. And the family-
group, whether large or small, preserves its ancient
constitution and character; it is still a religious
society, exacting obedience, on the part of all its
members, to traditional custom.

So much having been explained, the customs
regarding marriage and adoption, in their relation

to the family hierarchy, can be clearly understood. But a word first regarding this hierarchy, as it exists to-day. Theoretically the power of the head of the family is still supreme in the household. All must obey the head. Furthermore the females must obey the males — the wives, the husbands; and the younger members of the family are subject to the elder members. The children must not only obey the parents and grandparents, but must observe among themselves the domestic law of seniority: thus the younger brother should obey the elder brother, and the younger sister the elder sister. The rule of precedence is enforced gently, and is cheerfully obeyed even in small matters: for example, at meal-time, the elder boy is served first, the second son next, and so on, — an exception being made in the case of a very young child, who is not obliged to wait. This custom accounts for an amusing popular term often applied in jest to a second son, " Master Cold-Rice " (*Hiaméshi-San*); as the second son, having to wait until both infants and elders have been served, is not likely to find his portion desirably hot when it reaches him. . . . Legally, the family can have but one responsible head. It may be the grandfather, the father, or the eldest son; and it is generally the eldest son, because according to a custom of Chinese origin, the old folks usually resign their active authority as soon as the eldest son is able to take charge of affairs.

The subordination of young to old, and of females
to males, — in fact the whole existing constitution
of the family, — suggests a great deal in regard to
the probably stricter organization of the patriarchal
family, whose chief was at once ruler and priest, with
almost unlimited powers. The organization was
primarily, and still remains, religious: the marital
bond did not constitute the family; and the relation
of the parent to the household depended upon his
or her relation to the family as a religious body.
To-day also, the girl adopted into a household as
wife ranks only as an adopted child: marriage signifies adoption. She is called "flower-daughter"
(*hana-yomê*). In like manner, and for the same
reasons, the young man received into a household
as a husband of one of the daughters, ranks merely
as an adopted son. The adopted bride or bridegroom is necessarily subject to the elders, and may
be dismissed by their decision. As for the adopted
husband, his position is both delicate and difficult,
— as an old Japanese proverb bears witness:
Konuka san-go arêba, mukoyoshi to naruna ("While
you have even three *gō*[1] of rice-bran left, do not become a son-in-law"). Jacob does not have to wait
for Rachel: he is given to Rachel on demand; and
his service then begins. And after twice seven
years of service, Jacob may be sent away. In that
event his children do not any more belong to him.

[1] A *gō* is something more than a pint.

but to the family. His adoption may have had nothing to do with affection ; and his dismissal may have nothing to do with misconduct. Such matters, however they may be settled in law, are really decided by family interests — interests relating to the maintenance of the house and of its cult.[1]

It should not be forgotten that, although a daughter-in-law or a son-in-law could in former times be dismissed almost at will, the question of marriage in the old Japanese family was a matter of religious importance, — marriage being one of the chief duties of filial piety. This was also the case in the early Greek and Roman family ; and the marriage ceremony was performed, as it is now performed in Japan, not at a temple, but in the home. It was a rite of the family religion, — the rite by which the bride was adopted into the cult in the supposed presence of the ancestral spirits. Among the primitive Japanese there was probably no corresponding ceremony ; but after the establishment of the domestic cult, the marriage ceremony became a religious rite, and this it still remains. Ordinary marriages are not, however, performed before the household shrine or in front of the ancestral tablets, except under certain circumstances. The rule, as regards such ordinary marriages, seems to be that

---

[1] Recent legislation has been in favour of the *mukoyoshi* ; but, as a rule, the law is seldom resorted to except by men dismissed from the family for misconduct, and anxious to make profit by the dismissal.

if the parents of the bridegroom are yet alive, this is not done; but if they are dead, then the bridegroom leads his bride before their mortuary tablets, where she makes obeisance.   Among the nobility, in former times at least, the marriage ceremony appears to have been more distinctly religious, — judging from the following curious relation in the book *Shōrei-Hikki*, or "Record of Ceremonies" [1]: "At the weddings of the great, the bridal-chamber is composed of three rooms thrown into one [*by removal of the sliding-screens ordinarily separating them*], and newly decorated. . . . The shrine for the image of the family-god is placed upon a shelf adjoining the sleeping-place."   It is noteworthy also that Imperial marriages are always officially announced to the ancestors; and that the marriage of the heir-apparent, or other male offspring of the Imperial house, is performed before the *Kashiko-dokoro*, or imperial temple of the ancestors, which stands within the palace-grounds. [2]   As a general rule it would appear that the evolution of the marriage-ceremony in Japan chiefly followed Chinese precedent; and in the Chinese patriarchal family the ceremony is in its own way quite as much of a religious rite as the early Greek or Roman marriage.   And though the relation of the Japanese

---

[1] The translation is Mr. Mitford's.   There are no "images" of the family-god, and I suppose that the family's Shintō-shrine is meant, with its ancestral tablets.

[2] This was the case at the marriage of the present Crown-Prince.

rite to the family cult is less marked, it becomes sufficiently clear upon investigation. The alternate drinking of rice-wine, by bridegroom and bride, from the same vessels, corresponds in a sort to the Roman *confarreatio*. By the wedding-rite the bride is adopted into the family religion. She is adopted not only by the living but by the dead; she must thereafter revere the ancestors of her husband as her own ancestors; and should there be no elders in the household, it will become her duty to make the offerings, as representative of her husband. With the cult of her own family she has nothing more to do; and the funeral ceremonies performed upon her departure from the parental roof, — the solemn sweeping-out of the house-rooms, the lighting of the death-fire before the gate, — are significant of this religious separation.

Speaking of the Greek and Roman marriage, M. de Coulanges observes: "*Une telle religion ne pouvait pas admettre la polygamie.*" As relating to the highly developed domestic cult of those communities considered by the author of *La Cité Antique*, his statement will scarcely be called in question. But as regards ancestor-worship in general, it would be incorrect; since polygamy or polygyny, and polyandry may coexist with ruder forms of ancestor-worship. The Western-Aryan societies, in the epoch studied by M. de Coulanges, were practically

monogamic. The ancient Japanese society was
polygynous ; and polygyny persisted, after the establishment of the domestic cult. In early times, the
marital relation itself would seem to have been in-
definite. No distinction was made between the wife
and the concubines : " they were classed together as
' women.' " [1] Probably under Chinese influence the
distinction was afterwards sharply drawn ; and with
the progress of civilization, the general tendency
was towards monogamy, although the ruling classes
remained polygynous. In the 54th article of Iyeyasu's legacy, this phase of the social condition is
clearly expressed,—a condition which prevailed down
to the present era : —

> "The position a wife holds towards a concubine is the
> same as that of a lord to his vassal. The Emperor has
> twelve imperial concubines. The princes may have eight
> concubines. Officers of the highest class may have five
> mistresses. A Samurai may have two handmaids. All
> below this are ordinary married men."

This would suggest that concubinage had long
been (with some possible exceptions) an exclusive
privilege ; and that it should have persisted down to
the period of the abolition of the daimiates and of
the military class, is sufficiently explained by the
militant character of the ancient society.[2] Though

---

[1] Satow : *The Revival of Pure Shintau.*

[2] See especially Herbert Spencer's chapter, " The Family," in Vol. I, *Principles of Sociology*, § 315.

it is untrue that domestic ancestor-worship cannot coexist with polygamy or polygyny (Mr. Spencer's term is the most inclusive), it is at least true that such worship is favoured by the monogamic relation, and tends therefore to establish it, — since monogamy insures to the family succession a stability that no other relation can offer. We may say that, although the old Japanese society was not monogamic, the natural tendency was towards monogamy, as the condition best according with the religion of the family, and with the moral feeling of the masses.

Once that the domestic ancestor-cult had become universally established, the question of marriage, as a duty of filial pity, could not be judiciously left to the will of the young people themselves. It was a matter to be decided by the family, not by the children; for mutual inclination could not be suffered to interfere with the requirements of the household religion. It was not a question of affection, but of religious duty; and to think otherwise was impious. Affection might and ought to spring up from the relation. But any affection powerful enough to endanger the cohesion of the family would be condemned. A wife might therefore be divorced because her husband had become too much attached to her; an adopted husband might be divorced because of his power to exercise, through affection, too great an influence upon the daughter of the house. Other causes would probably be found for the divorce in either case — but they would not be difficult to find.

For the same reason that connubial affection could be tolerated only within limits, the natural rights of parenthood (as we understand them) were necessarily restricted in the old Japanese household. Marriage being for the purpose of obtaining heirs to perpetuate the cult, the children were regarded as belonging to the family rather than to the father and mother. Hence, in case of divorcing the son's wife, or the adopted son-in-law, — or of disinheriting the married son, — the children would be retained by the family. For the natural right of the young parents was considered subordinate to the religious rights of the house. In opposition to those rights, no other rights could be tolerated. Practically, of course, according to more or less fortunate circumstances, the individual might enjoy freedom under the paternal roof; but theoretically and legally there was no freedom in the old Japanese family for any member of it, — not excepting even its acknowledged chief, whose responsibilities were great. Every person, from the youngest child up to the grandfather, was subject to somebody else; and every act of domestic life was regulated by traditional custom.

Like the Greek or Roman father, the patriarch of the Japanese family appears to have had in early times powers of life and death over all the members of the household. In the ruder ages the father might either kill or sell his children; and afterwards, among the ruling classes his powers remained almost unlimited until modern times. Allowing for certain local exceptions, explicable by tradition, or class-exceptions, explicable by conditions of servitude, it may be said that originally the Japanese *pater-familias* was at once ruler, priest, and magistrate within the family. He could compel his children to marry or forbid them to marry; he could disinherit or repudiate them; he could ordain the profession or calling which they were to follow; and his power extended to all members of the family, and to the household dependents. At different epochs limits were placed to the exercise of this power, in the case of the ordinary people; but in the military class, the *patria potestas* was almost unrestricted. In its extreme form, the paternal power controlled everything, — the right to life and liberty, — the right to marry, or to keep the wife or husband already espoused, — the right to one's own children, — the right to hold property, — the right to hold office, — the right to choose or follow an occupation. The family was a despotism.

It should not be forgotten, however, that the absolutism prevailing in the patriarchal family has its justification in a religious belief, — in the conviction that everything should be sacrificed for the sake

of the cult, and every member of the family should
be ready to give up even life, if necessary, to assure
the perpetuity of the succession.   Remembering
this, it becomes easy to understand why, even in
communities otherwise advanced in civilization, it
should have seemed right that a father could kill or
sell his children.   The crime of a son might result
in the extinction of a cult through the ruin of the
family, — especially in a militant society like that
of Japan, where the entire family was held responsible for the acts of each of its members, so that a
capital offence would involve the penalty of death
on the whole of the household, including the children.   Again, the sale of a daughter, in time of extreme need, might save a house from ruin ; and filial
piety exacted submission to such sacrifice for the
sake of the cult.

As in the Aryan family,[1] property descended by
right of primogeniture from father to son ; the
eldest-born, even in cases where the other property
was to be divided among the children, always inheriting the homestead.   The homestead property was,
however, family property ; and it passed to the eldest
son as representative, not as individual.   Generally
speaking, sons could not hold property, without the
father's consent, during such time as he retained his

[1] The laws of succession in Old Japan differed considerably according to class,
place, and era ; the entire subject has not yet been fully treated ; and only a few
safe general statements can be ventured at the present time.

headship. As a rule, — to which there were various
exceptions, — a daughter could not inherit; and in
the case of an only daughter, for whom a husband
had been adopted, the homestead property would
pass to the adopted husband, because (until within
recent times) a woman could not become the head
of a family. This was the case also in the Western
Aryan household, in ancestor-worshipping times.

To modern thinking, the position of woman in
the old Japanese family appears to have been the
reverse of happy. As a child she was subject, not
only to the elders, but to all the male adults of
the household. Adopted into another household as
wife, she merely passed into a similar state of subjection, unalleviated by the affection which parental
and fraternal ties assured her in the ancestral home.
Her retention in the family of her husband did not
depend upon his affection, but upon the will of the
majority, and especially of the elders. Divorced,
she could not claim her children: they belonged to
the family of the husband. In any event her duties
as wife were more trying than those of a hired servant. Only in old age could she hope to exercise
some authority; but even in old age she was under
tutelage — throughout her entire life she was in tutelage. "A woman can have no house of her own
in the Three Universes," declared an old Japanese
proverb. Neither could she have a cult of her own:
there was no special cult for the women of a family

—no ancestral rite distinct from that of the husband.
And the higher the rank of the family into which
she entered by marriage, the more difficult would be
her position.   For a woman of the aristocratic class
no freedom existed: she could not even pass beyond
her own gate except in a palanquin (*kago*) or under
escort ; and her existence as a wife was likely to
be embittered by the presence of concubines in the
house.

Such was the patriarchal family in old times ; yet
it is probable that conditions were really better than
the laws and the customs would suggest.   The race
is a joyous and kindly one ; and it discovered, long
centuries ago, many ways of smoothing the difficulties of life, and of modifying the harsher exactions
of law and custom.   The great powers of the family-
head were probably but seldom exercised in cruel
directions.   He might have legal rights of the most
formidable character ; but these were required by
reason of his responsibilities, and were not likely
to be used against communal judgment.   It must
be remembered that the individual was not legally
considered in former times: the family only was
recognized ; and the head of it legally existed only
as representative.   If he erred, the whole family
was liable to suffer the penalty of his error.   Furthermore, every extreme exercise of his authority
involved proportionate responsibilities.   He could

divorce his wife, or compel his son to divorce the
adopted daughter-in-law; but in either case he
would have to account for this action to the family
of the divorced; and the divorce-right, especially
in the samurai class, was greatly restrained by the
fear of family resentment; the unjust dismissal of a
wife being counted as an insult to her kindred. He
might disinherit an only son; but in that event he
would be obliged to adopt a kinsman. He might
kill or sell either son or daughter; but unless he
belonged to some abject class, he would have to
justify his action to the community.[1] He might be
reckless in his management of the family property;
but in that case an appeal to communal authority
was possible, and the appeal might result in his
deposition. So far as we are able to judge from the
remains of old Japanese law which have been studied,
it would seem to have been the general rule that the
family-head could not sell or alienate the estate.
Though the family-rule was despotic, it was the
rule of a body rather than of a chief; the family-
head really exercising authority in the name of the
rest. . . . In this sense, the family still remains
a despotism; but the powers of its legal head are
now checked, from within as well as from without,

[1] Samurai fathers might kill a daughter convicted of unchastity, or kill a son
guilty of any action calculated to disgrace the family name. But they would not
sell a child. The sale of daughters was practised only by the abject classes, or by
families of other castes reduced to desperate extremities. A girl might, however,
sell herself for the sake of her family.

by later custom. The acts of adoption, disinherit-
ance, marriage, or divorce, are decided usually by
general consent; and the decision of the household
and kindred is required in the taking of any important step to the disadvantage of the individual.

Of course the old family-organization had certain
advantages which largely compensated the individual
for his state of subjection. It was a society of
mutual help; and it was not less powerful to give
aid, than to enforce obedience. Every member
could do something to assist another member in
case of need : each had a right to the protection of
all. This remains true of the family to-day. In a
well-conducted household, where every act is performed according to the old forms of courtesy and
kindness, — where no harsh word is ever spoken,
— where the young look up to the aged with affectionate respect, — where those whom years have inca-
pacitated for more active duty, take upon themselves
the care of the children, and render priceless service
in teaching and training, — an ideal condition has
been realized. The daily life of such a home, — in
which the endeavour of each is to make existence
as pleasant as possible for all, — in which the bond
of union is really love and gratitude, — represents
religion in the best and purest sense; and the place
is holy. . . .

It remains to speak of the dependants in the

ancient family. Though the fact has not yet been fully established, it is probable that the first domestics were slaves or serfs; and the condition of servants in later times, — especially of those in families of the ruling classes, — was much like that of slaves in the early Greek and Roman families. Though necessarily treated as inferiors, they were regarded as members of the household: they were trusted familiars, permitted to share in the pleasures of the family, and to be present at most of its reunions. They could legally be dealt with harshly; but there is little doubt that, as a rule, they were treated kindly, — absolute loyalty being expected from them. The best indication of their status in past times is furnished by yet surviving customs. Though the power of the family over the servant no longer exists in law or in fact, the pleasant features of the old relation continue; and they are of no little interest. The family takes a sincere interest in the welfare of its domestics, — almost such interest as would be shown in the case of poorer kindred. Formerly the family furnishing servants to a household of higher rank, stood to the latter in the relation of vassal to liege-lord; and between the two there existed a real bond of loyalty and kindliness. The occupation of servant was then hereditary; children were trained for the duty from an early age. After the man-servant or maid-servant had arrived at a certain age, permission to marry was accorded; and the relation of service then ceased, but not the bond of loyalty. The children of the married servants would be sent, when old enough, to work in the house of the master, and would leave it only when the time also came for them to marry. Relations of this kind still exist between certain aristocratic families and former vassal-families, and conserve some charming traditions and customs of hereditary service, unchanged for hundreds of years.

In feudal times, of course, the bond between master and servant was of the most serious kind; the latter being expected, in case of need, to sacrifice life and all else for the sake of the master or of the master's household. This also was the loyalty demanded of the Greek and Roman domestic, — before there had yet come into existence that inhuman form of servitude which reduced the toiler to the condition of a beast of burden; and the relation was partly a religious one. There does not seem to have been in ancient Japan any custom corresponding to that, described by M. de Coulanges, of adopting the Greek or Roman servant into the household cult. But as the Japanese vassal-families furnishing domestics were, as vassals, necessarily attached to the clan-cult of their lord, the relation of the servant to the family was to some extent a religious bond.

The reader will be able to understand, from the facts of this chapter, to what extent the individual was sacrificed to the family, as a religious body. From servant to master — up through all degrees of the household hierarchy — the law of duty was the same : obedience absolute to custom and tradition. The ancestral cult permitted no individual freedom : nobody could live according to his or her pleasure ; every one had to live according to rule. The individual did not even have a legal existence ; — the family was the unit of society. Even its patriarch existed in law as representative only, — responsible both to the living and the dead. His public responsibility, however, was not determined merely by civil law. It was determined by another religious bond, — that of the ancestral cult of ·the clan or tribe ; and this public form of ancestor-worship was even more exacting than the religion of the home.

The Communal Cult

AS by the religion of the household each individual was ruled in every action of domestic life, so, by the religion of the village or district the family was ruled in all its relations to the outer world. Like the religion of the home, the religion of the commune was ancestor-worship. What the household shrine represented to the family, the Shintō parish-temple represented to the community; and the deity there worshipped as tutelar god was called *Ujigami*, the god of the *Uji*, which term originally signified the patriarchal family or *gens*, as well as the family name.

Some obscurity still attaches to the question of the original relation of the community to the Uji-god. Hirata declares the god of the *Uji* to have been the common ancestor of the clan-family, — the ghost of the first patriarch; and this opinion (allowing for sundry exceptions) is almost certainly correct. But it is difficult to decide whether the *Uji-ko*, or "children of the family" (as Shintō parishioners are still termed) at first included only the descendants of the clan-ancestor, or also the whole of the inhabitants of the district ruled by the clan.   It is certainly not true at the present time that the tutelar deity of each Japanese district represents the common ancestor of its inhabitants, — though, to this general rule, there might be found exception in some of the remoter provinces. Most probably the god of the Uji was first worshipped by the people of the district rather as the spirit of a former ruler, or the patron-god of a ruling family, than as the spirit of a common ancestor. It has been tolerably well proved that the bulk of the Japanese people were in a state of servitude from before the beginning of the historic period, and so remained until within comparatively recent times. The subject-classes may not have had at first a cult of their own: their religion would most likely have been that of their masters. In later times the vassal was certainly attached to the cult of the lord. But it is difficult as yet to venture any general statement as to the earliest phase of the communal cult in Japan; for the history of the Japanese nation is not that of a single people of one blood, but a history of many clan-groups, of different origin, gradually brought together to form one huge patriarchal society.

However, it is quite safe to assume, with the best native authorities, that the Ujigami were originally clan-deities, and that they were usually, though not invariably, worshipped as clan-ancestors.

Some Ujigami belong to the historic period. The
war god Hachiman, for example, — to whom parish-
temples are dedicated in almost every large city, —
is the apotheosized spirit of the Emperor Ōjin,
patron of the famed Minamoto clan. This is an
example of Ujigami worship in which the clan-god is
not an ancestor. But in many instances the Ujigami is really the ancestor of an Uji; as in the
case of the great deity of Kasuga, from whom the
Fujiwara clan claimed descent. Altogether there
were in ancient Japan, after the beginning of the
historic era, 1182 clans, great and small; and these
appear to have established the same number of cults.
We find, as might be expected, that the temples
now called Ujigami — which is to say, Shintō parish-
temples in general — are always dedicated to a particular class of divinities, and never dedicated to
certain other gods. Also, it is significant that in
every large town there are Shintō temples dedicated
to the same Uji-gods, — proving the transfer of communal worship from its place of origin. Thus the
Izumo worshipper of Kasuga-Sama can find in
Osaka, Kyōto, Tōkyō, parish-temples dedicated to
his patron: the Kyūshū worshipper of Hachiman-
Sama can place himself under the protection of the
same deity in Musashi quite as well as in Higo or
Bungo. Another fact worth observing is that the
Ujigami temple is not necessarily the most important
Shintō temple in the parish: it is the parish-temple,

and important to the communal worship; but it may be outranked and overshadowed by some adjacent temple dedicated to higher Shintō gods. Thus in Kitzuki of Izumo, for example, the great Izumo temple is not the Ujigami, — not the parish-temple; the local cult is maintained at a much smaller temple. . . . Of the higher cults I shall speak further on; for the present let us consider only the communal cult, in its relation to communal life. From the social conditions represented by the worship of the Ujigami to-day, much can be inferred as to its influence in past times.

Almost every Japanese village has its Ujigami; and each district of every large town or city also has its Ujigami. The worship of the tutelar deity is maintained by the whole body of parishioners, — the Ujiko, or children of the tutelar god. Every such parish-temple has its holy days, when all Ujiko are expected to visit the temple, and when, as a matter of fact, every household sends at least one representative to the Ujigami. There are great festival-days and ordinary festival-days; there are processions, music, dancing, and whatever in the way of popular amusement can serve to make the occasion attractive. The people of adjacent districts vie with each other in rendering their respective temple-festivals (*matsuri*) enjoyable: every household contributes according to its means.

The Shintō parish-temple has an intimate relation to the life of the community as a body, and also to the individual existence of every Ujiko. As a baby he or she is taken to the Ujigami — (at the expiration of thirty-one days after birth if a boy, or thirty-three days after birth if a girl) — and placed under the protection of the god, in whose supposed presence the little one's name is recorded. Thereafter the child is regularly taken to the temple on holy days, and of course to all the big festivals, which are made delightful to young fancy by the display of toys on sale in temporary booths, and by the amusing spectacles to be witnessed in the temple grounds, — artists forming pictures on the pavement with coloured sands, — sweetmeat-sellers moulding animals and monsters out of sugar-paste, — conjurors and tumblers exhibiting their skill. . . . Later, when the child becomes strong enough to run about, the temple gardens and groves serve for a playground. School-life does not separate the Ujiko from the Ujigami (unless the family should permanently leave the district); the visits to the temple are still continued as a duty. Grown-up and married, the Ujiko regularly visits the guardian-god, accompanied by wife or husband, and brings the children to pay obeisance. If obliged to make a long journey, or to quit the district forever, the Ujiko pays a farewell visit to the Ujigami, as well as to the tombs of the family ancestors; and on returning to one's native place after prolonged absence, the first visit is to the god. . . . I have more than once been touched by the spectacle of soldiers at prayer before lonesome little temples in country places, — soldiers but just returned from Korea, China, or Formosa: their first thought on reaching home was to utter their thanks to the god of their childhood, whom they believed to have guarded them in the hour of battle and the season of pestilence.

The best authority on the local customs and laws of Old Japan, John Henry Wigmore, remarks that the Shintō cult had few relations with local administration. In his opinion the Ujigami were the deified ancestors of certain noble families of early times; and their temples continued to be in the patronage of those families. The office of the Shintō priest, or " god-master " (*kannushi*) was, and still is, hereditary; and, as a rule, any *kannushi* can trace back his descent from the family of which the Ujigami was originally the patron-god. But the Shintō priests, with some few exceptions, were neither magistrates nor administrators; and Professor Wigmore thinks that this may have been " due to the lack of administrative organization within the cult itself." [1]

[1] The vague character of the Shintō hierarchy is probably best explained by Mr. Spencer in Chapter VIII of the third volume of *Principles of Sociology*: " The establishment of an ecclesiastical organization separate from the political organization, but akin to it in its structure, appears to be largely determined by the rise of a decided distinction in thought between the affairs of this world and those of

This would be an adequate explanation. But in spite of the fact that they exercised no civil function, I believe it can be shown that Shintō priests had, and still have, powers above the law. Their relation to the community was of an extremely important kind: their authority was only religious; but it was heavy and irresistible.

To understand this, we must remember that the Shintō priest represented the religious sentiment of his district. The social bond of each community was identical with the religious bond, — the cult of the local tutelar god. It was to the Ujigami that prayers were made for success in all communal undertakings, for protection against sickness, for the triumph of the lord in time of war, for succour in the season of famine or epidemic. The Ujigami was the giver of all good things, — the special helper and guardian of the people. That this belief still prevails may be verified by any one who studies the peasant-life of Japan. It is not to the Buddhas that the farmer prays for bountiful harvests, or for rain in time of drought; it is not to the Buddhas

a supposed other world. Where the two are conceived as existing in continuity, or as intimately related, the organizations appropriate to their respective administrations remain either identical or imperfectly distinguished. . . . If the Chinese are remarkable for the complete absence of a priestly caste, it is because, along with their universal and active ancestor-worship, they have preserved that inclusion of the duties of priest in the duties of ruler, which ancestor-worship in its simple form shows us." Mr. Spencer remarks in the same paragraph on the fact that in ancient Japan "religion and government were the same." A distinct Shintō hierarchy was therefore never evolved.

that thanks are rendered for a plentiful rice-crop —
but to the ancient local god. And the cult of the
Ujigami embodies the moral experience of the community, — represents all its cherished traditions and
customs, its unwritten laws of conduct, its sentiment
of duty. . . . Now just as an offence against the
ethics of the family must, in such a society, be regarded as an impiety towards the family-ancestor,
so any breach of custom in the village or district
must be considered as an act of disrespect to its
Ujigami. The prosperity of the family depends,
it is thought, upon the observance of filial piety,
which is identified with obedience to the traditional
rules of household conduct; and, in like manner,
the prosperity of the commune is supposed to depend upon the observance of ancestral custom, —
upon obedience to those unwritten laws of the district, which are taught to all from the time of their
childhood. Customs are identified with morals.
Any offence against the customs of the settlement
is an öffence against the gods who protect it, and
therefore a menace to the public weal. The existence of the community is endangered by the crime
of any of its members: every member is therefore
held accountable by the community for his conduct.
Every action must conform to the traditional usages
of the Ujiko: independent exceptional conduct is a
public offence.

What the obligations of the individual to the

community signified in ancient times may therefore be imagined. He had certainly no more right to himself than had the Greek citizen three thousand years ago,—probably not so much. To-day, though laws have been greatly changed, he is practically in much the same condition. The mere idea of the right to do as one pleases (within such limits as are imposed on conduct by English and American societies, for example) could not enter into his mind. Such freedom, if explained to him, he would probably consider as a condition morally comparable to that of birds and beasts. Among ourselves, the social regulations for ordinary people chiefly settle what must *not* be done. But what one must not do in Japan—though representing a very wide range of prohibition — means much less than half of the common obligation : what one must do, is still more necessary to learn. . . . Let us briefly consider the restraints which custom places upon the liberty of the individual.

First of all, be it observed that the communal will reinforces the will of the household, — compels the observance of filial piety. Even the conduct of a boy, who has passed the age of childhood, is regulated not only by the family, but by the public. He must obey the household ; and he must also obey public opinion in regard to his domestic relations. Any marked act of disrespect, inconsistent with filial piety, would be judged and rebuked by all. When old enough to begin work or study, a lad's daily conduct is observed and criticised; and at the age when the household law first tightens about him, he also commences to feel the pressure of common opinion. On coming of age, he has to marry; and the idea of permitting him to choose a wife for himself is quite out of the question: he is expected to accept the companion selected for him. But should reasons be found for humouring him in the event of an irresistible aversion, then he must wait until another choice has been made by the family. The community would not tolerate insubordination in such matters: one example of filial revolt would constitute too dangerous a precedent. When the young man at last becomes the head of a household, and responsible for the conduct of its members, he is still constrained by public sentiment to accept advice in his direction of domestic affairs. He is not free to follow his own judgment, in certain contingencies. For example, he is bound by custom to furnish help to relatives; and he is obliged to accept arbitration in the event of trouble with them. He is not permitted to think of his own wife and children only, — such conduct would be deemed intolerably selfish: he must be able to act, to outward seeming at least, as if uninfluenced by paternal or marital affection in his public conduct. Even supposing that, later in life, he should be

appointed to the position of village or district headman, his right of action and judgment would be under
just as much restriction as before. Indeed, the
range of his personal freedom actually decreases
in proportion to his ascent in the social scale.
Nominally he may rule as headman : practically his
authority is only lent to him by the commune,
and it will remain to him just so long as the commune pleases. For he is elected to enforce the public will, not to impose his own, — to serve the
common interests, not to serve his own, — to maintain and confirm custom, not to break with it.
Thus, though appointed chief, he is only the public servant, and the least free man in his native place.

Various documents translated and published by
Professor Wigmore, in his " Notes on Land Tenure
and Local Institutions in Old Japan," give a startling idea of the minute regulation of communal life
in country-districts during the period of the Toku-
jawa Shōguns. Much of the regulation was certainly
imposed by higher authority ; but it is likely that
a considerable portion of the rules represented old
local custom. Such documents were called *Kumi-chō*
or "*Kumi* [1]-enactments ": they established the rules

[1] Down to the close of the feudal period, the mass of the population throughout
the country, in the great cities as well as in the villages, was administratively ordered
by groups of families, or rather of households, called *Kumi*, or " companies." The
general number of households in a *Kumi* was five ; but there were in some provinces
Kumi consisting of six, and of ten, households. The heads of the households
composing a *Kumi* elected one of their number as chief, — who became the respon-

of conduct to be observed by all the members of a village-community, and their social interest is very great.   By personal inquiry I have learned that in various parts oɪ the country, rules much like those recorded in the *Kumi-chō*, are still enforced by village custom.   I select a few examples from Professor Wigmore's translation : —

" If there be any of our number who are unkind to parents, or neglectful or disobedient, we will not conceal it or condone it, but will report it. . . ."

" We shall require children to respect their parents, servants to obey their masters, husbands and wives and brothers and sisters to live together in harmony, and the younger people to revere and to cherish their elders. . . . Each *kumi* [group of five households] shall carefully watch over the conduct of its members, so as to prevent wrong-doing."

" If any member of a *kumi*, whether farmer, merchant, or artizan, is lazy, and does not attend properly to his business, the *ban-gashira* [chief officer] will advise him, warn him, and lead him into better ways.   If the person does not listen to this advice, and becomes angry and obstinate, he is to be reported to the *toshiyori* [village elder]. . . ."

" When men who are quarrelsome and who like to

sible representative of all the members of the *Kumi*.   The origin and history of the *Kumi*-system is obscure : a similar system exists in China and in Korea.   (Professor Wigmore's reasons for doubting that the Japanese *Kumi*-system had a military origin, appear to be cogent.)   Certainly the system greatly facilitated administration.   To superior authority the *Kumi* was responsible, not the single household.

indulge in late hours away from home will not listen to admonition, we will report them. If any other *kumi* neglects to do this, it will be part of our duty to do it for them. . . ."

" All those who quarrel with their relatives, and refuse to listen to their good advice, or disobey their parents, or are unkind to their fellow-villagers, shall be reported [to the village officers]. . . ."

"Dancing, wrestling, and other public shows shall be forbidden. Singing and dancing-girls and prostitutes shall not be allowed to remain a single night in the *mura* [village]."

" Quarrels among the people shall be forbidden. In case of dispute the matter shall be reported. If this is not done, all parties shall be indiscriminately punished. . . ."

" Speaking disgraceful things of another man, or publicly posting him as a bad man, even if he is so, is forbidden."

" Filial piety and faithful service to a master should be a matter of course; but when there is any one who is especially faithful and diligent in these things, we promise to report him . . . for recommendation to the government. . . ."

" As members of a *kumi* we will cultivate friendly feeling even more than with our relatives, and will promote each other's happiness, as well as share each other's griefs. If there is an unprincipled or lawless person in a *kumi*, we will all share the responsibility for him." [1]

[1] "Notes on Land Tenure and Local Institutions in Old Japan " (*Transactions Asiatic Society of Japan*, Vol. XIX, Part I). I have chosen the quotations from different *kumi-cho*, and arranged them illustratively.

The above are samples of the moral regulations only : there were even more minute regulations about other duties, — for instance : —

" When a fire occurs, the people shall immediately hasten to the spot, each bringing a bucketful of water, and shall endeavour, under direction of the officers, to put the fire out. . . . Those who absent themselves shall be deemed culpable.

" When a stranger comes to reside here, enquiries shall be made as to the *mura* whence he came, and a surety shall be furnished by him. . . . No traveller shall lodge, even for a single night, in a house other than a public inn.

" News of robberies and night attacks shall be given by the ringing of bells or otherwise; and all who hear shall join in pursuit, until the offender is taken. Any one wilfully refraining, shall, on investigation, be punished."

From these same *Kumi-chō*, it appears that no one could leave his village even for a single night, without permission, — or take service elsewhere, or marry in another province, or settle in another place. Punishments were severe, — a terrible flogging being the common mode of chastisement by the higher authority. . . . To-day, there are no such punishments ; and, legally, a man can go where he pleases. But as a matter of fact he can nowhere do as he pleases ; for individual liberty is still largely restricted by the survival of communal sentiment and old-fashioned custom. In any country community it would be unwise to proclaim such a doctrine as that

a man has the right to employ his leisure and his
means as he may think proper. No man's time or
money or effort can be considered exclusively his
own, — nor even the body that his ghost inhabits.
His right to live in the community rests solely upon
his willingness to serve the community; and whoever may need his help or sympathy has the privilege of demanding it. That "a man's house is his
castle" cannot be asserted in Japan — except in the
case of some high potentate. No ordinary person
can shut his door to lock out the rest of the world.
Everybody's house must be open to visitors: to
close its gates by day would be regarded as an insult
to the community, — sickness affording no excuse.
Only persons in very great authority have the right
of making themselves inaccessible. And to displease
the community in which one lives, — especially if
the community be a rural one, — is a serious matter.
When a community is displeased, it acts as an individual. It may consist of five hundred, a thousand, or several thousand persons; but the thinking
of all is the thinking of one. By a single serious
mistake a man may find himself suddenly placed in
solitary opposition to the common will, — isolated,
and most effectively ostracized. The silence and
the softness of the hostility only render it all the
more alarming. This is the ordinary form of punishment for a grave offence against custom: violence
is rare, and when resorted to is intended (except in

some extraordinary cases presently to be noticed) as
a mere correction, the punishment of a blunder.   In
certain rough communities, blunders endangering
life are immediately punished by physical chastisement, — not in anger, but on traditional principle.
Once I witnessed at a fishing-settlement, a chastisement of this kind.   Men were killing tunny in the
surf; the work was bloody and dangerous; and in
the midst of the excitement, one of the fishermen
struck his killing-spike into the head of a boy.
Everybody knew that it was a pure accident; but
accidents involving danger to life are rudely dealt
with, and this blunderer was instantly knocked
senseless by the men nearest him, — then dragged out
of the surf and flung down on the sand to recover
himself as best he might.   No word was said about
the matter; and the killing went on as before.   Young
fishermen, I am told, are roughly handled by their
fellows on board a ship, in the case of any error
involving risk to the vessel.   But, as I have already
observed, only stupidity is punished in this fashion;
and ostracism is much more dreaded than violence.
There is, indeed, only one yet heavier punishment
than ostracism — namely, banishment, either for a
term of years or for life.

Banishment must in old feudal times have been
a very serious penalty; it is a serious penalty even
to-day, under the new order of things.   In former
years the man expelled from his native place by the

communal will — cast out from his home, his clan, his occupation — found himself face to face with misery absolute. In another community there would be no place for him, unless he happened to have relatives there; and these would be obliged to consult with the local authorities, and also with the officials of the fugitive's native place, before venturing to harbour him. No stranger was suffered to settle in another district than his own without official permission. Old documents are extant which record the punishments inflicted upon households for having given shelter to a stranger under pretence of relationship. A banished man was homeless and friendless. He might be a skilled craftsman; but the right to exercise his craft depended upon the consent of the guild representing that craft in the place to which he might go; and banished men were not received by the guilds. He might try to become a servant; but the commune in which he sought refuge would question the right of any master to employ a fugitive and a stranger. His religious connexions could not serve him in the least: the code of communal life was decided not by Buddhist, but by Shintō ethics. Since the gods of his birthplace had cast him out, and the gods of any other locality had nothing to do with his original cult, there was no religious help for him. Besides, the mere fact of his being a refugee was itself proof that he must have offended against his own cult.

In any event no stranger could look for sympathy among strangers. Even now to take a wife from another province is condemned by local opinion (it was forbidden in feudal times): one is still expected to live, work, and marry in the place where one has been born, — though, in certain cases, and with the public approval of one's own people, adoption into another community is tolerated. Under the feudal system there was incomparably less likelihood of sympathy for the stranger; and banishment signified hunger, solitude, and privation unspeakable. For be it remembered that the legal existence of the individual, at that period, ceased entirely outside of his relation to the family and to the commune. Everybody lived and worked for some household; every household for some clan; outside of the household, and the related aggregate of households, there was no life to be lived — except the life of criminals, beggars, and pariahs. Save with official permission, one could not even become a Buddhist monk. The very outcasts — such as the Eta classes — formed self-governing communities, with traditions of their own, and would not voluntarily accept strangers. So the banished man was most often doomed to become a *hinin*, — one of that wretched class of wandering pariahs who were officially termed " not-men," and lived by beggary, or by the exercise of some vulgar profession, such as that of ambulant musician or mountebank. In more ancient days a banished man could have sold himself into slavery ; but even this poor privilege seems to have been withdrawn during the Tokugawa era.

We can scarcely imagine to-day the conditions of such banishment : to find a Western parallel we must go back to ancient Greek and Roman times long preceding the Empire. Banishment then signified religious excommunication, and practically expulsion from all civilized society, — since there yet existed no idea of human brotherhood, no conception of any claim upon kindness except the claim of kinship. The stranger was everywhere the enemy. Now in Japan, as in the Greek city of old time, the religion of the tutelar god has always been the religion of a group only, the cult of a community : it never became even the religion of a province. The higher cults, on the other hand, did not concern themselves with the individual : his religion was only of the household and of the village or district ; the cults of other households and districts were entirely distinct ; one could belong to them only by adoption, and strangers, as a rule, were not adopted. Without a household or a clan-cult, the individual was morally and socially dead ; for other cults and clans excluded him. When cast out by the domestic cult that regulated his private life, and by the local cult that ordered his life in relation to the community, he simply ceased to exist in relation to human society.

How small were the chances in past times for personality to develop and assert itself may be imagined from the foregoing facts. The individual was completely and pitilessly sacrificed to the community. Even now the only safe rule of conduct in a Japanese settlement is to act in all things according to local custom; for the slightest divergence from rule will be observed with disfavour. Privacy does not exist; nothing can be hidden; everybody's vices or virtues are known to everybody else. Unusual behaviour is judged as a departure from the traditional standard of conduct; all oddities are condemned as departures from custom; and tradition and custom still have the force of religious obligations. Indeed, they really *are* religious and obligatory, not only by reason of their origin, but by reason of their relation also to the public cult, which signifies the worship of the past.

It is therefore easy to understand why Shintō never had a written code of morals, and why its greatest scholars have declared that a moral code is unnecessary. In that stage of religious evolution which ancestor-worship represents, there can be no distinction between religion and ethics, nor between ethics and custom. Government and religion are the same; custom and law are identified. The ethics of Shintō were all included in conformity to custom. The traditional rules of the household, the traditional laws of the commune — these were the morals of Shintō: to obey them was religion; to disobey them, impiety. . . . And, after all, the true significance of any religious code, written or unwritten, lies in its expression of social duty, its doctrine of the right and wrong of conduct, its embodiment of a people's moral experience. Really the difference between any modern ideal of conduct, such as the English, and the patriarchal ideal, such as that of the early Greeks or of the Japanese, would be found on examination to consist mainly in the minute extension of the older conception to all details of individual life. Assuredly the religion of Shintō needed no written commandment: it was taught to everybody from childhood by precept and example, and any person of ordinary intelligence could learn it. When a religion is capable of rendering it dangerous for anybody to act outside of rules, the framing of a code would be obviously superfluous. We ourselves have no written code of conduct as regards the higher social life, the exclusive circles of civilized existence, which are not ruled merely by the Ten Commandments. The knowledge of what to do in those zones, and of how to do it, can come only by training, by experience, by observation, and by the intuitive recognition of the reason of things.

And now to return to the question of the authority of the Shintō priest as representative of communal sentiment, — an authority which I believe to have been always very great. . . . Striking proof that the punishments inflicted by a community upon its erring members were originally inflicted in the name of the tutelar god is furnished by the fact that manifestations of communal displeasure still assume, in various country districts, a religious character. I have witnessed such manifestations, and I am assured that they still occur in most of the provinces. But it is in remote country-towns or isolated villages, where traditions have remained almost unchanged, that one can best observe these survivals of antique custom. In such places the conduct of every resident is closely watched and rigidly judged by all the rest. Little, however, is said about misdemeanours of a minor sort until the time of the great local Shintō festival, — the annual festival of the tutelar god. It is then that the community gives its warnings or inflicts its penalties : this at least in the case of conduct offensive to local ethics. The god, on the occasion of this festival, is supposed to visit the dwellings of his Ujiko ; and his portable shrine, — a weighty structure borne by thirty or forty men, — is carried through the principal streets. The bearers are supposed to act according to the will of the god, — to go whithersoever his divine spirit directs them. . . . I may describe the incidents of the procession as I saw it in a seacoast village, not once, but several times.

Before the procession a band of young men advance, leaping and wildly dancing in circles : these young men clear the way ; and it is unsafe to pass near them, for they whirl about as if moved by frenzy. . . . When I first saw such a band of dancers, I could imagine myself watching some old Dionysiac revel ; — their furious gyrations certainly realized Greek accounts of the antique sacred frenzy. There were, indeed, no Greek heads ; but the bronzed lithe figures, naked save for loin-cloth and sandals, and most sculpturesquely muscled, might well have inspired some vase-design of dancing fauns. After these god-possessed dancers — whose passage swept the streets clear, scattering the crowd to right and left — came the virgin priestess, white-robed and veiled, riding upon a horse, and followed by several mounted priests in white garments and high black caps of ceremony. Behind them advanced the ponderous shrine, swaying above the heads of its bearers like a junk in a storm. Scores of brawny arms were pushing it to the right ; other scores were pushing it to the left : behind and before, also, there was furious pulling and pushing ; and the roar of voices uttering invocations made it impossible to hear anything else. By immemorial custom the upper stories of all the dwellings had been tightly closed : woe to the Peeping Tom who should be detected, on such a day, in the impious act of *looking down upon the god !* . . .

Now the shrine-bearers, as I have said, are supposed to be moved by the spirit of the god — (probably by his Rough Spirit; for the Shintō god is multiple); and all this pushing and pulling and swaying signifies only the deity's inspection of the dwellings on either hand. He is looking about to see whether the hearts of his worshippers are pure, and is deciding whether it will be necessary to give a warning, or to inflict a penalty. His bearers will carry him whithersoever he chooses to go — through solid walls if necessary. If the shrine strike against any house, — even against an awning only, — that is a sign that the god is not pleased with the dwellers in that house. If the shrine breaks part of the house, that is a serious warning. But it may happen that the god wills to enter a house, — breaking his way. Then woe to the inmates, unless they flee at once through the back-door; and the wild procession, thundering in, will wreck and rend and smash and splinter everything on the premises before the god consents to proceed upon his round.

Upon enquiring into the reasons of two wreckings of which I witnessed the results, I learned enough to assure me that from the communal point of view, both aggressions were morally justifiable. In one case a fraud had been practised; in the other, help had been refused to the family of a drowned resident. Thus one offence had been legal; the other only moral. A country commu-

nity will not hand over its delinquents to the police
except in case of incendiarism, murder, theft, or
other serious crime. It has a horror of law, and
never invokes it when the matter can be settled by
any other means. This was the rule also in ancient
times, and the feudal government encouraged its
maintenance. But when the tutelar deity has been
displeased, *he* insists upon the punishment or disgrace of the offender ; and the offender's entire
family, as by feudal custom, is held responsible.
The victim can invoke the new law, if he dares, and
bring the wreckers of his home into court, and
recover damages, for the modern police-courts are
not ruled by Shintō. But only a very rash man
will invoke the new law against the communal judgment, for that action in itself would be condemned
as a gross breach of custom. The community is
always ready, through its council, to do justice in
cases where innocence can be proved. But if a man
really guilty of the faults charged to his account
should try to avenge himself by appeal to a non-
religious law, then it were well for him to remove
himself and his family, as soon as possible thereafter, to some far-away place.

We have seen that, in Old Japan, the life of the
individual was under two kinds of religious control.
All his acts were regulated according to the traditions either of the domestic or of the communal

cult; and these conditions probably began with the establishment of a settled civilization. We have also seen that the communal religion took upon itself to enforce the observance of the household religion. The fact will not seem strange if we remember that the underlying idea in either cult was the same, — the idea that the welfare of the living depended upon the welfare of the dead. Neglect of the household rite would provoke, it was believed, the malevolence of the spirits; and their malevolence might bring about some public misfortune. The ghosts of the ancestors controlled nature; — fire and flood, pestilence and famine were at their disposal as means of vengeance. One act of impiety in a village might, therefore, bring about misfortune to all. And the community considered itself responsible to the dead for the maintenance of filial piety in every home.

Developments of Shintō

THE teaching of Herbert Spencer that the greater gods of a people — those figuring in popular imagination as creators, or as particularly directing certain elemental forces — represent a later development of ancestor-worship, is generally accepted to-day. Ancestral ghosts, considered as more or less alike in the time when primitive society had not yet developed class distinctions of any important character, subsequently become differentiated, as the society itself differentiates, into greater and lesser. Eventually the worship of some one ancestral spirit, or group of spirits, overshadows that of all the rest ; and a supreme deity, or group of supreme deities, becomes evolved. But the differentiations of the ancestor-cult must be understood to proceed in a great variety of directions. Particular ancestors of families engaged in hereditary occupations may develop into tutelar deities presiding over those occupations — patron gods of crafts and guilds. Out of other ancestral cults, through various processes of mental association, may be evolved the worship of deities of strength, of health, of long life, of particular products, of particular localities.

When more light shall have been thrown upon the question of Japanese origins, it will probably be found that many of the lesser tutelar or patron gods now worshipped in the country were originally the gods of Chinese or Korean craftsmen; but I think that Japanese mythology, as a whole, will prove to offer few important exceptions to the evolutional law. Indeed, Shintō presents us with a mythological hierarchy of which the development can be satisfactorily explained by that law alone.

Besides the Ujigami, there are myriads of superior and of inferior deities. There are the primal deities, of whom only the names are mentioned, — apparitions of the period of chaos; and there are the gods of creation, who gave shape to the land. There are the gods of earth and sky, and the gods of the sun and moon. Also there are gods, beyond counting, supposed to preside over all things good or evil in human life, — birth and marriage and death, riches and poverty, strength and disease. . . . It can scarcely be supposed that all this mythology was developed out of the old ancestor-cult in Japan itself: more probably its evolution began on the Asiatic continent. But the evolution of the national cult — that form of Shintō which became the state religion — seems to have been Japanese, in the strict meaning of the word. This cult is the worship of the gods from whom the emperors claim descent, — the worship of the "imperial ancestors."

It appears that the early emperors of Japan — the "heavenly sovereigns," as they are called in the old records — were not emperors at all in the true meaning of the term, and did not even exercise universal authority. They were only the chiefs of the most powerful clan, or Uji, and their special ancestor-cult had probably in that time no dominant influence. But eventually, when the chiefs of this great clan really became supreme rulers of the land, their clan-cult spread everywhere, and overshadowed, without abolishing, all the other cults. Then arose the national mythology.

We therefore see that the course of Japanese ancestor-worship, like that of Aryan ancestor-worship, exhibits those three successive stages of development before mentioned. It may be assumed that on coming from the continent to their present island-home, the race brought with them a rude form of ancestor-worship, consisting of little more than rites and sacrifices performed at the graves of the dead. When the land had been portioned out among the various clans, each of which had its own ancestor-cult, all the people of the district belonging to any particular clan would eventually adopt the religion of the clan ancestor; and thus arose the thousand cults of the Ujigami. Still later, the special cult of the most powerful clan developed into a national religion, — the worship of the goddess of the sun, from whom the supreme ruler claimed descent. Then, under Chinese influence, the domestic form of ancestor-worship was established in lieu of the primitive family-cult: thereafter offerings and prayers were made regularly in the home, where the ancestral tablets represented the tombs of the family dead. But offerings were still made, on special occasions, at the graves; and the three Shintō forms of the cult, together with later forms of Buddhist introduction, continued to exist; and they rule the life of the nation to-day.

It was the cult of the supreme ruler that first gave to the people a written account of traditional beliefs. The mythology of the reigning house furnished the scriptures of Shintō, and established ideas linking together all the existing forms of ancestor-worship. All Shintō traditions were by these writings blended into one mythological history, — explained upon the basis of one legend. The whole mythology is contained in two books, of which English translations have been made. The oldest is entitled *Ko-ji-ki*, or "Records of Ancient Matters"; and it is supposed to have been compiled in the year 712 A.D. The other and much larger work is called *Nihongi*, "Chronicles of Nihon [Japan]," and dates from about 720 A.D. Both works profess to be histories; but a large portion of them is mythological, and either begins with a story of creation.

They were compiled, mostly, from oral tradition we
are told, by imperial order. It is said that a yet
earlier work, dating from the seventh century, may
have been drawn upon; but this has been lost. No
great antiquity can, therefore, be claimed for the
texts as they stand; but they contain traditions
which must be very much older, — possibly thousands of years older. The *Ko-ji-ki* is said to have
been written from the dictation of an old man of
marvellous memory; and the Shintō theologian
Hirata would have us believe that traditions thus
preserved are especially trustworthy. " It is probable," he wrote, " that those ancient traditions, preserved for us by exercise of memory, have for that
very reason come down to us in greater detail than
if they had been recorded in documents. Besides,
men must have had much stronger memories in the
days before they acquired the habit of trusting to
written characters for facts which they wished to
remember, — as is shown at the present time in the
case of the illiterate, who have to depend on memory
alone." We must smile at Hirata's good faith in
the changelessness of oral tradition; but I believe
that folk-lorists would discover in the character of
the older myths, intrinsic evidence of immense antiquity. Chinese influence is discernible in both
works; yet certain parts have a particular quality
not to be found, I imagine, in anything Chinese, —
a primeval artlessness, a weirdness, and a strangeness

having nothing in common with other mythical literature. For example, we have, in the story of Izanagi, the world-maker, visiting the shades to recall his dead spouse, a myth that seems to be purely Japanese. The archaic naïveté of the recital must impress anybody who studies the literal translation. I shall present only the substance of the legend, which has been recorded in a number of different versions : [1] —

When the time came for the Fire-god, Kagu-Tsuchi, to be born, his mother, Izanami-no-Mikoto, was burnt, and suffered change, and departed. Then Izanagi-no-Mikoto was wroth and said, " Oh ! that I should have given my loved younger sister in exchange for a single child ! " He crawled at her head and he crawled at her feet, weeping and lamenting ; and the tears which he shed fell down and became a deity. . . . Thereafter Izanagi-no-Mikoto went after Izanami-no-Mikoto into the Land of Yomi, the world of the dead. Then Izanami-no-Mikoto, appearing still as she was when alive, lifted the curtain of the palace (of the dead), and came forth to meet him ; and they talked together. And Izanagi-no-Mikoto said to her : " I have come because I sorrowed for thee, my lovely younger sister. O my lovely younger sister, the lands that I and thou were making together are not

[1] See for these different versions Aston's translation of the *Nihongi*, Vol I.

yet finished; therefore come back!" Then Izanami-no-Mikoto made answer, saying, " My august
lord and husband, lamentable it is that thou didst
not come sooner, — for now I have eaten of the
cooking-range of Yomi.   Nevertheless, as I am
thus delightfully honoured by thine entry here, my
lovely elder brother, I wish to return with thee to
the living world.   Now I go to discuss the matter
with the gods of Yomi.   Wait thou here, and look
not upon me."   So having spoken, she went back;
and Izanagi waited for her.   But she tarried so long
within that he became impatient.   Then, taking
the wooden comb that he wore in the left bunch of
his hair, he broke off a tooth from one end of the
comb and lighted it, and went in to look for Izanami-no-Mikoto.   But he saw her lying swollen and
festering among worms; and eight kinds of Thunder-Gods sat upon her. . . .   And Izanagi, being
overawed by that sight, would have fled away; but
Izanami rose up, crying: "Thou hast put me to
shame!   Why didst thou not observe that which I
charged thee? . . .   Thou hast seen my nakedness;
now I will see thine!"   And she bade the Ugly
Females of Yomi to follow after him, and slay him;
and the eight Thunders also pursued him, and
Izanami herself pursued him. . . .   Then Izanagi-
no-Mikoto drew his sword, and flourished it behind
him as he ran.   But they followed close upon him.
He took off his black headdress and flung it down;

and it became changed into grapes; and while the Ugly Ones were eating the grapes, he gained upon them. But they followed quickly; and he then took his comb and cast it down, and it became changed into bamboo sprouts; and while the Ugly Ones were devouring the sprouts, he fled on until he reached the mouth of Yomi. Then taking a rock which it would have required the strength of a thousand men to lift, he blocked therewith the entrance as Izanami came up. And standing behind the rock, he began to pronounce the words of divorce. Then, from the other side of the rock, Izanami cried out to him, " My dear lord and master, if thou dost so, in one day will I strangle to death a thousand of thy people!" And Izanagi-no-Mikoto answered her, saying, " My beloved younger sister, if thou dost so, I will cause in one day to be born fifteen hundred. . . ." But the deity Kukuri-himé-no-Kami then came, and spake to Izanami some word which she seemed to approve, and thereafter she vanished away. . . .

The strange mingling of pathos with nightmare-terror in this myth, of which I have not ventured to present all the startling naivete, sufficiently proves its primitive character. It is a dream that some one really dreamed, — one of those bad dreams in which the figure of a person beloved becomes horribly transformed; and it has a particular interest as expressing that fear of death and of the dead informing all primitive ancestor-worship. The whole pathos and weirdness of the myth, the vague monstrosity of the fancies, the formal use of terms of endearment in the moment of uttermost loathing and fear, — all impress one as unmistakably Japanese. Several other myths scarcely less remarkable are to be found in the *Ko-ji-ki* and *Nihongi;* but they are mingled with legends of so light and graceful a kind that it is scarcely possible to believe these latter to have been imagined by the same race. The story of the magical jewels and the visit to the sea-god's palace, for example, in the second book of the *Nihongi,* sounds oddly like an Indian fairy-tale; and it is not unlikely that the *Ko-ji-ki* and *Nihongi* both contain myths derived from various alien sources. At all events their mythical chapters present us with some curious problems which yet remain unsolved. Otherwise the books are dull reading, in spite of the light which they shed upon ancient customs and beliefs; and, generally speaking, Japanese mythology is unattractive. But to dwell here upon the mythology, at any length, is unnecessary; for its relation to Shintō can be summed up in the space of a single brief paragraph: —

In the beginning neither force nor form was manifest; and the world was a shapeless mass that floated

like a jelly-fish upon water. Then, in some way —
we are not told how — earth and heaven became
separated; dim gods appeared and disappeared;
and at last there came into existence a male and a
female deity, who gave birth and shape to things.
By this pair, Izanagi and Izanami, were produced
the islands of Japan, and the generations of the
gods, and the deities of the Sun and Moon. The
descendants of these creating deities, and of the gods
whom they brought into being, were the eight thousand (or eighty thousand) myriads of gods worshipped by Shintō. Some went to dwell in the
blue Plain of High Heaven; others remained on
earth and became the ancestors of the Japanese
race.

Such is the mythology of the *Ko-ji-ki* and the
Nihongi, stated in the briefest possible way. At
first it appears that there were two classes of gods
recognized: Celestial and Terrestrial; and the old
Shintō rituals (*norito*) maintain this distinction. But
it is a curious fact that the celestial gods of this
mythology do not represent celestial forces; and
that the gods who are really identified with celestial
phenomena are classed as terrestrial gods, — having
been born or "produced" upon earth. The Sun
and Moon, for example, are said to have been born
in Japan, — though afterwards placed in heaven;
the Sun-goddess, Ama-terasu-no-oho-Kami, having
been produced from the left eye of Izanagi, and the

Moon-god, Tsuki-yomi-no-Mikoto, having been produced from the right eye of Izanagi when, after his visit to the under-world, he washed himself at the mouth of a river in the island of Tsukushi. The Shintō scholars of the eighteenth and nineteenth centuries established some order in this chaos of fancies by denying all distinction between the Celestial and Terrestrial gods, except as regarded the accident of birth. They also denied the old distinction between the so-called Age of the Gods (*Kami-yo*), and the subsequent period of the Emperors. It was true, they said, that the early rulers of Japan were gods; but so were also the later rulers. The whole Imperial line, the "Sun's Succession," represented one unbroken descent from the Goddess of the Sun. Hirata wrote: "There exists no hard and fast line between the Age of the Gods and the present age · and there exists no justification whatever for drawing one, as the *Nihongi* does." Of course this position involved the doctrine of a divine descent for the whole race,—inasmuch as, according to the old mythology, the first Japanese were all descendants of gods,—and that doctrine Hirata boldly accepted. All the Japanese, he averred, were of divine origin, and for that reason superior to the people of all other countries. He even held that their divine descent could be proved without difficulty. These are his words: "The descendants of the gods who accompanied Ninigi-no-Mikoto [*grandson of the Sun-god-*

dess, and supposed founder of the Imperial house,] — as
well as the offspring of the successive Mikados, who
entered the ranks of the subjects of the Mikados,
with the names of Taira, Minamoto, and so forth, —
have gradually increased and multiplied.   Although
numbers of Japanese cannot state with certainty from
what gods they are descended, all of them have tribal
names (*kabanê*), which were originally bestowed on
them by the Mikados ; and those who make it their
province to study genealogies can tell from a man's
ordinary surname, who his remotest ancestor must
have been."   All the Japanese were gods in this
sense ; and their country was properly called the
Land of the Gods, — *Shinkoku* or *Kami-no-kuni*.
Are we to understand Hirata literally ?   I think
so — but we must remember that there existed in
feudal times large classes of people, outside of the
classes officially recognized as forming the nation,
who were not counted as Japanese, nor even as
human beings :   these were pariahs, and reckoned
as little better than animals.   Hirata probably
referred to the four great classes only — samurai,
farmers, artizans, and merchants.   But even in that
case what are we to think of his ascription of divinity to the race, in view of the moral and physical
feebleness of human nature?   The moral side of the
question is answered by the Shintō theory of evil
deities, " gods of crookedness," who were alleged to
have " originated from the impurities contracted by

Izanagi during his visit to the under-world." As
for the physical weakness of men, that is explained
by a legend of Ninigi-no-Mikoto, divine founder
of the imperial house. The Goddess of Long Life,
Iha-naga-himé (Rock-long-princess), was sent to him
for wife; but he rejected her because of her ugli-
ness; and that unwise proceeding brought about
"the present shortness of the lives of men." Most
mythologies ascribe vast duration to the lives of early
patriarchs or rulers: the farther we go back into
mythological history, the longer-lived are the sovereigns. To this general rule Japanese mythology presents no exception. The son of Ninigi-no-Mikoto is
said to have lived five hundred and eighty years at
his palace of Takachiho; but that, remarks Hirata,
"was a short life compared with the lives of those
who lived before him." Thereafter men's bodies
declined in force; life gradually became shorter and
shorter; yet in spite of all degeneration the Japanese still show traces of their divine origin. After
death they enter into a higher divine condition,
without, however, abandoning this world. . . . Such
were Hirata's views. Accepting the Shintō theory
of origins, this ascription of divinity to human nature
proves less inconsistent than it appears at first sight;
and the modern Shintōist may discover a germ of
scientific truth in the doctrine which traces back the
beginnings of life to the Sun.

More than any other Japanese writer, Hirata has
enabled us to understand the hierarchy of Shintō
mythology, — corresponding closely, as we might
have expected, to the ancient ordination of Japanese
society.   In the lowermost ranks are the spirits of
common people, worshipped only at the household
shrine or at graves.   Above these are the gentile
gods or Ujigami, — ghosts of old rulers now worshipped as tutelar gods.   All Ujigami, Hirata tells
us, are under the control of the Great God of Izumo,
— Oho-kuni-nushi-no-Kami, — and, " acting as his
agents, they rule the fortunes of human beings before their birth, during their life, and after their
death."   This means that the ordinary ghosts obey,
in the world invisible, the commands of the clan-
gods or tutelar deities ; that the conditions of communal worship during life continue after death.
The following extract from Hirata will be found of
interest, — not only as showing the supposed relation of the individual to the Ujigami, but also as
suggesting how the act of abandoning one's birthplace was formerly judged by common opinion : —

" When a person removes his residence, his original
Ujigami has to make arrangements with the Ujigami of the
place whither he transfers his abode.   On such occasions
it is proper to take leave of the old god, and to pay a visit
to the temple of the new god as soon as possible after
coming within his jurisdiction.   The apparent reasons
which a man imagines to have induced him to change his

abode may be many ; *but the real reasons cannot be otherwise than that either he has offended his Ujigami, and is therefore expelled, or that the Ujigami of another place has negotiated his transfer. . . ."* [1]

It would thus appear that every person was supposed to be the subject, servant, or retainer of some Ujigami, both during life and after death.

There were, of course, various grades of these clan-gods, just as there were various grades of living rulers, lords of the soil. Above ordinary Ujigami ranked the deities worshipped in the chief Shintō temples of the various provinces, which temples were termed *Ichi-no-miya*, or temples of the first grade. These deities appear to have been in many cases spirits of princes or greater daimyō, formerly ruling extensive districts ; but all were not of this category. Among them were deities of elements or elemental forces, — Wind, Fire, and Sea, — deities also of longevity, of destiny, and of harvests, — clan-gods, perhaps, originally, though their real history had been long forgotten. But above all other Shintō divinities ranked the gods of the Imperial Cult, — the supposed ancestors of the Mikados.

Of the higher forms of Shintō worship, that of the imperial ancestors proper is the most important, being the State cult ; but it is not the oldest. There are two supreme cults : that of the Sun-goddess, represented by the famous shrines of Ise ; and the Izumo cult, represented by the great temple of Kitzuki. This Izumo temple is the centre of the more ancient cult. It is dedicated to Oho-kuni-nushi-no-Kami, first ruler of the Province of the Gods, and offspring of the brother of the Sun-goddess. Dispossessed of his realm in favour of the founder of the imperial dynasty, Oho-kuni-nushi-no-Kami became the ruler of the Unseen World, — that is to say the World of Ghosts. Unto his shadowy dominion the spirits of all men proceed after death ; and he rules over all of the Ujigami. We may therefore term him the Emperor of the Dead. "You cannot hope," Hirata says, "to live more than a hundred years, under the most favourable circumstances ; but as you will go to the Unseen Realm of Oho-kuni-nushi-no-Kami after death, and be subject to him, learn betimes to bow down before him." . . . That weird fancy expressed in the wonderful fragment by Coleridge, "The Wanderings of Cain," would therefore seem to have actually formed an article of ancient Shintō faith : "*The Lord is God of the living only: the dead have another God.*" . . .

The God of the Living in Old Japan was, of course, the Mikado, — the deity incarnate, *Arahitogami,* — and his palace was the national sanctuary, the Holy of Holies. Within the precincts of that palace was the *Kashiko-Dokoro* (" Place of Awe "), the private shrine of the Imperial Ancestors, where only the court could worship, — the public form of the same cult being maintained .at Isé. But the Imperial House worshipped also by deputy (and still so worships) both at Kitzuki and Isé, and likewise at various other great sanctuaries. Formerly a great number of temples were maintained, or partly maintained, from the imperial revenues. All Shintō temples of importance used to be classed as greater and lesser shrines. There were 304 of the first rank, and 2828 of the second rank. But multitudes of temples were not included in this official classification, and depended upon local support. The recorded total of Shintō shrines to-day is upwards of 195,000.

We have thus — without counting the great Izumo cult of Oho-kuni-nushi-no-Kami — four classes of ancestor-worship : the domestic religion, the religion of the Ujigami, the worship at the chief shrines [*Ichi-no-miya*] of the several provinces, and the national cult at Isé. All these cults are now linked together by tradition ; and the devout Shintōist worships the divinit:es of all, collectively, in his daily morning prayer. Occasionally he visits the chief shrine of his province ; and he makes a pilgrimage to Isé if he can. Every Japanese is expected to visit the shrines of Isé once in his life-

time, or to send thither a deputy. Inhabitants of
remote districts are not all able, of course, to make
the pilgrimage; but there is no village which does
not, at certain intervals, send pilgrims either to
Kitzuki or to Isé on behalf of the community, —
the expense of such representation being defrayed
by local subscription. And, furthermore, every
Japanese can worship the supreme divinities of
Shintō in his own house, where upon a " god-shelf "
(*Kamidana*) are tablets inscribed with the assurance
of their divine protection, — holy charms obtained
from the priests of Isé or of Kitzuki. In the case
of the Isé cult, such tablets are commonly made
from the wood of the holy shrines themselves, which,
according to primal custom, must be rebuilt every
twenty years, — the timber of the demolished structures being then cut into tablets for distribution
throughout the country.

Another development of ancestor-worship — the
cult of gods presiding over crafts and callings —
deserves special study. Unfortunately we are as
yet little informed upon the subject. Anciently this
worship must have been more definitely ordered
and maintained than it is now. Occupations were
hereditary; artizans were grouped into guilds —
perhaps we might even say castes; — and each guild
or caste then probably had its patron-deity. In
some cases the craft-gods may have been ancestors

of Japanese craftsmen; in other cases they were
perhaps of Korean or Chinese origin,—ancestral
gods of immigrant artizans, who brought their cults
with them to Japan. Not much is known about
them. But it is tolerably safe to assume that most,
if not all of the guilds, were at one time religiously
organized, and that apprentices were adopted not
only in a craft, but into a cult. There were corpo-
rations of weavers, potters, carpenters, arrow-makers,
bow-makers, smiths, boat-builders, and other trades-
men; and the past religious organization of these is
suggested by the fact that certain occupations assume
a religious character even to-day. For example, the
carpenter still builds according to Shintō tradition:
he dons a priestly costume at a certain stage of the
work, performs rites, and chants invocations, and
places the new house under the protection of the
gods. But the occupation of the swordsmith was in
old days the most sacred of crafts: he worked in
priestly garb, and practised Shintō rites of purification while engaged in the making of a good blade.
Before his smithy was then suspended the sacred
rope of rice-straw (*shimé-nawa*), which is the oldest
symbol of Shintō: none even of his family might
enter there, or speak to him; and he ate only of
food cooked with holy fire.

The 195,000 shrines of Shintō represent, however, more than clan-cults or guild-cults or national-

cults. . . . Many are dedicated to different spirits
of the same god; for Shintō holds that the spirit
of either a man or a god may divide itself into
several spirits, each with a different character. Such
separated spirits are called waka-mi-tama ("august-
divided-spirits"). Thus the spirit of the Goddess
of Food, Toyo-uké-bimé, separated itself into the
God of Trees, Kukunochi-no-Kami, and into the
Goddess of Grasses, Kayanu-himé-no-Kami. Gods
and men were supposed to have also a Rough
Spirit and a Gentle Spirit; and Hirata remarks that
the Rough Spirit of Oho-kuni-nushi-no-Kami was
worshipped at one temple, and his Gentle Spirit at
another.[1] . . . Also we have to remember that
great numbers of Ujigami temples are dedicated to
the same divinity. These duplications or multiplications are again offset by the fact that in some of
the principal temples a multitude of different deities
are enshrined. Thus the number of Shintō temples
in actual existence affords no indication whatever of
the actual number of gods worshipped, nor of the
variety of their cults. Almost every deity mentioned in the *Ko-ji-ki* or *Nihongi* has a shrine somewhere; and hundreds of others — including many
later apotheoses — have their temples. Numbers
of temples have been dedicated, for example, to

---

[1] Even men had the Rough and the Gentle Spirit; but a god had three distinct
spirits, — the Rough, the Gentle, and the Bestowing, — respectively termed *Ara-
mi-tama*, *Nigi-mi-tama*, ard *Saki-mi-tama*. — [See SATOW's *Revival of Pure
Shintau*.]

historical personages, — to spirits of great ministers, captains, rulers, scholars, heroes, and statesmen. The famous minister of the Empress Jingō, Take-no-uji-no-Sukuné, — who served under six successive sovereigns, and lived to the age of three hundred years, — is now invoked in many a temple as a giver of long life and great wisdom. The spirit of Sugiwara-no-Michizané, once minister to the Emperor Daigō, is worshipped as the god of calligraphy, under the name of Tenjin, or Temmangu : children everywhere offer to him the first examples of their handwriting, and deposit in receptacles, placed before his shrine, their worn-out writing-brushes. The Soga brothers, victims and heroes of a famous twelfth-century tragedy, have become gods to whom people pray for the maintenance of fraternal harmony. Kato Kiyomasa, the determined enemy of Jesuit Christianity, and Hidéyoshi's greatest captain, has been apotheosized both by Buddhism and by Shintō. Iyéyasu is worshipped under the appellation of Tōshōgu. In fact most of the great men of Japanese history have had temples erected to them ; and the spirits of the daimyō were, in former years, regularly worshipped by the subjects of their descendants and successors.

Besides temples to deities presiding over industries and agriculture, — or deities especially invoked by the peasants, such as the goddess of silkworms, the goddess of rice, the gods of wind and weather, — there are to be found in almost every part of the country what I may call propitiatory temples. These latter Shintō shrines have been erected by way of compensation to spirits of persons who suffered great injustice or misfortune. In these cases the worship assumes a very curious character, the worshipper always appealing for protection against the same kind of calamity or trouble as that from which the apotheosized person suffered during life. In Izumo, for example, I found a temple dedicated to the spirit of a woman, once a prince's favourite. She had been driven to suicide by the intrigues of jealous rivals. The story is that she had very beautiful hair; but it was not quite black, and her enemies used to reproach her with its color. Now mothers having children with brownish hair pray to her that the brown may be changed to black; and offerings are made to her of tresses of hair and Tōkyō coloured prints, for it is still remembered that she was fond of such prints. In the same province there is a shrine erected to the spirit of a young wife, who pined away for grief at the absence of her lord. She used to climb a hill to watch for his return, and the shrine was built upon the place where she waited; and wives pray there to her for the safe return of absent husbands. . . . An almost similar kind of propitiatory worship is practised in cemeteries. Public pity seeks to apotheosize those urged to suicide by cruelty, or those executed for offences which, although legally criminal, were inspired by patriotic or other motives commanding sympathy. Before their graves offerings are laid and prayers are murmured. Spirits of unhappy lovers are commonly invoked by young people who suffer from the same cause. . . . And, among other forms of propitiatory worship I must mention the old custom of erecting small shrines to spirits of animals, — chiefly domestic animals, — either in recognition of dumb service rendered and ill-rewarded, or as a compensation for pain unjustly inflicted.

Yet another class of tutelar divinities remains to be noticed, — those who dwell within or about the houses of men. Some are mentioned in the old mythology, and are probably developments of Japanese ancestor-worship; some are of alien origin; some do not appear to have any temples; and some represent little more than what is called Animism. This class of divinities corresponds rather to the Roman *dii genitales* than to the Greek δαίμονες. Suijin-Sama, the God of Wells; Kojin, the God of the Cooking-range (in almost every kitchen there is either a tiny shrine for him, or a written charm bearing his name); the gods of the Cauldron and Saucepan, Kudo-no-Kami and Kobé-no-Kami (anciently called Okitsuhiko and Okitsuhimé); the Master of Ponds, Iké-no-Nushi,

supposed to make apparition in the form of a
serpent; the Goddess of the Rice-pot, O-Kama-
Sama; the Gods of the Latrina, who first taught
men how to fertilize their fields (these are commonly
represented by little figures of paper, having the
forms of a man and a woman, but faceless); the
Gods of Wood and Fire and Metal; the Gods likewise of Gardens, Fields, Scarecrows, Bridges, Hills,
Woods, and Streams; and also the Spirits of Trees
(for Japanese mythology has its dryads): most of
these are undoubtedly of Shintō. On the other
hand, we find the roads under the protection of
Buddhist deities chiefly. I have not been able to
learn anything regarding gods of boundaries, — *ter-
mes*, as the Latins called them; and one sees only
images of the Buddhas at the limits of village territories. But in almost every garden, on the north
side, there is a little Shintō shrine, facing what is
called the *Ki-Mon*, or " Demon-Gate," — that is to
say, the direction from which, according to Chinese
teaching, all evils come; and these little shrines,
dedicated to various Shintō deities, are supposed to
protect the home from evil spirits. The belief in
the Ki-Mon is obviously a Chinese importation.

One may doubt, however, if Chinese influence
alone developed the belief that every part of a
house, — every beam of it, — and every domestic
utensil has its invisible guardian. Considering this
belief, it is not surprising that the building of a

house—unless the house be in foreign style—is still a religious act, and that the functions of a master-builder include those of a priest.

This brings us to the subject of Animism. (I doubt whether any evolutionist of the contemporary school holds to the old-fashioned notion that animism preceded ancestor-worship,—a theory involving the assumption that belief in the spirits of inanimate objects was evolved before the idea of a human ghost had yet been developed.)   In Japan it is now as difficult to draw the line between animistic beliefs and the lowest forms of Shintō, as to establish a demarcation between the vegetable and the animal worlds; but the earliest Shintō literature gives no evidence of such a developed animism as that now existing.   Probably the development was gradual, and largely influenced by Chinese beliefs.   Still, we read in the *Ko-ji-ki* of "evil gods who glittered like fireflies or were disorderly as mayflies," and of "demons who made rocks, and stumps of trees, and the foam of the green waters to speak,"— showing that animistic or fetichistic notions were prevalent to some extent before the period of Chinese influence.   And it is significant that where animism is associated with persistent worship (as in the matter of the reverence paid to strangely shaped stones or trees), the form of the worship is, in most cases, Shintō.   Before such objects there is usually to be seen the model of a Shintō gateway, — *torii.* . . . With the development of animism, under Chinese and Korean influence, the man of Old Japan found himself truly in a world of spirits and demons. They spoke to him in the sound of tides and of cataracts, in the moaning of wind and the whispers of leafage, in the crying of birds, and the trilling of insects, in all the voices of nature. For him all visible motion — whether of waves or grasses or shifting mist or drifting cloud — was ghostly; and the never moving rocks — nay, the very stones by the wayside — were informed with viewless and awful being.

Worship and Purification

WE have seen that, in Old Japan, the world of the living was everywhere ruled by the world of the dead, — that the individual, at every moment of his existence, was under ghostly supervision. In his home he was watched by the spirits of his fathers; without it, he was ruled by the god of his district. All about him, and above him, and beneath him were invisible powers of life and death. In his conception of nature all things were ordered by the dead, — light and darkness, weather and season, winds and tides, mist and rain, growth and decay, sickness and health. The viewless atmosphere was a phantom-sea, an ocean of ghost; the soil that he tilled was pervaded by spirit-essence; the trees were haunted and holy; even the rocks and the stones were infused with conscious life. . . . How might he discharge his duty to the infinite concourse of the invisible?

Few scholars could remember the names of all the greater gods, not to speak of the lesser; and no mortal could have found time to address those greater gods by their respective names in his daily

prayer. The later Shintō teachers proposed to
simplify the duties of the faith by prescribing one
brief daily prayer to the gods in general, and special
prayers to a few gods in particular; and in thus
doing they were most likely confirming a custom
already established by necessity. Hirata wrote:
" As the number of the gods who possess different
functions is very great, it will be convenient to
worship by name the most important only, and
to include the rest in a general petition." He prescribed ten prayers for persons having time to
repeat them, but lightened the duty for busy folk,
— observing: " Persons whose daily affairs are
so multitudinous that they have not time to go
through all the prayers, may content themselves
with adoring (1) the residence of the Emperor, (2)
the domestic god-shelf, — *kamidana*, (3) the spirits
of their ancestors, (4) their local patron-god, —
Ujigami, (5) the deity of their particular calling."
He advised that the following prayer should be
daily repeated before the " god-shelf " : —

" Reverently adoring the great god of the two palaces
of Isé in the first place, — the eight hundred myriads of
celestial gods, — the eight hundred myriads of terrestrial
gods, — the fifteen hundred myriads of gods to whom are
consecrated the great and small temples in all provinces, all
islands, and all places of the Great Land of Eight Islands,
— the fifteen hundred myriads of gods whom they cause to
serve them, and the gods of branch-palaces and branch-

temples, — and Sohodo-no-Kami [1] whom I have invited to the shrine set up on this divine shelf, and to whom I offer praises day by day, — I pray with awe that they will deign to correct the unwilling faults which, heard and seen by them, I have committed; and that, blessing and favouring me according to the powers which they severally wield, they will cause me to follow the divine example, and to perform good works in the Way." [2]

This text is interesting as an example of what Shintō's greatest expounder thought a Shintō prayer should be; and, excepting the reference to So-ho-do-no-Kami, the substance of it is that of the morning prayer still repeated in Japanese households. But the modern prayer is very much shorter. . . . In Izumo, the oldest Shintō province, the customary morning worship offers perhaps the best example of the ancient rules of devotion. Immediately upon rising, the worshipper performs his ablutions; and after having washed his face and rinsed his mouth, he turns to the sun, claps his hands, and with bowed head reverently utters the simple greeting: " Hail to thee this day, August One!" In thus adoring the sun he is also fulfilling his duty as a subject, — paying obeisance to the Imperial Ancestor. . . . The act is performed out of doors, not kneeling, but standing; and the spectacle of this simple worship is impressive. I can now see in memory, —

[1] Sohodo-no-Kami is the god of scarecrows, — protector of the fields.
[2] Translated by Satow.

just as plainly as I saw with my eyes many years ago, off the wild Oki coast, — the naked figure of a young fisherman erect at the prow of his boat, clapping his hands in salutation to the rising sun, whose ruddy glow transformed him into a statue of bronze. Also I retain a vivid memory of pilgrim-figures poised upon the topmost crags of the summit of Fuji, clapping their hands in prayer, with faces to the East. . . . Perhaps ten thousand — twenty thousand — years ago all humanity so worshipped the Lord of Day. . . .

After having saluted the sun, the worshipper returns to his house, to pray before the *Kamidana* and before the tablets of the ancestors. Kneeling, he invokes the great gods of Isé or of Izumo, the gods of the chief temples of his province, the god of his parish-temple also (*Ujigami*), and finally all the myriads of the deities of Shintō. These prayers are not said aloud. The ancestors are thanked for the foundation of the home; the higher deities are invoked for aid and protection. . . . As for the custom of bowing in the direction of the Emperor's palace, I am not able to say to what extent it survives in the remoter districts; but I have often seen the reverence performed. Once, too, I saw reverence done immediately in front of the gates of the palace in Tōkyō by country-folk on a visit to the capital. They knew me, because I had often sojourned in their village; and on reaching Tōkyō

they sought me out, and found me. I took them
to the palace; and before the main entrance they
removed their hats, and bowed, and clapped their
hands, — just as they would have done when salut-
ing the gods or the rising sun, — and this with a
simple and dignified reverence that touched me not
a little.

The duties of morning worship, which include
the placing of offerings before the tablets, are not
the only duties of the domestic cult. In a Shintō
household, where the ancestors and the higher gods
are separately worshipped, the ancestral shrine may
be said to correspond with the Roman *lararium*;
while the " god-shelf," with its *taima* or *o-nusa* (symbols of those higher gods especially revered by the
family), may be compared with the place accorded
by Latin custom to the worship of the Penates.
Both Shintō cults have their particular feast-days;
and, in the case of the ancestor-cult, the feast-days
are occasions of religious assembly, — when the
relatives of the family should gather to celebrate
the domestic rite. . . . The Shintōist must also
take part in the celebration of the festivals of the
Ujigami, and must at least aid in the celebration of
the nine great national holidays related to the national
cult; these nine, out of a total eleven, being occasions of imperial ancestor-worship.

The nature of the public rites varied according to

the rank of the gods. Offerings and prayers were made to all; but the greater deities were worshipped with exceeding ceremony. To-day the offerings usually consist of food and rice-wine, together with symbolic articles representing the costlier gifts of woven stuffs presented by ancient custom. The ceremonies include processions, music, singing, and dancing. At the very small shrines there are few ceremonies, — only offerings of food are presented. But at the great temples there are hierarchies of priests and priestesses (*miko*) — usually daughters of priests; and the ceremonies are elaborate and solemn. It is particularly at the temples of Isé (where, down to the fourteenth century the high-priestess was a daughter of emperors), or at the great temple of Izumo, that the archaic character of the ceremonial can be studied to most advantage. There, in spite of the passage of that huge wave of Buddhism, which for a period almost submerged the more ancient faith, all things remain as they were a score of centuries ago; — Time, in those haunted precincts, would seem to have slept, as in the enchanted palaces of fairy-tale. The mere shapes of the buildings, weird and tall, startle by their unfamiliarity. Within, all is severely plain and pure: there are no images, no ornaments, no symbols visible — except those strange paper-cuttings (*gohei*), suspended to upright rods, which are symbols of offerings and also tokens of the view-

less.   By the number of them in the sanctuary, you
know the number of the deities to whom the place
is consecrate.   There is nothing imposing but the
space, the silence, and the suggestion of the past.
The innermost shrine is veiled : it contains, perhaps,
a mirror of bronze, an ancient sword, or other object enclosed in multiple wrappings : that is all.
For this faith, older than icons, needs no images :
its gods are ghosts ; and the void stillness of its
shrines compels more awe than tangible representation could inspire.   Very strange, to Western eyes
at least, are the rites, the forms of the worship, the
shapes of sacred objects.   Not by any modern
method must the sacred fire be lighted, — the fire
that cooks the food of the gods : it can be kindled
only in the most ancient of ways, with a wooden
fire-drill.   The chief priests are robed in the sacred
colour, — white, — and wear headdresses of a shape
no longer seen elsewhere : high caps of the kind
formerly worn by lords and princes.   Their assist-
ants wear various colours, according to grade ; and
the faces of none are completely shaven ; — some
wear full beards, others the mustache only.   The
actions and attitudes of these hierophants are dignified, yet archaic, in a degree difficult to describe.
Each movement is regulated by tradition ; and to
perform well the functions of a *Kannushi*, a long
disciplinary preparation is necessary.   The office is
hereditary ; the training begins in boyhood ; and

the impassive deportment eventually acquired is really a wonderful thing. Officiating, the Kannushi seems rather a statue than a man, — an image moved by invisible strings; — and, like the gods, he never winks. Not at least observably. . . . Once, during a great Shintō procession, several Japanese friends, and I myself, undertook to watch a young priest on horseback, in order to see how long he could keep from winking; and none of us were able to detect the slightest movement of eyes or eyelids, notwithstanding that the priest's horse became restive during the time that we were watching.

The principal incidents of the festival ceremonies within the great temples are the presentation of the offerings, the repetition of the ritual, and the dancing of the priestesses. Each of these performances retains a special character rigidly fixed by tradition. The food-offerings are served upon archaic vessels of unglazed pottery (red earthenware mostly): boiled rice pressed into cones of the form of a sugar-loaf, various preparations of fish and of edible sea-weed, fruits and fowls, rice-wine presented in jars of immemorial shape. These offerings are carried into the temple upon white wooden trays of curious form, and laid upon white wooden tables of equally curious form; — the faces of the bearers being covered, below the eyes, with sheets of white paper, in order that their breath may not contaminate the food of the gods; and the trays, for like reason, must be borne at arms' length. . . . In ancient times the offerings would seem to have included things much more costly than food, — if we may credit the testimony of what are probably the oldest documents extant in the Japanese tongue, the Shintō rituals, or *norito*.[1]   The following excerpt from Satow's translation of the ritual prayer to the Wind-gods of Tatsuta is interesting, not only as a fine example of the language of the *norito*, but also as indicating the character of the great ceremonies in early ages, and the nature of the offerings: —

" As the great offerings set up for the Youth-god, I set up various sorts of offerings: for Clothes, bright cloth, glittering cloth, soft cloth, and coarse cloth, — and the five kinds of things, a mantlet, a spear, a horse furnished with a saddle; — for the Maiden-god I set up various sorts of offerings — providing Clothes, a golden thread-box, a golden *tatari*, a golden skein-holder, bright cloth, glittering cloth, soft cloth, and coarse cloth, and the five kinds of things, a horse furnished with a saddle; — as to Liquor, I raise high the beer-jars, fill and range-in-a-row the bellies of the beer-jars; soft grain and coarse grain; — as to things which dwell in the hills, things soft of hair and things coarse of hair; — as to things which grow in the great field-plain, sweet herbs and bitter herbs; — as to things which dwell in the blue sea-plain, things broad of fin and things narrow of fin — down to the weeds of the offing and weeds of the

---

[1] Several have been translated by Satow, whose opinion of their antiquity is here cited; and translations have also been made into German.

shore.   And if the sovran gods will take these great offerings which I set up, — piling them up like a range of hills,
— peacefully in their hearts, as peaceful offerings and satisfactory offerings ; and if the sovran gods, deigning not
to visit the things produced by the great People of the
region under heaven with bad winds and rough waters, will
ripen and bless them, — I will at the autumn service set up
the first fruits, raising high the beer-jars, filling and rang-
ing-in-rows the bellies of the beer-jars, — and drawing
them hither in juice and in ear, in many hundred rice-
plants and a thousand rice-plants.   And for this purpose
the princes and councillors and all the functionaries, the
servants of the six farms of the country of Yamato —
even to the males and females of them — have all come
and assembled in the fourth month of this year, and, plung-
ing down the root of the neck cormorant-wise in the presence
of the sovran gods, fulfil their praise as the Sun of to-day
rises in glory." . . .

The offerings are no longer piled up "like a
range of hills," nor do they include "all things
dwelling in the mountains and in the sea " ; but the
imposing ritual remains, and the ceremony is always
impressive.   Not the least interesting part of it is
the sacred dance.   While the gods are supposed to
be partaking of the food and wine set out before
their shrines, the girl-priestesses, robed in crimson
and white, move gracefully to the sound of drums
and flutes, — waving fans, or shaking bunches of tiny
bells as they circle about the sanctuary.   According
to our Western notions, the performance of the

miko could scarcely be called dancing; but it is a graceful spectacle, and very curious, — for every step and attitude is regulated by traditions of unknown antiquity. As for the plaintive music, no Western ear can discern in it anything resembling a real melody; but the gods should find delight in it, because it is certainly performed for them to-day exactly as it used to be performed twenty centuries ago.

I speak of the ceremonies especially as I have witnessed them in Izumo: they vary somewhat according to cult and province. At the shrines of Isé, Kasuga, Kompira, and several others which I visited, the ordinary priestesses are children; and when they have reached the nubile age, they retire from the service. At Kitzuki the priestesses are grown-up women: their office is hereditary; and they are permitted to retain it even after marriage.

Formerly the Miko was more than a mere officiant: the songs which she is still obliged to learn indicate that she was originally offered to the gods as a bride. Even yet her touch is holy; the grain sown by her hand is blessed. At some time in the past she seems to have been also a pythoness: the spirits of the gods possessed her and spoke through her lips. All the poetry of this most ancient of religions centres in the figure of its little Vestal, — child-bride of ghosts, — as she flutters, like some wonderful white-and-crimson butterfly, before the shrine of the Invisible. Even in these years of change, when she must go to the public school, she continues to represent all that is delightful in Japanese girlhood; for her special home-training keeps her reverent, innocent, dainty in all her little ways, and worthy to remain the pet of the gods.

The history of the higher forms of ancestor-worship in other countries would lead us to suppose that the public ceremonies of the Shintō-cult must include some rite of purification. As a matter of fact, the most important of all Shintō ceremonies is the ceremony of purification, — *o-harai*, as it is called, which term signifies the casting-out or expulsion of evils. . . . In ancient Athens a corresponding ceremony took place every year; in Rome, every four years. The *o-harai* is performed twice every year, — in the sixth month and the twelfth month by the ancient calendar. It used to be not less obligatory than the Roman lustration; and the idea behind the obligation was the same as that which inspired the Roman laws on the subject. . . . So long as men believe that the welfare of the living depends upon the will of the dead, — that all happenings in the world are ordered by spirits of different characters, evil as well as good, — that every bad action lends additional power to the viewless forces of destruction, and therefore endangers the public prosperity, — so long will the necessity of a public purification remain an article of common faith.   The presence in any community of even one person who has offended the gods, consciously or unwillingly, is a public misfortune, a public peril. Yet it is not possible for all men to live so well as never to vex the gods by thought, word, or deed, — through passion or ignorance or carelessness. "Every one," declares Hirata, "is certain to commit accidental offences, however careful he may be. . . .   Evil acts and words are of two kinds: those of which we are conscious, and those of which we are not conscious. . . .   It is better to assume that we have committed such unconscious offences." Now it should be remembered that for the man of Old Japan, — as for the Greek or the Roman citizen of early times, — religion consisted chiefly in the exact observance of multitudinous custom; and that it was therefore difficult to know whether, in performing the duties of the several cults, one had not inadvertently displeased the Unseen.   As a means of maintaining and assuring the religious purity of the people, periodical lustration was consequently deemed indispensable.

From the earliest period Shintō exacted scrupulous cleanliness — indeed, we might say that it regarded physical impurity as identical with moral impurity, and intolerable to the gods.   It has always been, and still remains, a religion of ablutions. The Japanese love of cleanliness — indicated by the universal practice of daily bathing, and by the irreproachable condition of their homes — has been maintained, and was probably initiated, by their religion. Spotless cleanliness being required by the rites of ancestor-worship, — in the temple, in the person of the officiant, and in the home, — this rule of purity was naturally extended by degrees to all the conditions of existence. And besides the great periodical ceremonies of purification, a multitude of minor lustrations were exacted by the cult. This was the case also, it will be remembered, in the early Greek and Roman civilizations: the citizen had to submit to purification upon almost every important occasion of existence. There were lustrations indispensable at birth, marriage, and death; lustrations on the eve of battle; lustrations, at regular periods, of the dwelling, estate, district, or city. And, as in Japan, no one could approach a temple without a preliminary washing of hands. But ancient Shintō exacted more than the Greek or the Roman cult: it required the erection of special houses for birth, — "parturition-houses"; special houses for the consummation of marriage, — 'nuptial huts"; and special buildings for the dead, — "mourning-houses." Formerly women were obliged during the period of menstruation, as well as during the time of confinement, to live apart. These harsher archaic customs

have almost disappeared, except in one or two
remote districts, and in the case of certain priestly
families; but the general rules as to purification,
and as to the times and circumstances forbidding
approach to holy places, are still everywhere obeyed.
Purity of heart is not less insisted upon than
physical purity; and the great rite of lustration,
performed every six months, is of course a moral
purification. It is performed not only at the great
temples, and at all the Ujigami, but likewise in
every home.[1]

The modern domestic form of the *harai* is very
simple. Each Shintō parish-temple furnishes to all
its Ujiko, or parishioners, small paper-cuttings called
hitogata ("mankind-shapes"), representing figures
of men, women, and children as in silhouette, —
only that the paper is white, and folded curiously.
Each household receives a number of *hitogata* corresponding to the number of its members, — "men-
shapes" for the men and boys, "women-shapes"

---

[1] On the *kamidana*, "or god-shelf," there is usually placed a kind of oblong
paper-box containing fragments of the wands used by the priests of Isé at the great
national purification-ceremony, or *o-barai*. This box is commonly called by the
name of the ceremony, *o-barai*, or "august purification," and is inscribed with
the names of the great gods of Isé. The presence of this object is supposed to protect the home; but it should be replaced by a new *o-barai* at the expiration of six
months; for the virtue of the charm is supposed to last only during the interval
between two official purifications. This distribution to thousands of homes of fragments of the wands, used to "drive away evils" at the time of the Isé lustration,
represents of course the supposed extension of the high-priest's protection to those
homes until the time of the next *o-barai*.

for the women and girls. Each person in the house touches his head, face, limbs, and body with one of these *hitogata*; repeating the while a Shintō invocation, and praying that any misfortune or sickness incurred by reason of offences involuntarily committed against the gods (for in Shintō belief sickness and misfortune are divine punishments) may be mercifully taken away. Upon each *hitogata* is then written the age and sex (not the name) of the person for whom it was furnished; and when this has been done, all are returned to the parish-temple, and there burnt, with rites of purification. Thus the community is "lustrated" every six months.

In the old Greek and Latin cities lustration was accompanied with registration. The attendance of every citizen at the ceremony was held to be so necessary that one who wilfully failed to attend might be whipped and sold as a slave. Non-attendance involved loss of civic rights. It would seem that in Old Japan also every member of a community was obliged to be present at the rite; but I have not been able to learn whether any registration was made upon such occasions. Probably it would have been superfluous: the Japanese individual was not officially recognized; the family-group alone was responsible, and the attendance of the several members would have been assured by the responsibility of the group. The use of the *hitogata*, on which the name is not written, but only the sex and age

of the worshipper, is probably modern, and of
Chinese origin.   Official registration existed, even in
early times ; but it appears to have had no particular relation to the *o-harai;* and the registers were
kept, it seems, not by the Shintō, but by the Buddhist parish-priests. . . .   In concluding these remarks about the *o-harai,* I need scarcely add that
special rites were performed in cases of accidental
religious defilement, and that any person judged to
have sinned against the rules of the public cult had
to submit to ceremonial purification.

   Closely related by origin to the rites of purification are sundry ascetic practices of Shintō.   It is not
an essentially ascetic religion : it offers flesh and
wine to its gods ; and it prescribes only such forms
of self-denial as ancient custom and decency require.
Nevertheless, some of its votaries perform extraordinary austerities on special occasions, — austerities
which always include much cold-water bathing.   It
is not uncommon for the very fervent worshipper
to invoke the gods as he stands naked under the
ice-cold rush of a cataract in midwinter. . . .   But
the most curious phase of this Shintō asceticism is
represented by a custom still prevalent in remote
districts.   According to this custom a community
yearly appoints one of its citizens to devote himself
wholly to the gods on behalf of the rest.   During
the term of his consecration, this communal repre-

sentative must separate from his family, must not
approach women, must avoid all places of amusement, must eat only food cooked with sacred fire,
must abstain from wine, must bathe in fresh cold
water several times a day, must repeat particular
prayers at certain hours, and must keep vigil upon
certain nights. When he has performed these
duties of abstinence and purification for the specified
time, he becomes religiously free; and another man
is then elected to take his place. The prosperity
of the settlement is supposed to depend upon the
exact observance by its representative of the duties
prescribed: should any public misfortune occur, he
would be suspected of having broken his vows.
Anciently, in the case of a common misfortune, the
representative was put to death. In the little town
of Mionoséki, where I first learned of this custom,
the communal representative is called *ichi-nen-
gannushi* ("one-year god-master"); and his full
term of vicarious atonement is twelve months. I
was told that elders are usually appointed for this
duty,—young men very seldom. In ancient times
such a communal representative was called by a name
signifying "abstainer." References to the custom
have been found in Chinese notices of Japan dating from a time before the beginning of Japanese
authentic history.

Every persistent form of ancestor-worship has its

system or systems of divination; and Shintō exemplifies the general law.   Whether divination ever
obtained in ancient Japan the official importance
which it assumed among the Greeks and the Romans
is at present doubtful.   But long before the introduction of Chinese astrology, magic, and fortune-
telling, the Japanese practised various kinds of
divination, as is proved by their ancient poetry,
their records, and their rituals.   We find mention
also of official diviners, attached to the great cults.
There was divination by bones, by birds, by rice,
by barley-gruel, by footprints, by rods planted in
the ground, and by listening in public ways to the
speech of people passing by.   Nearly all — probably
all — of these old methods of divination are still in
popular use.   But the earliest form of official divination was performed by scorching the shoulder-blade
of a deer, or other animal, and observing the cracks
produced by the heat.[1]   Tortoise-shells were afterwards used for the same purpose.   Diviners were
especially attached, it appears, to the imperial palace;
and Motowori, writing in the latter half of the eighteenth century, speaks of divination as still being, in
that epoch, a part of the imperial function.   "To

[1] Concerning this form of divination, Satow remarks that it was practised by the
Mongols in the time of Genghis Khan, and is still practised by the Khirghiz
Tartars, — facts of strong interest in view of the probable origin of the early
Japanese tribes.

For instances of ancient official divination see Aston's translation of the *Nibongi*,
Vol. I, pp. 157, 189, 227, 229, 237.

the end of time," he said, "the Mikado is the child
of the Sun-goddess. His mind is in perfect harmony of thought and feeling with hers. He does
not seek out new inventions; but he rules in
accordance with precedents which date from the
Age of the Gods; and if he is ever in doubt, he
has recourse to divination, which reveals to him the
mind of the great goddess."

Within historic times at least, divination would
not seem to have been much used in warfare, —
certainly not to the extent that it was used by the
Greek and Roman armies. The greatest Japanese
captains, — such as Hidéyoshi and Nobunaga —
were decidedly irreverent as to omens. Probably
the Japanese, at an early period of their long military history, learned by experience that the general
who conducts his campaign according to omens
must always be at a hopeless disadvantage in dealing with a skilful enemy who cares nothing about
omens.

Among the ancient popular forms of divination
which still survive, the most commonly practised
in households is divination by dry rice. For the
public, Chinese divination is still in great favour;
but it is interesting to observe that the Japanese
fortune-teller invariably invokes the Shintō gods
before consulting his Chinese books, and maintains
a Shintō shrine in his reception-room.

We have seen that the developments of ancestor-worship in Japan present remarkable analogies with the developments of ancestor-worship in ancient Europe, — especially in regard to the public cult, with its obligatory rites of purification.

But Shintō seems nevertheless to represent conditions of ancestor-worship less developed than those which we are accustomed to associate with early Greek and Roman life; and the coercion which it exercised appears to have been proportionally more rigid. The existence of the individual worshipper was ordered not merely in relation to the family and the community, but even in relation to inanimate things. Whatever his occupation might be, some god presided over it; whatever tools he might use, they had to be used in such manner as tradition prescribed for all admitted to the craft-cult. It was necessary that the carpenter should so perform his work as to honour the deity of carpenters, — that the smith should fulfil his daily task so as to honour the god of the bellows, — that the farmer should never fail in respect to the earth-god, and the food-god, and the scare-crow god, and the spirits of the trees about his habitation. Even the domestic utensils were sacred : the servant could not dare to forget the presence of the deities of the cooking-range, the hearth, the cauldron, the brazier, — or the supreme necessity of keeping the fire pure. The professions, not less

than the trades, were under divine patronage: the
physician, the teacher, the artist — each had his
religious duties to observe, his special traditions to
obey. The scholar, for example, could not dare to
treat his writing-implements with disrespect, or put
written paper to vulgar uses: such conduct would
offend the god of calligraphy. Nor were women
ruled less religiously than men in their various
occupations: the spinners and weaving-maidens
were bound to revere the Weaving-goddess and the
Goddess of Silkworms; the sewing-girl was taught
to respect her needles; and in all homes there was
observed a certain holiday upon which offerings
were made to the Spirits of Needles. In Samurai
families the warrior was commanded to consider his
armour and his weapons as holy things: to keep
them in beautiful order was an obligation of which
the neglect might bring misfortune in the time of
combat; and on certain days offerings were set
before the bows and spears, arrows and swords, and
other war-implements, in the alcove of the family
guest-room. Gardens, too, were holy; and there
were rules to be observed in their management, lest
offence should be given to the gods of trees and
flowers. Carefulness, cleanliness, dustlessness, were
everywhere enforced as religious obligations.

. . . It has often been remarked in these latter
days that the Japanese do not keep their public
offices, their railway stations, their new factory-build-

ings, thus scrupulously clean.   But edifices built in foreign style, with foreign material, under foreign supervision, and contrary to every local tradition, must seem to old-fashioned thinking God-forsaken places ; and servants amid such unhallowed sur-roundings do not feel the invisible about them, the weight of pious custom, the silent claim of beautiful and simple things to human respect.

The Rule of the Dead

IT should now be evident to the reader that the ethics of Shintō were all comprised in the doctrine of unqualified obedience to customs originating, for the most part, in the family cult. Ethics were not different from religion; religion was not different from government; and the very word for government signified "matters-of-religion." All government ceremonies were preceded by prayer and sacrifice; and from the highest rank of society to the lowest every person was subject to the law of tradition. To obey was piety; to disobey was impious; and the rule of obedience was enforced upon each individual by the will of the community to which he belonged. Ancient morality consisted in the minute observance of rules of conduct regarding the household, the community, and the higher authority.

But these rules of behaviour mostly represented the outcome of social experience; and it was scarcely possible to obey them faithfully, and yet to remain a bad man. They commanded reverence toward the Unseen, respect for authority, affection to parents, tenderness to wife and children, kindness to neighbours, kindness to dependants, diligence and exactitude in labour, thrift and cleanliness in habit. Though at first morality signified no more than obedience to tradition, tradition itself gradually became identified with true morality. To imagine the consequent social condition is, of course, somewhat difficult for the modern mind. Among ourselves, religious ethics and social ethics have long been practically dissociated; and the latter have become, with the gradual weakening of faith, more imperative and important than the former. Most of us learn, sooner or later in life, that it is not enough to keep the ten commandments, and that it is much less dangerous to break most of the commandments in a quiet way than to violate social custom. But in Old Japan there was no distinction tolerated between ethics and custom — between moral requirements and social obligations: convention identified both, and to conceal a breach of either was impossible, — as privacy did not exist. Moreover the unwritten commandments were not limited to ten; they were numbered by hundreds, and the least infringement was punishable, not merely as a blunder, but as a sin. Neither in his own home nor anywhere else could the ordinary person do as he pleased; and the extraordinary person was under the surveillance of zealous dependants whose constant duty was to reprove any breach of usage. The religion capable of regulating every act of existence by the force of common opinion requires no catechism.

Early moral custom must be coercive custom. But as many habits, at first painfully formed under compulsion only, become easy through constant repetition, and at last automatic, so the conduct compelled through many generations by religious and civil authority, tends eventually to become almost instinctive. Much depends, no doubt, upon the degree to which religious compulsion is hindered by exterior causes, — by long-protracted war, for example, — and in Old Japan there was interference extraordinary. Nevertheless, the influence of Shintō accomplished wonderful things, — evolved a national type of character worthy, in many ways, of earnest admiration. The ethical sentiment developed in that character differed widely from our own; but it was exactly adapted to the social requirements. For this national type of moral character was invented the name *Yamato-damashi* (or *Yamato-gokoro*), — the Soul of Yamato (or Heart of Yamato), — the appellation of the old province of Yamato, seat of the early emperors, being figuratively used for the entire country. We might correctly, though less literally, interpret the expression *Yamato-damashi* as "The Soul of Old Japan."

It was in reference to this "Soul of Old Japan" that the great Shintō scholars of the eighteenth

and nineteenth centuries put forth their bold assertion that conscience alone was a sufficient ethical
guide.   They declared the high quality of the
Japanese conscience a proof of the divine origin
of the race.   " Human beings," wrote Motowori,
"having been produced by the spirits of the two
Creative Deities, are naturally endowed with the
knowledge of what they ought to do, and of what
they ought to refrain from doing.   It is unnecessary for them to trouble their minds with systems
of morality.   If a system of morals were necessary,
men would be inferior to animals, — all of whom
are endowed with the knowledge of what they
ought to do, only in an inferior degree to
men." [1] . . .   Mabuchi, at an earlier day, had made
a comparison between Japanese and Chinese morality, greatly to the disadvantage of the latter.   " In
ancient times," said Mabuchi, "when men's dispositions were straightforward, a complicated system of
morals was unnecessary.   It would naturally happen that bad actions might be occasionally committed ; but the straightforwardness of men's
dispositions would prevent the evil from being
concealed and so growing in extent.   So in those
days it was unnecessary to have a doctrine of right
and wrong.   But the Chinese, being bad at heart,
in spite of the teaching which they got, were good

[1] All of these extracts are quoted from Satow's great essay on the Shintō
revival.

only on the outside; so their bad acts became of such magnitude that society was thrown into disorder. The Japanese, being straightforward, could do without teaching." Motowori repeated these ideas in a slightly different way: "It is because the Japanese were truly moral in their practice that they required no theory of morals; and the fuss made by the Chinese about theoretical morals is owing to their laxity in practice. . . . To have learned that there is no Way [*ethical system*] to be learned and practised, is really to have learned to practise the Way of the Gods." At a later day Hirata wrote: "Learn to stand in awe of the Unseen, and that will prevent you from doing wrong. Cultivate the conscience implanted in you: then you will never wander from the Way."

Though the sociologist may smile at these declarations of moral superiority (especially as based on the assumption that the race had been better in primeval times, when yet fresh from the hands of the gods), there was in them a grain of truth. When Mabuchi and Motowori wrote, the nation had been long subjected to a discipline of almost incredible minuteness in detail, and of extraordinary rigour in application. And this discipline had actually brought into existence a wonderful average of character,—a character of surprising patience, unselfishness, honesty, kindliness, and docility combined with high courage. But only the evolutionist can imagine what the cost of developing that character must have been.

It is necessary here to observe that the discipline to which the nation had been subjected up to the age of the great Shintō writers, seems to have had a curious evolutional history of its own.   In primitive times it had been much less uniform, less complex, less minutely organized, though not less implacable ; and it had continued to develop and elaborate more and more with the growth and consolidation of society, until, under the Tokugawa Shōgunate the possible maximum of regulation was reached.   In other words, the yoke had been made heavier and heavier in proportion to the growth of the national strength, — in proportion to the power of the people to bear it. . . . We have seen that, from the beginning of this civilization, the whole life of the citizen was ordered for him : his occupation, his marriage, his rights of fatherhood, his rights to hold or to dispose of property, — all these matters were settled by religious custom.   We have also seen that outside as well as inside of his home, his actions were under supervision, and that a single grave breach of usage might cause his social ruin, — in which case he would be given to understand that he was not merely a social, but also a religious offender ; that the communal god was angry with him ; and that to pardon his fault might provoke the divine vengeance against the entire settlement. But it yet remains to be seen what rights were left him by the central authority ruling his district, — which authority represented a third form of religious despotism from which there was no appeal in ordinary cases.

Material for the study of the old laws and customs have not yet been collected in sufficient quantity to yield us full information as to the conditions of all classes before Meiji. But a great deal of precious work has been accomplished in this direction by American scholars; and the labours of Professor Wigmore and of the late Dr. Simmons have furnished documentary evidence from which much can be learned about the legal status of the masses during the Tokugawa period. This, as I have said, was the period of the most elaborated regulation. The extent to which the people were controlled can be best inferred from the nature and number of the sumptuary laws to which they were subjected. Sumptuary laws in Old Japan probably exceeded in multitude and minuteness anything of which Western legal history yields record. Rigidly as the family-cult dictated behaviour in the home, strictly as the commune enforced its standards of communal duty, — just so rigidly and strictly did the rulers of the nation dictate how the individual — man, woman, or child — should dress, walk, sit, speak, work, eat, drink. Amusements were not less unmercifully regulated than were labours.

Every class of Japanese society was under sumptuary regulation, — the degree of regulation varying in different centuries; and this kind of legislation appears to have been established at an early period. It is recorded that, in the year 681 A.D., the Emperor Temmu regulated the costumes of all classes, — " from the Princes of the Blood down to the common people, — and the wearing of head-dresses and girdles, as well as of all kinds of coloured stuffs, — according to a scale." [1] The costumes and the colours to be worn by priests and nuns had been already fixed, by an edict issued in 679 A.D. Afterwards these regulations were greatly multiplied and detailed. But it was under the Tokugawa rulers, a thousand years later, that sumptuary laws obtained their most remarkable development; and the nature of them is best indicated by the regulations applying to the peasantry. Every detail of the farmer's existence was prescribed for by law, — from the size, form, and cost of his dwelling, down even to such trifling matters as the number and the quality of the dishes to be served to him at meal-times. A farmer with an income of 100 *koku* of rice — (let us say 90 to £100 per annum) — might build a house 60 feet long, but no longer: he was forbidden to construct it with a room containing an alcove; and he was not

[1] See *Nihongi* Aston's translation, Vol. II, pp 343, 348, 350.

allowed — except by special permission — to roof it with tiles. None of his family were permitted to wear silk; and in case of the marriage of his daughter to a person legally entitled to wear silk, the bridegroom was to be requested not to wear silk at the wedding. Three kinds of viands only were to be served at the wedding of such a farmer's daughter or son; and the quality as well as the quantity of the soup, fish, or sweetmeats offered to the wedding-guests, were legally fixed. So likewise the number of the wedding-gifts: even the cost of the presents of rice-wine and dried fish was prescribed, and the quality of the single fan which it was permissible to offer the bride. At no time was a farmer allowed to make any valuable presents to his friends. At a funeral he might serve the guests with certain kinds of plain food; but if rice-wine were served it was not to be served in wine-cups, — only in soup-cups! [The latter regulation probably referred to Shintō funerals in especial.] On the occasion of a child's birth, the grandparents were allowed to make only four presents (according to custom), — including " one cotton baby-dress "; and the values of the presents were fixed. On the occasion of the Boy's Festival, the presents to be given to the child by the whole family, including grandparents, were limited by law to " one paper-flag," and " two toy-spears." . . . A farmer whose property was assessed at 50 *koku* was forbidden to build a house more than 45 feet long. At the wedding of his daughter the gift-girdle was not to exceed 50 *sen* in value ; and it was forbidden to serve more than one kind of soup at the wedding-feast. . . . A farmer with a property assessed at 20 *koku* was not allowed to build a house more than 36 feet long, or to use in building it such superior qualities of wood as *keyaki* or *hinoki*. The roof of his house was to be made of bamboo-thatch or straw ; and he was strictly forbidden the comfort of floor-mats. On the occasion of the wedding of his daughter he was forbidden to have fish or any roasted food served at the wedding-feast. The women of his family were not allowed to wear leather sandals : they might wear only straw-sandals or wooden clogs ; and the thongs of the sandals or the clogs were to be made of cotton. The women were further forbidden to wear hair-bindings of silk, or hair-ornaments of tortoise-shells ; but they might wear wooden combs and combs of bone — not ivory. The men were forbidden to wear stockings, and their sandals were to be made of bamboo.[1] They were also forbidden to use sun-shades — *hi-gasa* — or paper-umbrellas. . . . A farmer assessed at 10 *koku* was forbidden to build a house more than 30 feet long. The women of his family were required to wear sandals with thongs of bam-

---

[1] There are sandals or clogs made of bamboo-wood, but the meaning here is bamboo-grass.

boo-grass. At the wedding of his son or daughter one present only was allowed, — a quilt-chest. At the birth of his child one present only was to be made : namely, one toy-spear, in the case of a boy ; or one paper-doll, or one " mud-doll," in the case of a girl. . . . As for the more unfortunate class of farmers, having no land of their own, and officially termed *mizunomi*, or "water-drinkers," it is scarcely necessary to remark that these were still more severely restricted in regard to food, apparel, etc. They were not even allowed, for example, to have a quilt-chest as a wedding-present. But a fair idea of the complexity of these humiliating restrictions can only be obtained by reading the documents published by Professor Wigmore, which chiefly consist of paragraphs like these : —

"The collar and the sleeve-ends of the clothes may be ornamented with silk, and an *obi* (soft girdle) of silk or crêpe-silk may be worn — but not in public." . . .

"A family ranking less than 20 *koku* must use the *Takéda-wan* (Takéda rice-bowl), and the *Nikkō-zen* (Nikkō tray)." . . . [These were utensils of the cheapest kind of lacquer-ware.]

"Large farmers or chiefs of *Kumi* may use umbrellas ; but small farmers and farm-labourers must use only *mino* (straw-raincoats), and broad straw-hats." . . .

These documents published by Professor Wigmore contain only the regulations issued for the daimiate of Maizuru ; but regulations equally minute and vexatious appear to have been enforced throughout the whole country.   In Izumo I found that, prior to Meiji, there were sumptuary laws prescribing not only the material of the dresses to be worn by the various classes, but even the colours of them, and the designs of the patterns.   The size of rooms, as well as the size of houses, was fixed there by law, — also the height of buildings and of fences, the number of windows, the material of construction. . . .   It is difficult for the Western mind to understand how human beings could patiently submit to laws that regulated not only the size of one's dwelling, and the cost of its furniture, but even the substance and character of clothing, — not only the expense of a wedding outfit, but the quality of the marriage-feast, and the quality of the vessels in which the food was to be served, — not only the kind of ornaments to be worn in a woman's hair, but the material of the thongs of her sandals, — not only the price of presents to be made to friends, but the character and the cost of the cheapest toy to be given to a child.   And the peculiar constitution of society made it possible to enforce this sumptuary legislation by communal will; the people were obliged to coerce themselves!   Each community, as we have seen, had been organized in groups of five or more households, called *kumi;* and the heads of the households forming a *kumi* elected one of their number as *kumi-gashira,* or group-chief, directly responsible to the higher authority.   The *kumi* was accountable for the conduct of each and all of its members; and each member was in some sort responsible for the rest.   "Every member of a *kumi*," declares one of the documents above mentioned, "must carefully watch the conduct of his fellow-members.   If any one violates these regulations, without due excuse, he is to be punished; and his *kumi* will also be held responsible."   Responsible even for the serious offence of giving more than one paper-doll to a child! . . .   But we should remember that in early Greek and Roman societies there was much legislation of a similar kind.   The laws of Sparta regulated the way in which a woman should dress her hair; the laws of Athens fixed the number of her robes.   At Rome, in early times, women were forbidden to drink wine; and a similar law existed in the Greek cities of Miletus and Massilia.   In Rhodes and Byzantium the citizen was forbidden to shave; in Sparta he was forbidden to wear a moustache.   (I need scarcely refer to the later Roman laws regulating the cost of marriage-feasts, and the number of guests that might be invited to a banquet; for this legislation was directed chiefly against luxury.)   The astonishment evoked by Japanese sumptuary laws, particularly as inflicted upon the peasantry, is justified less by their general character than by their implacable minuteness, — their ferocity of detail. . . .

Where a man's life was legally ordered even to the least particulars, — even to the quality of his foot-gear and head-gear, the cost of his wife's hair-pins, and the price of his child's doll, — one could hardly suppose that freedom of speech would have been tolerated. It did not exist; and the degree to which speech became regulated can be imagined only by those who have studied the spoken tongue. The hierarchical organization of society was faithfully reflected in the conventional organization of language, — in the ordination of pronouns, nouns, and verbs, — in the grades conferred upon adjectives by prefixes or suffixes. With the same merciless exactitude which prescribed rules for dress, diet, and manner of life, all utterance was regulated both negatively and positively, — but positively much more than negatively. There was little insistence upon what was not to be said; but rules innumerable decided exactly what should be said, — the word to be chosen, the phrase to be used. Early training enforced caution in this regard: everybody had to learn that only certain verbs and nouns and pronouns were lawful when addressing superiors, and other words permissible only when speaking to equals or to inferiors. Even the un-educated were obliged to learn something about this. But education cultivated a system of verbal etiquette so multiform that only the training of years could enable any one to master it. Among the higher classes this etiquette developed almost inconceivable complexity.   Grammatical modifications of language, which, by implication, exalted the person addressed or humbly depreciated the person addressing, must have come into general use at some very early period ; but under subsequent Chinese influence these forms of propitiatory speech multiplied exceedingly.   From the Mikado himself — who still makes use of personal pronouns, or at least pronominal expressions, forbidden to any other mortal — down through all the grades of society, each class had an " I " peculiarly its own.   Of terms corresponding to " you " or " thou " there are still sixteen in use ; but formerly there were many more. There are yet eight different forms of the second person singular used only in addressing children, pupils, or servants.[1]   Honorific or humble forms of nouns indicating relationship were similarly multiplied and graded : there are still in use nine terms signifying " father," nine terms signifying " mother," eleven terms for " wife," eleven terms for " son," nine terms for " daughter," and seven terms for " husband."   The rules of the verb, above all, were complicated by the exigencies of etiquette to a

[1] The sociologist will of course understand that these facts are not by any means inconsistent with that very sparing use of pronouns so amusingly discussed in Percival Lowell's " Soul of the Far East." In societies where subjection is extreme "there is an avoidance of the use of personal pronouns," though, as Herbert Spencer points out in illustrating this law, it is just among such societies that the most elaborate distinctions in pronominal forms of address are to be found.

degree of which no idea can be given in any brief statement. . . . At nineteen or twenty years of age a person carefully trained from childhood might have learned all the necessary verbal usages of respectable society ; but for a mastery of the etiquette of superior converse many more years of study and experience were required. With the unceasing multiplication of ranks and classes there came into existence a corresponding variety of forms of language : it was possible to ascertain to what class a man or a woman belonged by listening to his or to her conversation. The written, like the spoken tongue, was regulated by strict convention : the forms used by women were not those used by men ; and those differences in verbal etiquette arising from the different training of the sexes resulted in the creation of a special epistolary style, — a "woman's language," which remains in use. And this sex-differentiation of language was not confined to letter-writing : there was a woman's language also of converse, varying according to class. Even to-day, in ordinary conversation, an educated woman makes use of words and phrases not employed by men. Samurai women especially had their particular forms of expression in feudal times ; and it is still possible to decide, from the speech of any woman brought up according to the old home-training, whether she belongs to a Samurai family.

Of course the matter as well as the manner of converse was restricted; and the nature of the restraints upon free speech can be inferred from the nature of the restraints upon freedom of demeanour. Demeanour was most elaborately and mercilessly regulated, not merely as to obeisances, of which there were countless grades, varying according to sex as well as class, — but even in regard to facial expression, the manner of smiling, the conduct of the breath, the way of sitting, standing, walking, rising. Everybody was trained from infancy in this etiquette of expression and deportment. At what period it first became a mark of disrespect to betray, by look or gesture, any feeling of grief or pain in the presence of a superior, we cannot know; there is reason to believe that the most perfect self-control in this regard was enforced from prehistoric times. But there was gradually developed — partly, perhaps, under Chinese teaching — a most elaborate code of deportment which exacted very much more than impassiveness. It required not only that any sense of anger or pain should be denied all outward expression, but that the sufferer's face and manner should indicate the contrary feeling. Sullen submission was an offence; mere impassive obedience inadequate: the proper degree of submission should manifest itself by a pleasant smile, and by a soft and happy tone of voice. The smile, however, was also regulated.

One had to be careful about the quality of the smile:
it was a mortal offence, for example, so to smile in
addressing a superior, that the back teeth could be
seen.   In the military class especially this code of
demeanour was ruthlessly enforced.   Samurai women
were required, like the women of Sparta, to show
signs of joy on hearing that their husbands or sons
had fallen in battle: to betray any natural feeling
under the circumstances was a grave breach of decorum.   And in all classes demeanour was regulated so
severely that even to-day the manners of the people
everywhere still reveal the nature of the old discipline.   The strangest fact is that the old-fashioned
manners appear natural rather than acquired, instinctive rather than made by training.   The bow, — the
sibilant indrawing of the breath which accompanies
the prostration, and is practised also in praying to
the gods, — the position of the hands upon the floor
in the moment of greeting or of farewell, — the way
of sitting or rising or walking in presence of a guest,
— the manner of receiving or presenting anything,
— all these ordinary actions have a charm of seeming naturalness that mere teaching seems incapable
of producing.   And this is still more true of the
higher etiquette, — the exquisite etiquette of the
old-time training in cultivated classes, — particularly
as displayed by women.   We must suppose that the
capacity to acquire such manners depends considerably upon inheritance, — that it could only have

been formed by the past experience of the race under discipline.

What such discipline, as regards politeness, must have signified for the mass of the people, may be inferred from the enactment of Iyéyasu authorizing a Samurai to kill any person of the three inferior classes guilty of rudeness. Be it observed that Iyéyasu was careful to qualify the meaning of " rude " : he said that the Japanese term for a rude fellow signified " an other-than-expected person " — so that to commit an offence worthy of death it was only necessary to act in an " unexpected manner " ; that is to say, contrary to prescribed etiquette : —

" The Samurai are the masters of the four classes. Agriculturists, artizans, and merchants may not behave in a rude manner towards Samurai. The term for a rude man is ' other-than-expected fellow ' ; and a Samurai is not to be interfered with in cutting down a fellow who has behaved to him in a manner other than is expected. The Samurai are grouped into direct retainers, secondary retainers, and nobles and retainers of high and low grade ; but the same line of conduct is equally allowable to them all towards an other-than-expected fellow."— [*Art.* 45.]

But there is little reason to suppose that Iyéyasu created any new privilege of slaughter : he probably did no more than confirm by enactment certain long established military rights. Stern rules about the conduct of inferiors to superiors would seem to have been pitilessly enforced long before the rise of the military power. We read that the Emperor Yūriaku, in the latter part of the fifth century, killed a steward for the misdemeanour of remaining silent, through fear, when spoken to: we also find it recorded that he struck down a maid-of-honour who had brought him a cup of wine, and that he would have cut off her head but for the extraordinary presence of mind which enabled her to improvise a poetical appeal for mercy.   Her only fault had been that, in carrying the wine-cup, she failed to notice that a leaf had fallen into it, — probably because court-custom obliged her to carry the cup in such a way as not to breathe upon it: for emperors and high nobles were served after the manner of gods. It is true that Yūriaku was in the habit of killing people for little mistakes; but it is evident that, in the cases cited, such mistakes were regarded as breaches of long-established decorum.

Probably before as well as after the introduction of the Chinese penal codes, — the so-called Ming and Tsing codes, by which the country was ruled under the Shōguns, — the bulk of the nation was literally under the rod. Common folk were punished by cruel whippings for the most trifling offences.   For serious offences, death by torture was an ordinary penalty; and there were extraordinary penalties as savage, or almost as savage, as those established during our own medieval period, —

burnings and crucifixions and quarterings and boil-
ing alive in oil. The documents regulating the life
of village-folk do not contain any indication of the
severity of legal discipline: the *Kumi-chō* declarations that such and such conduct "shall be punished" suggest nothing terrible to the reader who
has not made himself familiar with the ancient codes.
As a matter of fact the term "punishment" in a
Japanese legal document might signify anything
from a trifling fine up to burning alive. . . . Some
evidence of the severity used to repress quarrelling
even as late as the time of Iyeyasu, may be found in
a curious letter of Captain Saris, who visited Japan
in 1613. "The first of Iuly," wrote the Captain,
"two of our Company happened to quarrell the one
with the other, and were very likely to haue gone
into the field [*i.e. to have fought a duel*] to the
endangering of vs all. For it is a custome here that
whosoever drawes a weapon in anger, although he
do noe harme therewith, hee is presently cut in
peeces; and, doing but small hurt, not only them-
selues are so executed, but their whole generation." . . . The literal meaning of "cut in
peeces" he explains later on, when recounting in
the same letter an execution that came under his
observation: —

"The eighth, three *Iaponians* were executed, viz., two
men and one woman: the cause this, — the woman, none
of the honestest (her husband being trauelled from home)

had appointed these two their several hours to repair vnto her. The latter man, not knowing of the former, and comming in before the houre appointed, found the first man, and enraged thereat, he whipped out his cattan [*katana*] and wounded both of them very sorely, — hauing very neere hewn the chine of the mans back in two. But as well as hee might he cleared himselfe, and recouering his cattan, wounded the other. The street, taking notice of the fray, forthwith seased vpon them, led them aside, and acquainted King *Foyne* therewith, and sent to know his pleasure, (for according to his will, the partie is executed), who presently gaue order that they should cut off their heads : which done, euery man that listed (as very many did) came to try the sharpness of their cattans vpon the corps, so that, before they left off, they had hewne them all three into peeces as small as a mans hand, — and yet notwithstanding, did not then giue over, but, placing the peeces one vpon another, would try how many of them they could strike through at a blow; and the peeces are left to the fowles to deuoure." . . . .

Evidently the execution was in this case ordered for cause more serious than the offence of fighting ; but it is true that quarrels were strictly forbidden and rigorously punished.

Though privileged to cut down " other-than-expected " people of inferior rank, the military class itself had to endure a discipline even more severe than that which it maintained. The penalty for a word or a look that displeased, or for a trifling mistake in performance of duty, might be death. In most cases the Samurai was permitted to be his own executioner; and the right of self-destruction was deemed a privilege; but the obligation to thrust a dagger deeply into one's belly on the left side, and then draw the blade slowly and steadily across to the right side, so as to sever all the entrails, was certainly not less cruel than the vulgar punishment of crucifixion, or rather, double-transfixion.

Just as all matters relating to the manner of the individual's life were regulated by law, so were all matters relating to his death, — the quality of his coffin, the expenses of his interment, the order of his funeral, the form of his tomb. In the seventh century laws were passed to the effect that no one should be buried with unseemly expense; and these laws fixed the cost of funerals according to rank and grade. Subsequent edicts decided the dimensions and material of coffins, and the size of graves. In the eighth century every detail of funerals, for all classes of persons from prince to peasant, was fixed by decree. Other laws, and modifications of laws, were made upon the subject in later centuries; but there appears to have always been a general tendency to extravagance in the matter of funerals, — a tendency so strong that, in spite of centuries of sumptuary legislation, it remains to-day a social danger. This can easily be understood if we remember the beliefs regarding duty to the dead, and the conse-

quent desire to honour and to please the spirit even
at the risk of family impoverishment.

Most of the legislation to which reference has
already been made must appear to modern minds
tyrannical ; and some of the regulations seem to us
strangely cruel. There was, moreover, no way of
evading or shirking these obligations of law and custom : whoever failed to fulfil them was doomed to
perish or to become an outcast; implicit obedience
was the condition of survival. The tendency of such
regulation was necessarily to suppress all mental and
moral differentiation, to numb personality, to establish one uniform and unchanging type of character;
and such was the actual result. To this day every
Japanese mind reveals the lines of that antique mould
by which the ancestral mind was compressed and
limited. It is impossible to understand Japanese
psychology without knowing something of the laws
that helped to form it, — or, rather, to crystallize it
under pressure.

Yet, on the other hand, the ethical effects of this
iron discipline were unquestionably excellent. It
compelled each succeeding generation to practise the
frugality of the forefathers; and that compulsion was
partly justified by the great poverty of the nation.
It reduced the cost of living to a figure far below
our Western comprehension of the necessary ; it
cultivated sobriety, simplicity, economy ; it enforced

cleanliness, courtesy, and hardihood.   And—strange as the fact may seem—it did *not* make the people miserable: they found the world beautiful in spite of all their trouble; and the happiness of the old life was reflected in the old Japanese art, much as the joyousness of Greek life yet laughs to us from the vase-designs of forgotten painters.

And the explanation is not difficult.   We must remember that the coercion was not exercised only from without: it was really maintained from within. The discipline of the race was self-imposed.   The people had gradually created their own social conditions, and therefore the legislation conserving those conditions; and they believed that legislation the best possible.   They believed it to be the best possible for the excellent reason that it had been founded upon their own moral experience; and they could greatly endure because they had great faith.   Only religion could have enabled any people to bear such discipline without degenerating into mopes and cowards; and the Japanese never so degenerated: the traditions that compelled self-denial and obedience, also cultivated courage, and insisted upon cheerfulness.   The power of the ruler was unlimited because the power of all the dead supported him. " Laws," says Herbert Spencer, " whether written or unwritten, formulate the rule of the dead over the living.   In addition to that power which past generations exercise over present generations, by transmitting their natures, — bodily and mental, — and in addition to the power they exercise over them by bequeathed habits and modes of life, — there is the power they exercise through their regulations for public conduct, handed down orally, or in writing. . . . I emphasize these truths," — he adds, — " for the purpose of showing that they imply a tacit ancestor-worship." . . . Of no other laws in the history of human civilization are these observations more true than of the laws of Old Japan. Most strikingly did they " formulate the rule of the dead over the living." And the hand of the dead was heavy : it is heavy upon the living even to-day.

The Introduction of Buddhism

THE nature of the opposition which the ancient religion of Japan could offer to the introduction of any hostile alien creed, should now be obvious. The family being founded upon ancestor-worship, the commune being regulated by ancestor-worship, the clan-group or tribe being governed by ancestor-worship, and the Supreme Ruler being at once the high-priest and deity of an ancestral cult which united all the other cults in one common tradition, it must be evident that the promulgation of any religion essentially opposed to Shintō would have signified nothing less than an attack upon the whole system of society. Considering these circumstances, it may well seem strange that Buddhism should have succeeded, after some preliminary struggles (which included one bloody battle), in getting itself accepted as a second national faith. But although the original Buddhist doctrine was essentially in disaccord with Shintō beliefs, Buddhism had learned in India, in China, in Korea, and in divers adjacent countries, how to meet the spiritual needs of peoples maintaining a persistent ancestor-worship. In-

tolerance of ancestor-worship would have long ago
resulted in the extinction of Buddhism; for its
vast conquests have all been made among ancestor-
worshipping races.   Neither in India nor in China
nor in Korea,.— neither in Siam nor Burmah nor
Annam, — did it attempt to extinguish ancestor-
worship.   Everywhere it made itself accepted as
an ally, nowhere as an enemy, of social custom.
In Japan it adopted the same policy which had
secured its progress on the continent; and in order
to form any clear conception of Japanese religious
conditions, this fact must be kept in mind.

As the oldest extant Japanese texts — with the
probable exception of some Shintō rituals — date
from the eighth century, it is only possible to surmise the social conditions of that earlier epoch in
which there was no form of religion but ancestor-
worship.   Only by imagining the absence of all
Chinese and Korean influences, can we form
some vague idea of the state of things which existed
during the so-called Age of the Gods, — and it is
difficult to decide at what period these influences
began to operate.   Confucianism appears to have
preceded Buddhism by a considerable interval; and
its progress, as an organizing power, was much
more rapid.   Buddhism was first introduced from
Korea, about 552 A.D.; but the mission accomplished little.   By the end of the eighth century

the whole fabric of Japanese administration had been
reorganized upon the Chinese plan, under Confucian
influence; but it was not until well into the ninth
century that Buddhism really began to spread
throughout the country. Eventually it overshadowed the national life, and coloured all the
national thought. Yet the extraordinary conservatism of the ancient ancestor-cult — its inherent
power of resisting fusion — was exemplified by the
readiness with which the two religions fell apart on
the disestablishment of Buddhism in 1871. After
having been literally overlaid by Buddhism for
nearly a thousand years, Shintō immediately re-
assumed its archaic simplicity, and reëstablished
the unaltered forms of its earliest rites.

But the attempt of Buddhism to absorb Shintō
seemed at one period to have almost succeeded.
The method of the absorption is said to have been
devised, about the year 800, by the famous founder
of the Shingon sect, Kūkai or " Kōbōdaishi "
(as he is popularly called), who first declared the
higher Shintō gods to be incarnations of various
Buddhas. But in this matter, of course, Kōbōdaishi
was merely following precedents of Buddhist policy.
Under the name of Ryōbu-Shintō,[1] the new com-
pound of Shintō and Buddhism obtained imperial
approval and support. Thereafter, in hundreds of

[1] The term " Ryobu " signifies "two-departments " or " two religions."

places, the two religions were domiciled within the
same precinct — sometimes even within the same
building: they seemed to have been veritably
amalgamated. And nevertheless there was no
real fusion; — after ten centuries of such contact
they separated again, as lightly as if they had never
touched. It was only in the domestic form of the
ancestor-cult that Buddhism really affected permanent modifications; yet even these were neither
fundamental nor universal. In certain provinces
they were not made; and almost everywhere a considerable part of the population preferred to follow
the Shintō form of the ancestor-cult. Yet another
large class of persons, converts to Buddhism, continued to profess the older creed as well; and, while
practising their ancestor-worship according to the
Buddhist rite, maintained separately also the domestic worship of the elder gods. In most Japanese
houses to-day, the "god-shelf" and the Buddhist
shrine can both be found; both cults being maintained under the same roof.[1] . . . But I am mentioning these facts only as illustrating the conservative
vitality of Shintō, not as indicating any weakness
in the Buddhist propaganda. Unquestionably the
influence which Buddhism exerted upon Japanese

[1] The ancestor-worship and the funeral rites are Buddhist, as a general rule, if
the family be Buddhist; but the Shintō gods are also worshipped in most Buddhist
households, except those attached to the Shin sect. Many followers of even the
Shin sect, however, appear to follow the ancient religion likewise; and they have
their Ujigami.

civilization was immense, profound, multiform, incalculable; and the only wonder is that it should not have been able to stifle Shintō forever. To state, as various writers have carelessly stated, that Buddhism became the popular religion, while Shintō remained the official religion, is altogether misleading. As a matter of fact Buddhism became as much an official religion as Shintō itself, and influenced the lives of the highest classes not less than the lives of the poor. It made monks of Emperors, and nuns of their daughters; it decided the conduct of rulers, the nature of decrees, and the administration of laws. In every community the Buddhist parish-priest was a public official as well as a spiritual teacher: he kept the parish register, and made report to the authorities upon local matters of importance.

By introducing the love of learning, Confucianism had partly prepared the way for Buddhism. As early even as the first century there were some Chinese scholars in Japan; but it was toward the close of the third century that the study of Chinese literature first really became fashionable among the ruling classes. Confucianism, however, did not represent a new religion: it was a system of ethical teachings founded upon an ancestor-worship much like that of Japan. What it had to offer was a kind of social philosophy,— an explanation of the

eternal reason of things. It reinforced and expanded
the doctrine of filial piety ; it regulated and elaborated preëxisting ceremonial ; and it systematized all
the ethics of government. In the education of the
ruling classes it became a great power, and has so
remained down to the present day. Its doctrines
were humane, in the best meaning of the word ; and
striking evidence of its humanizing effect on government policy may be found in the laws and the
maxims of that wisest of Japanese rulers — Iyeyasu.

But the religion of the Buddha brought to Japan
another and a wider humanizing influence, — a new
gospel of tenderness, —together with a multitude of
new beliefs that were able to accommodate themselves to the old, in spite of fundamental dissimi-
larity. In the highest meaning of the term, it was a
civilizing power. Besides teaching new respect for
life, the duty of kindness to animals as well as to all
human beings, the consequence of present acts upon
the conditions of a future existence, the duty of resignation to pain as the inevitable result of forgotten
error, it actually gave to Japan the arts and the
industries of China. Architecture, painting, sculpture, engraving, printing, gardening — in short,
every art and industry that helped to make life
beautiful — developed first in Japan under Buddhist
teaching.

There are many forms of Buddhism ; and in

modern Japan there are twelve principal Buddhist
sects ; but, for present purposes, it will be enough
to speak, in the most general way, of popular
Buddhism only, as distinguished from philosophical
Buddhism, which I shall touch upon in a subsequent
chapter. The higher Buddhism could not, at any
time or in any country, have had a large popular
following ; and it is a mistake to suppose that its
particular doctrines — such as the doctrine of Nirvâna — were taught to the common people. Only
such forms of doctrine were preached as could be
made intelligible and attractive to very simple
minds.   There is a Buddhist proverb : " First observe the person ; then preach the Law,"—that is to
say, Adapt your instruction to the capacity of the
listener. In Japan, as in China, Buddhism had to
adapt its instruction to the mental capacity of large
classes of people yet unaccustomed to abstract ideas.
Even to this day the masses do not know so much
as the meaning of the word "Nirvâna" (*Nêhan*) : they
have been taught only the simpler forms of the religion ; and in dwelling upon these, it will be needless
to consider differences of sect and dogma.

To appreciate the direct influence of Buddhist
teaching upon the minds of the common people, we
must remember that in Shintō there was no doctrine
of metempsychosis. As I have said before, the
spirits of the dead, according to ancient Japanese
thinking, continued to exist in the world : they

mingled somehow with the viewless forces of nature, and acted through them. Everything happened by the agency of these spirits — evil or good. Those who had been wicked in life remained wicked after death; those who had been good in life became good gods after death; but all were to be propitiated. No idea of future reward or punishment existed before the coming of Buddhism : there was no notion of any heaven or hell. The happiness of ghosts and gods alike was supposed to depend upon the worship and the offerings of the living.

With these ancient beliefs Buddhism attempted to interfere only by expanding and expounding them, — by interpreting them in a totally new light. Modifications were effected, but no suppressions : we might even say that Buddhism accepted the whole body of the old beliefs. It was true, the new teaching declared, that the dead continued to exist invisibly ; and it was not wrong to suppose that they became divinities, since all of them were destined, sooner or later, to enter upon the way to Buddhahood — the divine condition. Buddhism acknowledged likewise the greater gods of Shintō, with all their attributes and dignities, — declaring them incarnations of Buddhas or Bodhisattvas : thus the goddess of the sun was identified with *Dai-Nichi-Nyōrai* (the Tathâgata Mahâvairokana) ; the deity Hachiman was identified with *Amida* (Amitâbha). Nor did Buddhism deny the existence of goblins

and evil gods : these were identified with the Pretas
and the Mârakâyikas ; and the Japanese popular
term for goblin, *Ma*, to-day reminds us of this iden-
tification. As for wicked ghosts, they were to be
thought of as Pretas only, — *Gaki*, — self-doomed by
the errors of former lives to the Circle of Perpetual
Hunger. The ancient sacrifices to the various gods
of disease and pestilence — gods of fever, small-pox,
dysentery, consumption, coughs, and colds — were
continued with Buddhist approval ; but converts
were bidden to consider such maleficent beings as
Pretas, and to present them with only such food-
offerings as are bestowed upon Pretas — not for
propitiation, but for the purpose of relieving ghostly
pain. In this case, as in the case of the ancestral
spirits, Buddhism prescribed that the prayers to be
repeated were to be said *for* the sake of the haunters,
rather than *to* them. . . . The reader may be reminded of the fact that Roman Catholicism, by
making a similar provision, still practically tolerates
a continuance of the ancient European ancestor-
worship. And we cannot consider that worship
extinct in any of those Western countries where the
peasants still feast their dead upon the Night of All
Souls.

Buddhism, however, did more than tolerate the
old rites. It cultivated and elaborated them.
Under its teaching a new and beautiful form of
the domestic cult came into existence ; and all the

touching poetry of ancestor-worship in modern
Japan can be traced to the teaching of the Buddhist missionaries. Though ceasing to regard their
dead as gods in the ancient sense, the Japanese con
verts were encouraged to believe in their presence,
and to address them in terms of reverence and
affection. It is worthy of remark that the doctrine
of Pretas gave new force to the ancient fear of
neglecting the domestic rites. Ghosts unloved
might not become " evil gods " in the Shintō meaning of the term; but the malevolent *Gaki* was even
more to be dreaded than the malevolent *Kami*, —
for Buddhism defined in appalling ways the nature
of the *Gaki's* power to harm. In various Buddhist
funeral-rites, the dead are actually addressed as
Gaki, — beings to be pitied but also to be feared, —
much needing human sympathy and succour, but
able to recompense the food-giver by ghostly help.

One particular attraction of Buddhist teaching
was its simple and ingenious interpretation of
nature. Countless matters which Shintō had never
attempted to explain, and could not have explained,
Buddhism expounded in detail, with much apparent
consistency. Its explanations of the mysteries of
birth, life, and death were at once consoling to pure
minds, and wholesomely discomforting to bad con-
sciences. It taught that the dead were happy or
unhappy not directly because of the attention or the

neglect shown them by the living, but because of their past conduct while in the body.[1] It did not attempt to teach the higher doctrine of successive rebirths, — which the people could not possibly have understood, — but the merely symbolic doctrine of transmigration, which everybody could understand. To die was not to melt back into nature, but to be reincarnated; and the character of the new body, as well as the conditions of the new existence, would depend upon the quality of one's deeds and thoughts in the present body. All states and conditions of being were the consequence of past actions. Such a man was now rich and powerful, because in previous lives he had been generous and kindly; such another man was now sickly and poor, because in some previous existence he had been sensual and selfish. This woman was happy in her husband and her children, because in the time of a former birth she had proved herself a loving daughter and a faithful spouse; this other was wretched and childless, because in some anterior existence she had been a jealous wife and a cruel mother. "To hate your enemy," the Buddhis preacher would proclaim, "is

[1] The reader will doubtless wonder how Buddhism could reconcile its doctrine of successive rebirths with the ideas of ancestor-worship. If one died only to be born again, what could be the use of offering food or addressing any kind of prayer to the reincarnated spirit? This difficulty was met by the teaching that the dead were not immediately reborn in most cases, but entered into a particular condition called *Chū-U*. They might remain in this disembodied condition for the time of one hundred years, after which they were reincarnated. The Buddhist services for the dead are consequently limited to the time of one hundred years.

foolish as well as wrong: he is now your enemy only because of some treachery that you practised upon him in a previous life, when he desired to be your friend. Resign yourself to the injury which he now does you: accept it as the expiation of your forgotten fault. . . . The girl whom you hoped to marry has been refused you by her parents, — given away to another. But once, in another existence, she was yours by promise; and you broke the pledge then given. . . . Painful indeed the loss of your child; but this loss is the consequence of having, in some former life, refused affection where affection was due. . . . Maimed by mishap, you can no longer earn your living as before. Yet this mishap is really due to the fact that in some previous existence you wantonly inflicted bodily injury. Now the evil of your own act has returned upon you: repent of your crime, and pray that its Karma may be exhausted by this present suffering." . . . All the sorrows of men were thus explained and consoled. Life was expounded as representing but one stage of a measureless journey, whose way stretched back through all the night of the past, and forward through all the mystery of the future, — out of eternities forgotten into the eternities to be; and the world itself was to be thought of only as a traveller's resting-place, an inn by the roadside.

Instead of preaching to the people about Nirvâna,

Buddhism discoursed to them of blisses to be won and pains to be avoided: the Paradise of Amida, Lord of Immeasurable Light; the eight hot hells called To-kwatsu, and the eight icy hells called Abuda. On the subject of future punishment the teaching was very horrible: I should advise no one of delicate nerves to read the Japanese, or rather the Chinese accounts of hell. But hell was the penalty for supreme wickedness only: it was not eternal; and the demons themselves would at last be saved. . . . Heaven was to be the reward of good deeds: the reward might indeed be delayed, through many successive rebirths, by reason of lingering Karma; but, on the other hand, it might be attained by virtue of a single holy act in this present life. Besides, prior to the period of supreme reward, each succeeding rebirth could be made happier than the preceding one by persistent effort in the holy Way. Even as regarded conditions in this transitory world, the results of virtuous conduct were not to be despised. The beggar of to-day might to-morrow be reborn in the palace of a daimyō; the blind shampooer might become, in his very next life, an imperial minister. Always the recompense would be proportionate to the sum of merit. In this lower world to practise the highest virtue was difficult; and the great rewards were hard to win. But for all good deeds a recompense was sure; and there was no one who could not acquire merit.

Even the Shintō doctrine of conscience — the god-given sense of right and wrong — was not denied by Buddhism. But this conscience was interpreted as the essential wisdom of the Buddha dormant in every human creature, — wisdom darkened by ignorance, clogged by desire, fettered by Karma, but destined sooner or later to fully awaken, and to flood the mind with light.

It would seem that the Buddhist teaching of the duty of kindness to all living creatures, and of pity for all suffering, had a powerful effect upon national habit and custom, long before the new religion found general acceptance. As early as the year 675, a decree was issued by the Emperor Temmu forbidding the people to eat " the flesh of kine, horses, dogs, monkeys, or barn-door fowls," and prohibiting the use of traps or the making of pitfalls in catching game.[1] The fact that all kinds of flesh-meat were not forbidden is probably explained by this Emperor's zeal for the maintenance of both creeds ; — an absolute prohibition might have interfered with Shintō usages, and would certainly have been incompatible with Shintō traditions. But, although fish never ceased to be an article of food for the laity, we may say that from about this time the mass of the nation abandoned its habits of diet, and forswore the eating of meat, in accordance with

[1] See Aston's translation of the *Nihongi*, Vol. II, p. 328.

Buddhist teaching. . . .   This teaching was based upon the doctrine of the unity of all sentient existence.   Buddhism explained the whole visible world by its doctrine of Karma, — simplifying that doctrine so as to adapt it to popular comprehension.   The forms of all creatures, — bird, reptile, or mammal; insect or fish, — represented only different results of Karma: the ghostly life in each was one and the same; and, in even the lowest, some spark of the divine existed.   The frog or the serpent, the bird or the bat, the ox or the horse, — all had had, at some past time, the privilege of human (perhaps even superhuman) shape: their present conditions represented only the consequence of ancient faults. Any human being also, by reason of like faults, might hereafter be reduced to the same dumb state, — might be reborn as a reptile, a fish, a bird, or a beast of burden.   The consequence of wanton cruelty to any animal might cause the perpetrator of that cruelty to be reborn as an animal of the same kind, destined to suffer the same cruel treatment.   Who could even be sure that the goaded ox, the over-driven horse, or the slaughtered bird, had not formerly been a human being of closest kin, — ancestor, parent, brother, sister, or child? . . .

Not by words only were all these things taught. It should be remembered that Shintō had no art: its ghost-houses, silent and void, were not even decorated.   But Buddhism brought in its train all the arts of carving, painting, and decoration.   The images of its Bodhisattvas, smiling in gold, — the figures of its heavenly guardians and infernal judges, its feminine angels and monstrous demons, — must have startled and amazed imaginations yet unaccustomed to any kind of art.   Great paintings hung in the temples, and frescoes limned upon their walls or ceilings, explained better than words the doctrine of the Six States of Existence, and the dogma of future rewards and punishments.   In rows of *kakémono*, suspended side by side, were displayed the incidents of a Soul's journey to the realm of judgment, and all the horrors of the various hells.   One pictured the ghosts of faithless wives, for ages doomed to pluck, with bleeding fingers, the rasping bamboo-grass that grows by the Springs of Death; another showed the torment of the slanderer, whose tongue was torn by demon-pincers; in a third appeared the spectres of lustful men, vainly seeking to flee the embraces of women of fire, or climbing, in frenzied terror, the slopes of the Mountain of Swords.   Pictured also were the circles of the Preta-world, and the pangs of the Hungry Ghosts, and likewise the pains of rebirth in the form of reptiles and of beasts.   And the art of these early representations— many of which have been preserved — was an art of no mean order. We can hardly conceive the effect upon inexperienced imagination of the crimson frown of Emma

(*Yama*), Judge of the dead, — or the vision of that weird Mirror which reflected to every spirit the misdeeds of its life in the body, — or the monstrous fancy of that double-faced Head before the judgment seat, representing the visage of the woman Mirumé, whose eyes behold all secret sin; and the vision of the man Kaguhana, who smells all odours of evil-doing. . . . Parental affection must have been deeply touched by the painted legend of the world of children's ghosts, — the little ghosts that must toil, under demon-surveillance, in the Dry Bed of the River of Souls. . . . But pictured terrors were offset by pictured consolations, — by the beautiful figure of Kwannon, white Goddess of Mercy, — by the compassionate smile of Jizō, the playmate of infant-ghosts, — by the charm also of celestial nymphs, floating on iridescent wings in light of azure. The Buddhist painter opened to simple fancy the palaces of heaven, and guided hope, through gardens of jewel-trees, even to the shores of that lake where the souls of the blessed are reborn in lotos-blossoms, and tended by angel-nurses.

Moreover, for people accustomed only to such simple architecture as that of the Shintō *miya*, the new temples erected by the Buddhist priests must have been astonishments. The colossal Chinese gates, guarded by giant statues; the lions and lanterns of bronze and stone; the enormous suspended bells, sounded by swinging-beams; the swarming of dragon-shapes under the eaves of the vast roofs; the glimmering splendour of the altars; the ceremonial likewise, with its chanting and its incense-burning and its weird Chinese music, — cannot have failed to inspire the wonder-loving with delight and awe. It is a noteworthy fact that the earliest Buddhist temples in Japan still remain, even to Western eyes, the most impressive. The Temple of the Four Deva Kings at Ōsaka — which, though more than once rebuilt, preserves the original plan — dates from 600 A.D.; the yet more remarkable temple called Hōryūji, near Nara, dates from about the year 607.

Of course the famous paintings and the great statues could be seen at the temples only; but the Buddhist image-makers soon began to people even the most desolate places with stone images of Buddhas and of Bodhisattvas. Then first were made those icons of Jizō, which still smile upon the traveller from every roadside, — and the images of Kōshin, protector of highways, with his three symbolic Apes, — and the figure of that Batō-Kwannon, who protects the horses of the peasant, — with other figures in whose rude but impressive art suggestions of Indian origin are yet recognizable. Gradually the graveyards became thronged with dreaming Buddhas or Bodhisattvas, — holy guardians of the dead, throned upon lotos-flowers of stone, and smiling with closed eyes the smile of the Calm Supreme. In the cities everywhere Buddhist sculptors opened shops, to furnish pious households with images of the chief divinities worshipped by the various Buddhist sects; and the makers of *ihai*, or Buddhist mortuary tablets, as well as the makers of household shrines, multiplied and prospered.

Meanwhile the people were left free to worship their ancestors according to either creed; and if a majority eventually gave preference to the Buddhist rite, this preference was due in large measure to the peculiar emotional charm which Buddhism had infused into the cult. Except in minor details, the two rites differed scarcely at all; and there was no conflict whatever between the old ideas of filial piety and the Buddhist ideas attaching to the new ancestor-worship. Buddhism taught that the dead might be helped and made happier by prayer, and that much ghostly comfort could be given them by food-offerings. They were not to be offered flesh or wine; but it was proper to gratify them with fruits and rice and cakes and flowers and the smoke of incense. Besides, even the simplest food-offerings might be transmuted, by force of prayer, into celestial nectar and ambrosia. But what especially helped the new ancestor-cult to popular favour, was the fact that it included many beautiful and touching customs not known to the old. Everywhere

the people soon learned to kindle the hundred and
eight fires of welcome for the annual visit of their
dead, — to supply the spirits with little figures made
of straw, or made out of vegetables, to serve for
oxen or horses,[1] — also to prepare the ghost-ships
(*shōryōbuné*), in which the souls of the ancestors
were to return, over the sea, to their under-world.
Then too were instituted the *Bon-odori*, or Dances
of the Festival of the Dead,[2] and the custom of
suspending white lanterns at graves, and coloured
lanterns at house-gates, to light the coming and
the going of the visiting dead.

But perhaps the greatest value of Buddhism to
the nation was educational. The Shintō priests
were not teachers. In early times they were mostly
aristocrats, religious representatives of the clans;
and the idea of educating the common people could
not even have occurred to them. Buddhism, on

[1] An eggplant, with four pegs of wood stuck into it, to represent legs, usually
stands for an ox; and a cucumber, with four pegs, serves for a horse. . . . One
is reminded of the fact that, at some of the ancient Greek sacrifices, similar substi-
tutes for real animals were used. In the worship of Apollo, at Thebes, apples with
wooden pegs stuck into them, to represent feet and horns, were offered as substi-
tutes for sheep.

[2] The dances themselves — very curious and very attractive to witness — are
much older than Buddhism; but Buddhism made them a feature of the festival referred to, which lasts for three days. No person who has not witnessed a
Bon-odori can form the least idea of what Japanese dancing means: it is something
utterly different from what usually goes by the name, — something indescribably
archaic, weird, and nevertheless fascinating. I have repeatedly sat up all night to
watch the peasants dancing. Japanese dancing girls, be it observed, do not dance:
they pose. The peasants dance.

the other hand, offered the boon of education to all, — not merely a religious education, but an education in the arts and the learning of China. The Buddhist temples eventually became common schools, or had schools attached to them; and at each parish temple the children of the community were taught, at a merely nominal cost, the doctrines of the faith, the wisdom of the Chinese classics, calligraphy, drawing, and much besides. By degrees the education of almost the whole nation came under Buddhist control; and the moral effect was of the best. For the military class indeed there was another and special system of education; but Samurai scholars sought to perfect their knowledge under Buddhist teachers of renown; and the imperial household itself employed Buddhist instructors. For the common people everywhere the Buddhist priest was the schoolmaster; and by virtue of his occupation as teacher, not less than by reason of his religious office, he ranked with the samurai. Much of what remains most attractive in Japanese character — the winning and graceful aspects of it — seems to have been developed under Buddhist training.

It was natural enough that to his functions of public instructor, the Buddhist priest should have added those of a public registrar. Until the period of disendowment, the Buddhist clergy remained, throughout the country, public as well as religious officials. They kept the parish records, and fur-

nished at need certificates of birth, death, or family
descent.

To give any just conception of the immense
civilizing influence which Buddhism exerted in
Japan would require many volumes. Even to
summarize the results of that influence by stating
only the most general facts, is scarcely possible, —
for no general statement can embody the whole
truth of the work accomplished. As a moral force,
Buddhism strengthened authority and cultivated
submission, by its capacity to inspire larger hopes
and fears than the more ancient religion could create. As teacher, it educated the race, from the
highest to the humblest, both in ethics and in
esthetics. All that can be classed under the name
of art in Japan was either introduced or developed
by Buddhism; and the same may be said regarding
nearly all Japanese literature possessing real literary
quality,— excepting some Shintō rituals, and some
fragments of archaic poetry. Buddhism introduced
drama, the higher forms of poetical composition,
and fiction, and history, and philosophy. All the
refinements of Japanese life were of Buddhist introduction, and at least a majority of its diversions and
pleasures. There is even to-day scarcely one interesting or beautiful thing, produced in the country,
for which the nation is not in some sort indebted to
Buddhism. Perhaps the best and briefest way of

stating the range of such indebtedness, is simply to say that Buddhism brought the whole of Chinese civilization into Japan, and thereafter patiently modified and reshaped it to Japanese requirements. The elder civilization was not merely superimposed upon the social structure, but fitted carefully into it, combined with it so perfectly that the marks of the welding, the lines of the juncture, almost totally disappeared.

The Higher Buddhism

PHILOSOPHICAL Buddhism requires some brief consideration in this place, — for two reasons. The first is that misapprehension or ignorance of the subject has rendered possible the charge of atheism against the intellectual classes of Japan. The second reason is that some persons imagine the Japanese common people — that is to say, the greater part of the nation — believers in the doctrine of Nirvâna as extinction (though, as a matter of fact, even the meaning of the word is unknown to the masses), and quite resigned to vanish from the face of the earth, because of that incapacity for struggle which the doctrine is supposed to create. A little serious thinking ought to convince any intelligent man that no such creed could ever have been the religion of either a savage or a civilized people. But myriads of Western minds are ready at all times to accept statements of impossibility without taking the trouble to think about them; and if I can show some of my readers how far beyond popular comprehension the doctrines of the higher Buddhism really are, something will have been accomplished for the cause of truth and common-sense. And besides the reasons already given for dwelling upon the subject, there is this third and special reason, — that it is one of extraordinary interest to the student of modern philosophy.

Before going further, I must remind you that the metaphysics of Buddhism can be studied anywhere else quite as well as in Japan, since the more important sûtras have been translated into various European languages, and most of the untranslated texts edited and published. The texts of Japanese Buddhism are Chinese; and only Chinese scholars are competent to throw light upon the minor special phases of the subject. Even to read the Chinese Buddhist canon of 7000 volumes is commonly regarded as an impossible feat, — though it has certainly been accomplished in Japan. Then there are the commentaries, the varied interpretations of different sects, the multiplications of later doctrine, to heap confusion upon confusion. The complexities of Japanese Buddhism are incalculable; and those who try to unravel them soon become, as a general rule, hopelessly lost in the maze of detail. All this has nothing to do with my present purpose. I shall have very little to say about Japanese Buddhism as distinguished from other Buddhism, and nothing at all to say about sect-differences. I shall keep to general facts as regards the higher doctrine, — selecting from among such facts only those most suitable for the illustration of that doctrine. And I shall not take up the subject of Nirvâna, in spite of its great importance, — having treated it as fully as I was able in my *Gleanings in Buddha-Fields*, — but confine myself to the topic of certain analogies between the conclusions of Buddhist metaphysics and the conclusions of contemporary Western thought.

In the best single volume yet produced in English on the subject of Buddhism,[1] the late Mr. Henry Clarke Warren observed: "A large part of the pleasure that I have experienced in the study of Buddhism has arisen from what I may call the strangeness of the intellectual landscape. All the ideas, the modes of argument, even the postulates assumed and not argued about, have always seemed so strange, so different from anything to which I have been accustomed, that I felt all the time as though walking in Fairyland. Much of the charm that the Oriental thoughts and ideas have for me appears to be because they so seldom fit into Western categories." . . . The serious attraction of Buddhist philosophy could not be better suggested: it is indeed "the strangeness of the intellectual landscape," as of a world inside-out and upside-down, that has chiefly interested Western

---

[1] *Buddhism in Translations*, by Henry Clarke Warren (Cambridge, Massachusetts, 1896). Published by Harvard University.

thinkers heretofore.   Yet after all, there *is* a class of
Buddhist concepts which can be fitted, or very
nearly fitted, into Western categories.   The higher
Buddhism is a kind of Monism; and it includes
doctrines that accord, in the most surprising manner,
with the scientific theories of the German and the
English monists.   To my thinking, the most curious part of the subject, and its main interest, is
represented just by these accordances, — particularly
in view of the fact that the Buddhist conclusions
have been reached through mental processes unknown to Western thinking, and unaided by any
knowledge of science. . . .   I venture to call myself
a student of Herbert Spencer; and it was because
of my acquaintance with the Synthetic Philosophy
that I came to find in Buddhist philosophy a more
than romantic interest.   For Buddhism is also a
theory of evolution, though the great central idea of
our scientific evolution (the law of progress from
homogeneity to heterogeneity) is not correspondingly
implied by Buddhist doctrine as regards the life of
this world.   The course of evolution as we conceive
it, according to Professor Huxley, " must describe a
trajectory like that of a ball fired from a mortar;
and the sinking half of that course is as much a part
of the general process of evolution as the rising."
The highest point of the trajectory would represent
what Mr. Spencer calls Equilibration, — the supreme point of development preceding the period

of decline; but, in Buddhist evolution, this supreme point vanishes into Nirvâna. I can best illustrate the Buddhist position by asking you to imagine the trajectory line upside-down, — a course descending out of the infinite, touching ground, and ascending again to mystery. . . . Nevertheless, some Buddhist ideas do offer the most startling analogy with the evolutional ideas of our own time; and even those Buddhist concepts most remote from Western thought can be best interpreted by the help of illustrations and of language borrowed from modern science.

I think that we may consider the most remarkable teachings of the higher Buddhism, — excluding the doctrine of Nirvâna, for the reason already given, — to be the following : —

That there is but one Reality ; —

That the consciousness is not the real Self ; —

That Matter is an aggregate of phenomena created by the force of acts and thoughts ; —

That all objective and subjective existence is made by Karma, — the present being the creation of the past, and the actions of the present and the past, in combination, determining the conditions of the future. . . . (Or, in other words, that the universe of Matter, and the universe of [conditioned] Mind, represent in their evolution a strictly moral order.)

It will be worth while now to briefly consider

these doctrines in their relation to modern thought, — beginning with the first, which is Monism : —

All things having form or name, — Buddhas, gods, men, and all living creatures, — suns, worlds, moons, the whole visible cosmos, — are transitory phenomena. . . .   Assuming, with Herbert Spencer, that the test of reality is permanence, one can scarcely question this position; it differs little from the statement with which the closing chapter of the *First Principles* concludes : —

"Though the relation of subject and object renders necessary to us these antithetical conceptions of Spirit and Matter, the one is no less than the other to be regarded as but a sign of the Unknown Reality which underlies both." — *Edition of* 1894.

For Buddhism the sole reality is the Absolute, — Buddha as unconditioned and Infinite Being. There is no other veritable existence, whether of Matter or of Mind; there is no real individuality or personality; the "I" and the "Not-I" are essentially nowise different.   We are reminded of Mr. Spencer's position, that "it is one and the same Reality which is manifested to us both subjectively and objectively."   Mr. Spencer goes on to say : "Subject and Object, as actually existing, can never be contained in *the consciousness produced by the coöperation of the two*, though they are necessarily

implied by it; and the antithesis of Subject and
Object, never to be transcended while consciousness
lasts, renders impossible all knowledge of that Ultimate Reality in which Subject and Object are
united.". . . I do not think that a master of the
higher Buddhism would dispute Mr. Spencer's
doctrine of Transfigured Realism. Buddhism does
not deny the actuality of phenomena as phenomena,
but denies their permanence, and the truth of the
appearances which they present to our imperfect
senses. Being transitory, and not what they seem,
they are to be considered in the nature of illusions,
— impermanent manifestations of the only permanent Reality. But the Buddhist position is not
agnosticism: it is astonishingly different, as we shall
presently see. Mr. Spencer states that we cannot
know the Reality so long as consciousness lasts, —
because while consciousness lasts we cannot transcend
the antithesis of Object and Subject, and it is this
very antithesis which makes consciousness possible.
"Very true," the Buddhist metaphysician would
reply; "we cannot know the sole Reality while
consciousness lasts. *But destroy consciousness, and
the Reality becomes cognizable.* Annihilate the illusion of Mind, and the light will come." This destruction of consciousness signifies Nirvâna, — the
extinction of all that we call Self. Self is blindness:
destroy it, and the Reality will be revealed as
infinite vision and infinite peace.

We have now to ask what, according to Buddhist philosophy, is the meaning of the visible universe as phenomenon, and the nature of the consciousness that perceives. However transitory, the phenomenon makes an impression upon consciousness; and consciousness itself, though transitory, has existence; and its perceptions, however delusive, are perceptions of actual relation. Buddhism answers that both the universe and the consciousness are merely aggregates of Karma — complexities incalculable of conditions shaped by acts and thoughts through some enormous past. All substance and all conditioned mind (as distinguished from unconditioned mind) are products of acts and thoughts: by acts and thoughts the atoms of bodies have been integrated; and the affinities of those atoms — the polarities of them, as a scientist might say — represent tendencies shaped in countless vanished lives. I may quote here from a modern Japanese treatise on the subject: —

"The aggregate actions of all sentient beings give birth to the varieties of mountains, rivers, countries, etc. They are caused by aggregate actions, and so are called aggregate fruits. Our present life is the reflection of past actions. Men consider these reflections as their real selves. Their eyes, noses, ears, tongues, and bodies — as well as their gardens, woods, farms, residences, servants, and maids — men imagine to be their own possessions; but, in fact, they are only results endlessly produced by innumerable actions. In tracing every thing back to the ultimate limits of the past, we cannot find a beginning : hence it is said that death and birth have no beginning. Again, when seeking the ultimate limit of the future, we cannot find the end." [1]

This teaching that all things are formed by Karma — whatever is good in the universe repre-senting the results of meritorious acts or thoughts; and what ever is evil, the results of evil acts or thoughts — has the approval of five of the great sects; and we may accept it as a leading doctrine of Japanese Buddhism. . . . The cosmos is, then, an aggregate of Karma; and the mind of man is an aggregate of Karma , and the beginnings thereof are unknown, and the end cannot be imagined. There is a spiritual evolution, of which the goal is Nirvâna; but we have no declaration as to a final state of universal rest, when the shaping of substance and of mind will have ceased forever. . . . Now the Syn-thetic Philosophy assumes a very similar position as regards the evolution of phenomena : there is no beginning to evolution, nor any conceivable end. I quote from Mr. Spencer's reply to a critic in the *North American Review* : —

"That 'absolute commencement of organic life upon the globe,' which the reviewer says I 'cannot evade the admission of,' I distinctly deny. The affirmation of

[1] *Outlines of the Mahâyâna Philosophy*, by S. Kuroda.

universal evolution is in itself the negation of an absolute commencement of anything. Construed in terms of evolution, every kind of being is conceived as a product of modification wrought by insensible gradations upon a preëxisting kind of being; and this holds as fully of the supposed ' commencement of organic life ' as of all subsequent developments of organic life. . . . That organic matter was not produced all at once, but was reached through steps, we are well warranted in believing by the experiences of chemists." [1] . . .

Of course it should be understood that the Buddhist silence, as to a beginning and an end, concerns only the production of phenomena, not any particular existence of groups of phenomena. That of which no beginning or end can be predicated is simply the Eternal Becoming. And, like the older Indian philosophy from which it sprang, Buddhism teaches the alternate apparition and disparition of universes. At certain prodigious periods of time, the whole cosmos of " one hundred thousand times ten millions of worlds " vanishes away, — consumed by fire or otherwise destroyed, — but only to be reformed again. These periods are called " World-Cycles," and each World-Cycle is divided into four " Immensities," — but we need not here consider the details of the doctrine. It is only the fundamental idea of a evolutional rhythm that is really interesting. I need scarcely remind the reader that

[1] *Principles of Biology*, Vol. I, p. 482.

the alternate disintegration and reintegration of the cosmos is also a scientific conception, and a commonly accepted article of evolutional belief. I may quote, however, for other reasons, the paragraph expressing Herbert Spencer's views upon the subject : —

"Apparently the universally coexistent forces of attraction and repulsion, which, as we have seen, necessitate rhythm in all minor changes throughout the Universe, also necessitate rhythm in the totality of changes, — produce now an immeasurable period during which the attractive forces, predominating, cause universal concentration; and then an immeasurable period during which the repulsive forces, predominating, cause diffusion, — alternate eras of Evolution and Dissolution.   And thus there is suggested to us the conception of a past during which there have been successive Evolutions analogous to that which is now going on ; and a future during which successive other such Evolutions may go on — ever the same in principle, but never the same in concrete result." — *First Principles*, § 183.[1]

Further on, Mr. Spencer has pointed out the vast logical consequence involved by this hypothesis : —

"If, as we saw reason to think, there is an alternation of Evolution and Dissolution in the totality of things, — if, as we are obliged to infer from the Persistence of Force, the arrival at either limit of this vast rhythm brings about the conditions under which a counter-movement commences,

[1] This paragraph, from the fourth edition, has been considerably qualified in the definitive edition of 1900.

— if we are hence compelled to entertain the conception of Evolutions that have filled an immeasurable past, and Evolutions that will fill an immeasurable future,—we can no longer contemplate the visible creation as having a definite beginning or end, or as being isolated. It becomes unified with all existence before and after; and the Force which the Universe presents falls into the same category with its Space and Time as admitting of no limitation in thought." [1] — *First Principles*, § 190.

The foregoing Buddhist positions sufficiently imply that the human consciousness is but a temporary aggregate,—not an eternal entity. There is no permanent self: there is but one eternal principle in all life,—the supreme Buddha. Modern Japanese call this Absolute the "Essence of Mind." "The fire fed by faggots," writes one of these, "dies when the faggots have been consumed; but the essence of fire is never destroyed. . . . All things in the Universe are Mind." So stated, the position is unscientific; but as for the conclusion reached, we may remember that Mr. Wallace has stated almost exactly the same thing, and that there are not a few modern preachers of the doctrine of a "universe of mind-stuff." The hypothesis is "unthinkable." But the most serious thinker will agree with the Buddhist assertion that the relation of all phenomena to the unknowable is merely that of waves to sea. "Every

[1] Condensed and somewhat modified in the definitive edition of 1900 ; but, for present purposes of illustration, the text of the fourth edition has been preferred.

feeling and thought being but transitory," says Mr.
Spencer, "an entire life made up of such feelings
and thoughts being but transitory, — nay, the objects
amid which life is passed, though less transitory,
being severally in course of losing their individuali-
ties quickly or slowly, — we learn that the one thing
permanent is the Unknown Reality hidden under
all these changing shapes." Here the English and
the Buddhist philosophers are in accord; but thereafter they suddenly part company. For Buddhism
is not agnosticism, but gnosticism, and professes
to know the unknowable. The thinker of Mr.
Spencer's school cannot make assumptions as to the
nature of the sole Reality, nor as to the reason of
its manifestations. He must confess himself in-
tellectually incapable of comprehending the nature
of force, matter, or motion. He feels justified in
accepting the hypothesis that all known elements
have been evolved from one primordial undif-
ferentiated substance, — the chemical evidence for
this hypothesis being very strong. But he certainly
would not call that primordial substance a substance
of mind, nor attempt to explain the character of the
forces that effected its integration. Again, though
Mr. Spencer would probably acknowledge that we
know of matter only as an aggregate of forces, and
of atoms only as force-centres, or knots of force, he
would not declare that an atom *is* a force-centre,
and nothing else. . . . But we find evolutionists

of the German school taking a position very similar to the Buddhist position, — which implies a universal sentiency, or, more strictly speaking, a universal potential-sentiency. Haeckel and other German monists assume such a condition for all substance. They are not agnostics, therefore, but gnostics; and their gnosticism very much resembles that of the higher Buddhism.

According to Buddhism there is no reality save Buddha: all things else are but Karma. There is but one Life, one Self: human individuality and personality are but phenomenal conditions of that Self. Matter is Karma; Mind is Karma — that is to say, mind as we know it: Karma, as visibility, represents to us mass and quality; Karma, as mentality, signifies character and tendency. The primordial substance — corresponding to the " protyle " of our Monists — is composed of Five Elements, which are mystically identified with Five Buddhas, all of whom are really but different modes of the One. With this idea of a primordial substance there is necessarily associated the idea of a universal sentiency. Matter is alive.

Now to the German monists also matter is alive. On the phenomena of cell-physiology, Haeckel claims to base his conviction that " even the atom is not without rudimentary form of sensation and will, — or, as it is better expressed, of feeling (*aesthesis*), and of inclination (*tropesis*), — that is to

say, a universal soul of the simplest kind." I
may quote also from Haeckel's *Riddle of the
Universe* the following paragraph expressing the
monistic notion of substance as held by Vogt and
others : —

" The two fundamental forms of substance, ponderable
matter and ether, are not dead and only moved by extrinsic
force ; but they are endowed with sensation and will (though,
naturally, of the lowest grade) ; they experience an inclination for condensation, a dislike of strain ; they strive
after the one, and struggle against the other."

Less like a revival of the dreams of the Alche-
mists is the very probable hypothesis of Schneider,
that sentiency begins with the formation of certain
combinations, — that feeling is evolved from the
non-feeling just as organic being has been evolved
from inorganic substance. But all these monist
ideas enter into surprising combination with the
Buddhist teaching about matter as integrated Karma ;
and for that reason they are well worth citing in this
relation. To Buddhist conception all matter is sentient, — the sentiency varying according to condition :
" even rocks and stones," a Japanese Buddhist
text declares, " can worship Buddha." In the German monism of Professor Haeckel's school, the
particular qualities and affinities of the atom represent feeling and inclination, " a soul of the simplest
kind " ; in Buddhism these qualities are made by

Karma, — that is to say, they represent tendencies formed in previous states of existence. The hypotheses appear to be very similar. But there is one immense, all-important difference, between the Occidental and the Oriental monism. The former would attribute the qualities of the atom merely to a sort of heredity, — to the persistency of tendencies developed under chance-influences operating throughout an incalculable past. The latter declares the history of the atom to be purely moral! All matter, according to Buddhism, represents aggregated sentiency, making, by its inherent tendencies, toward conditions of pain or pleasure, evil or good. " Pure actions," writes the author of *Outlines of the Mahâyâna Philosophy*, "bring forth the Pure Lands of all the quarters of the universe; while impure deeds produce the Impure Lands." That is to say, the matter integrated by the force of moral acts goes to the making of blissful worlds; and the matter formed by the force of immoral acts goes to the making of miserable worlds. All substance, like all mind, has its Karma; planets, like men, are shaped by the creative power of acts and thoughts; and every atom goes to its appointed place, sooner or later, according to the moral or immoral quality of the tendencies that inform it. Your good or bad thought or deed will not only affect your next rebirth, but will likewise affect in some sort the nature of worlds yet unevolved, wherein, after innumerable cycles,

you may have to live again. Of course, this tremendous idea has no counterpart in modern evolutional philosophy. Mr. Spencer's position is well
known; but I must quote him for the purpose of
emphasizing the contrast between Buddhist and
scientific thought : —

"... We have no ethics of nebular condensation, or of
sidereal movement, or of planetary evolution; the conception
is not relevant to inorganic matter. Nor, when we turn to
organized things, do we find that it has any relation to the
phenomena of plant-life; though we ascribe to plants
superiorities and inferiorities, leading to successes and failures in the struggle for existence, we do not associate
with them praise or blame. It is only with the rise of
sentiency in the animal world that the subject-matter of
ethics originates." — *Principles of Ethics*, Vol. II, § 326.

On the contrary, it will be seen, Buddhism
actually teaches what we may call, to borrow Mr.
Spencer's phrase, "the ethics of nebular condensation," — though to Buddhist astronomy, the scientific meaning of the term " nebular condensation "
was never known. Of course the hypothesis is beyond the power of human intelligence to prove or
to disprove. But it is interesting, for it proclaims
a purely moral order of the cosmos, and attaches
almost infinite consequence to the least of human
acts. Had the old Buddhist metaphysicians been
acquainted with the facts of modern chemistry, they

might have applied their doctrine, with appalling success, to the interpretation of those facts. They might have explained the dance of atoms, the affinities of molecules, the vibrations of ether, in the most fascinating and terrifying way by their theory of Karma. . . . Here is a universe of suggestion, — most weird suggestion — for anybody able and willing to dare the experiment of making a new religion, or at least a new and tremendous system of Alchemy, based upon the notion of a moral order in the inorganic world!

But the metaphysics of Karma in the higher Buddhism include much that is harder to understand than any alchemical hypothesis of atom-combinations. As taught by popular Buddhism, the doctrine of rebirth is simple enough, — signifying no more than transmigration: you have lived millions of times in the past, and you are likely to live again millions of times in the future, — all the conditions of each rebirth depending upon past conduct. The common notion is that after a certain period of bodiless sojourn in this world, the spirit is guided somehow to the place of its next incarnation. The people, of course, believe in souls. But there is nothing of all this in the higher doctrine, which denies transmigration, denies the existence of the soul, denies personality. There is no Self to be reborn; there is no transmigration — and yet there is rebirth! There is no real " I " that suffers or is glad — and yet there is new suffering to be borne or new happiness to be gained! What we call the Self, — the personal consciousness, — dissolves at the death of the body; but the Karma, formed during life, then brings about the integration of a new body and a new consciousness. You suffer in this existence because of acts done in a previous existence — yet the author of those acts was not identical with your present self! Are you, then, responsible for the faults of another person?

The Buddhist metaphysician would answer thus: " The form of your question is wrong, because it assumes the existence of personality, — and there is no personality. There is really no such individual as the 'you' of the inquiry. The suffering is indeed the result of errors committed in some anterior existence or existences; but there is no responsibility for the acts of another person, since there is no personality. The ' I ' that was and the ' I ' that is represent in the chain of transitory being aggregations momentarily created by acts and thoughts; and the pain belongs to the aggregates as condition resulting from quality." All this sounds extremely obscure: to understand the real theory we must put away the notion of personality, which is a very difficult thing to do. Successive births do not mean transmigration in the common sense of that word, but only the self-propagation of

Karma: the perpetual multiplying of certain conditions by a kind of ghostly gemmation, — if I may borrow a biological term. The Buddhist illustration, however, is that of flame communicated from one lamp-wick to another: a hundred lamps may thus be lighted from one flame, and the hundred flames will all be different, though the origin of all was the same. Within the hollow flame of each transitory life is enclosed a part of the only Reality; but this is not a soul that transmigrates. Nothing passes from birth to birth but Karma, — character or condition.

One will naturally ask how can such a doctrine exert any moral influence whatever? ·If the future being shaped by my Karma is to be in nowise identical with my present self, — if the future consciousness evolved by *my* Karma is to be essentially another consciousness, — how can I force myself to feel anxious about the sufferings of that unborn person? "Again your question is wrong," a Buddhist would answer: " to understand the doctrine you must get rid of the notion of individuality, and think, not of persons, but of successive states of feeling and consciousness, each of which buds out of the other, — a chain of existences interdependently united." . . . I may attempt another illustration. Every individual, as we understand the term, is continually changing. All the structures of the body are constantly undergoing waste and repair; and the

body that you have at this hour is not, as to substance, the same body that you had ten years ago.
Physically you are not the same person : yet you
suffer the same pains, and feel the same pleasures,
and find your powers limited by the same conditions.
Whatever disintegrations and reconstructions of
tissue have taken place within you, you have the
same physical and mental peculiarities that you had
ten years ago. Doubtless the cells of your brain
have been decomposed and recomposed : yet you
experience the same emotions, recall the same
memories, and think the same thoughts. Everywhere the fresh substance has assumed the qualities
and tendencies of the substance replaced. This
persistence of condition is like Karma. The trans-
mission of tendency remains, though the aggregate
is changed. . . .

These few glimpses into the fantastic world of
Buddhist metaphysics will suffice, I trust, to convince any intelligent reader that the higher Buddhism (to which belongs the much-discussed and
little-comprehended doctrine of Nirvâna) could
never have been the religion of millions almost
incapable of forming abstract ideas, — the religion
of a population even yet in a comparatively early
stage of religious evolution. It was never understood by the people at all, nor is it ever taught to
them to-day. It is a religion of metaphysicians, a

religion of scholars, a religion so difficult to be understood, even by persons of some philosophical training, that it might well be mistaken for a system of universal negation. Yet the reader should now be able to perceive that, because a man disbelieves in a personal God, in an immortal soul, and in any continuation of personality after death, it does not follow that we are justified in declaring him an irreligious person, — especially if he happen to be an Oriental. The Japanese scholar who believes in the moral order of the universe, the ethical responsibility of the present to all the future, the immeasurable consequence of every thought and deed, the ultimate disparition of evil, and the power of attainment to conditions of infinite memory and infinite vision, — cannot be termed either an atheist or a materialist, except by bigotry and ignorance. Profound as may be the difference between his religion and our own, in respect of symbols and modes of thought, the moral conclusions reached in either case are very much the same.

The Social Organization

THE late Professor Fiske, in his *Outlines of Cosmic Philosophy*, made a very interesting remark about societies like those of China, ancient Egypt, and ancient Assyria. "I am expressing," he said, "something more than an analogy, I am describing a real homology so far as concerns the process of development, — when I say that these communities simulated modern European nations, much in the same way that a tree-fern of the carboniferous period simulated the exogenous trees of the present time." So far as this is true of China, it is likewise true of Japan. The constitution of the old Japanese society was no more than an amplification of the constitution of the family, — the patriarchal family of primitive times. All modern Western societies have been developed out of a like patriarchal condition: the early civilizations of Greece and Rome were similarly constructed, upon a lesser scale. But the patriarchal family in Europe was disintegrated thousands of years ago: the *gens* and the *curia* dissolved and disappeared; the originally distinct classes became fused together; and a total reorganization of society was gradually effected, everywhere resulting in the substitution of voluntary for compulsory coöperation. Industrial types of society developed; and a state-religion overshadowed the ancient and exclusive local cults. But society in Japan never, till within the present era, became one coherent body, never developed beyond the clan-stage. It remained a loose agglomerate of clan-groups, or tribes, each religiously and administratively independent of the rest; and this huge agglomerate was kept together, not by voluntary coöperation, but by strong compulsion. Down to the period of Meiji, and even for some time afterward, it was liable to split and fall asunder at any moment that the central coercive power showed signs of weakness. We may call it a feudalism; but it resembled European feudalism only as a tree-fern resembles a tree.

Let us first briefly consider the nature of the ancient Japanese society. Its original unit was not the household, but the patriarchal family, — that is to say, the gens or clan, a body of hundreds or thousands of persons claiming descent from a common ancestor, and so religiously united by a common ancestor-worship, — the cult of the Ujigami. As I have said before, there were two classes of these patriarchal families: the Ō-uji, or Great Clans; and the Ko-uji, or Little Clans. The lesser were branches of the greater, and subordinate to

them, — so that the group formed by an Ō-uji with
its Ko-uji might be loosely compared with the
Roman curia or Greek phratry. Large bodies of
serfs or slaves appear to have been attached to the
various great Uji; and the number of these, even at
a very early period, seems to have exceeded that of
the members of the clans proper. The different
names given to these subject-classes indicate different grades and kinds of servitude. One name was
tomobé, signifying bound to a place, or district;
another was *yakabé*, signifying bound to a family;
a third was *kakibé*, signifying bound to a close, or
estate; yet another and more general term was
tami, which anciently signified " dependants," but is
now used in the meaning of the English word
"folk." . . . There is little doubt that the bulk
of the people were in a condition of servitude, and
that there were many forms of servitude. Mr.
Spencer has pointed out that a general distinction
between slavery and serfdom, in the sense commonly attached to each of those terms, is by no
means easy to establish; the real state of a subject-
class, especially in early forms of society, depending
much more upon the character of the master, and
the actual conditions of social development, than
upon matters of privilege and legislation. In
speaking of early Japanese institutions, the distinction is particularly hard to draw: we are still but
little informed as to the condition of the subject-

classes in ancient times.   It is safe to assert, however, that there were then really but two great
classes, — a ruling oligarchy, divided into many
grades ; and a subject population, also divided into
many grades.   Slaves were tattooed, either on the
face or some part of the body, with a mark indicating their ownership.   Until within recent years this
system of tattooing appears to have been maintained
in the province of Satsuma, — where the marks
were put especially upon the hands ; and in many
other provinces the lower classes were generally
marked by a tattoo on the face.   Slaves were
bought and sold like cattle in early times, or presented as tribute by their owners, — a practice constantly referred to in the ancient records.   Their
unions were not recognized : a fact which reminds
us of the distinction among the Romans between
connubium and *contubernium ;* and the children of a
slave-mother by a free father remained slaves.[1]   In
the seventh century, however, private slaves were
declared state-property, and great numbers were

[1] In the year 645, the Emperor Kōtoku issued the following edict on the
subject : —

"The law of men and women shall be that the children born of a free man and
a free woman shall belong to the father ; if a free man takes to wife a slave-woman,
her children shall belong to the mother ; if a free woman marries a slave-man, the
children shall belong to the father ; if they are slaves of two houses, the children
shall belong to the mother.   The children of temple-serfs shall follow the rule for
freemen.   But in regard to others who become slaves, they shall be treated according to the rule for slaves."— Aston's translation of the *Nihongi*, Vol. II,
p. 202.

then emancipated,—including nearly all—probably all—who were artizans or followed useful callings. Gradually a large class of freedmen came into existence; but until modern times the great mass of the common people appear to have remained in a condition analogous to serfdom. The greater number certainly had no family names,—which is considered evidence of a former slave-condition. Slaves proper were registered in the names of their owners: they do not seem to have had a cult of their own,—in early times, at least. But, prior to Meiji, only the aristocracy, samurai, doctors, and teachers — with perhaps a few other exceptions — could use a family name. Another queer bit of evidence on the subject, furnished by the late Dr. Simmons, relates to the mode of wearing the hair among the subject-classes. Up to the time of the Ashikaga shōgunate (1334 A.D.), all classes excepting the nobility, samurai, Shintō priests, and doctors, shaved the greater part of the head, and wore queues; and this fashion of wearing the hair was called *yakko-atama* or *dorei-atama* — terms signifying "slave-head," and indicating that the fashion originated in a period of servitude.

About the origin of Japanese slavery, much remains to be learned. There are evidences of successive immigrations; and it is possible that some, at least, of the earlier Japanese settlers were reduced by later invaders to the status of servitude. Again,

there was a considerable immigration of Koreans
and Chinese, some of whom might have voluntarily
sought servitude as a refuge from worse evils.   But
the subject remains obscure.   We know, however,
that degradation to slavery was a common punishment in early times; also, that debtors unable to
pay became the slaves of their creditors; also, that
thieves were sentenced to become the slaves of those
whom they had robbed.[1]   Evidently there were
great differences in the conditions of servitude.
The more unfortunate class of slaves were scarcely
better off than domestic animals; but there were
serfs who could not be bought or sold, nor employed at other than special work; these were of
kin to their lords, and may have entered voluntarily
into servitude for the sake of sustenance and protection.   Their relation to their masters reminds
us of that of the Roman client to the Roman
patron.

As yet it is difficult to establish any clear distinction between the freedmen and the freemen of
ancient Japanese society; but we know that the
free population, ranking below the ruling class,

[1] An edict issued by the Empress Jitō, in 690, enacted that a father could sell
his son into real slavery; but that debtors could be sold only into a kind of serfdom.
The edict ran thus : "If a younger brother of the common people is sold by his
elder brother, he should be classed with freemen; if a child is sold by his parents,
he should be classed with slaves; persons confiscated into slavery, by way of payment of interest on debts, are to be classed with freemen; and their children, though
born of a union with a slave, are to be all classed with freemen." — Aston's
Nihongi, Vol. II, p. 402.

consisted of two great divisions : the *kunitsuko* and
the *tomonotsuko*. The first were farmers, descendants perhaps of the earliest Mongol invaders, and
were permitted to hold their own lands independently of the central government : they were lords
of their own soil, but not nobles. The *tomonotsuko*
were artizans, — probably of Korean or Chinese
descent, for the most part, — and numbered no
less than 180 clans. They followed hereditary
occupations ; and their clans were attached to the
imperial clans, for which they were required to
furnish skilled labour.

Originally each of the Ō-uji and Ko-uji had its
own territory, chiefs, dependants, serfs, and slaves.
The chieftainships were hereditary, — descending
from father to son in direct succession from the
original patriarch. The chief of a great clan was
lord over the chiefs of the subclans attached to it :
his authority was both religious and military. It
must not be forgotten that religion and government
were considered identical.

All Japanese clan-families were classed under
three heads, — *Kōbétsu*, *Shinbétsu*, and *Bambétsu*.
The *Kōbétsu* (" Imperial Branch ") represented the
so-called imperial families, claiming descent from
the Sun-goddess ; the *Shinbétsu* (" Divine Branch ")
were clans claiming descent from other deities,
terrestrial or celestial ; the *Bambétsu* (" Foreign
Branch ") represented the mass of the people.

Thus it would seem that, by the ruling classes, the common people were originally considered strangers, — Japanese only by adoption. Some scholars think that the term *Bambêtsu* was at first given to serfs or freedmen of Chinese or Korean descent. But this has not been proved. It is only certain that all society was divided into three classes, according to ancestry; that two of these classes constituted a ruling oligarchy;[1] and that the third, or "foreign" class represented the bulk of the nation, — the *plebs*.

There was a division also into castes — *kabanê* or *sei*. (I use the term "castes," following Dr. Florenz, a leading authority on ancient Japanese civilization, who gives the meaning of *sei* as equivalent to that of the Sanscrit *varna*, signifying "caste" or "colour.") Every family in the three great divisions of Japanese society belonged to some caste; and each caste represented at first some occupation or calling. Caste would not seem to have developed any very rigid structure in Japan; and there were early tendencies to a confusion of the kabanê. In the seventh century the confusion became so great that the Emperor Temmu thought it necessary to reorganize the *sei;* and by him all the clan-families were regrouped into eight new castes.

[1] Dr. Florenz accounts for the distinction between *Kōbêtsu* and *Shinbêtsu* as due to the existence of two military ruling classes, — resulting from two successive waves of invasion or immigration. The *Kōbêtsu* were the followers of Jimmu Tennō; the *Shinbêtsu* were earlier conquerors who had settled in Yamato prior to the advent of Jimmu. These first conquerors, he thinks, were not dispossessed.

Such was the primal constitution of Japanese
society; and that society was, therefore, in no true
sense of the term, a fully formed nation. Nor can
the title of Emperor be correctly applied to its early
rulers. The German scholar, Dr. Florenz, was the
first to establish these facts, contrary to the assumption of Japanese historians. He has shown that the
" heavenly sovereign" of the early ages was the
hereditary chief of one Uji only, — which Uji, being
the most powerful of all, exercised influence over
many of the others. The authority of the " heavenly
sovereign" did not extend over the country. But
though not even a king, — outside of his own large
group of patriarchal families, — he enjoyed three
immense prerogatives. The first was the right of
representing the different Uji before the common
ancestral deity, — which implies the privileges and
powers of a high priest. The second was the right
of representing the different Uji in foreign relations :
that is to say, he could make peace or declare war in
the name of all the clans, and therefore exercised the
supreme military authority. His third prerogative
included the right to settle disputes between clans ;
the right to nominate a clan-patriarch, in case that
the line of direct succession to the chieftainship of
any Uji came to an end ; the right to establish new
Uji ; and the right to abolish an Uji guilty of so acting as to endanger the welfare of the rest. He was,
therefore, Supreme Pontiff, Supreme Military Com-

mander, Supreme Arbitrator, and Supreme Magistrate. But he was not yet supreme king: his powers were exercised only by consent of the clans. Later he was to become the Great Khan in very fact, and even much more, — the Priest-Ruler, the God-King, the Deity-Incarnate. But with the growth of his dominion, it became more and more difficult for him to exercise all the functions originally combined in his authority; and, as a consequence of deputing those functions, his temporal sway was doomed to decline, even while his religious power continued to augment.

The earliest Japanese society was not, therefore, even a feudalism in the meaning which we commonly attach to that word: it was a union of clans at first combined for defence and offence, — each clan having a religion of its own. Gradually one clan-group, by power of wealth and numbers, obtained such domination that it was able to impose its cult upon all the rest, and to make its hereditary chief Supreme High Pontiff. The worship of the Sun-goddess so became a race-cult; but this worship did not diminish the relative importance of the other clan-cults, — it only furnished them with a common tradition. Eventually a nation formed; but the clan remained the real unit of society; and not until the present era of Meiji was its disintegration effected — at least in so far as legislation could accomplish.

We may call that period during which the clans became really united under one head, and the national cult was established, the First Period of Japanese Social Evolution. However, the social organism did not develop to the limit of its type until the era of the Tokugawa shōguns, — so that, in order to study it as a completed structure, we must turn to modern times. Yet it had taken on the vague outline of its destined form as early as the reign of the Emperor Temmu, whose accession is generally dated 673 A.D. During that reign Buddhism appears to have become a powerful influence at court; for the Emperor practically imposed a vegetarian diet upon the people — proof positive of supreme power in fact as well as in theory. Even before this time society had been arranged into ranks and grades, — each of the upper grades being distinguished by the form and quality of the official head-dresses worn; but the Emperor Temmu established many new grades, and reorganized the whole administration, after the Chinese manner, in one hundred and eight departments. Japanese society then assumed, as to its upper ranks, nearly all the hierarchical forms which it presented down to the era of the Tokugawa shōguns, who consolidated the system without seriously changing its fundamental structure. We may say that from the close of the First Period of its social evolution, the nation remained practically separated into two classes: the governing class, including all orders of the nobility and military; and the producing class, comprising all the rest. The chief event of the Second Period of the social evolution was the rise of the military power, which left the imperial religious authority intact, but usurped all the administrative functions — (this subject will be considered in a later chapter). The society eventually crystallized by this military power was a very complex structure — outwardly resembling a huge feudalism, as we understand the term, but intrinsically different from any European feudalism that ever existed. The difference lay especially in the religious organization of the Japanese communities, each of which, retaining its particular cult and patriarchal administration, remained essentially separate from every other. The national cult was a bond of tradition, not of cohesion: there was no religious unity. Buddhism, though widely accepted, brought no real change into this order of things; for, whatever Buddhist creed a commune might profess, the real social bond remained the bond of the Ujigami. So that, even as fully developed under the Tokugawa rule, Japanese society was still but a great aggregate of clans and subclans, kept together by military coercion.

At the head of this vast aggregate was the Heavenly Sovereign, the Living God of the race, — Priest-Emperor and Pontiff Supreme, — representing the oldest dynasty in the world.

Next to him stood the Kugé, or ancient nobility,
— descendants of emperors and of gods. There
were, in the time of the Tokugawa, 155 families of
this high nobility. One of these, the Nakatomi,
held, and still holds, the highest hereditary priesthood : the Nakatomi were, under the Emperor, the
chiefs of the ancestral cult. All the great clans of
early Japanese history — such as the Fujiwara, the
Taira, the Minamoto — were Kugé ; and most of
the great regents and shōguns of later history were
either Kugé or descendants of Kugé.

Next to the Kugé ranked the Buké, or military
class, — also called Monofufu, Wasaraü, or Samu-
rahi (according to the ancient writing of these names),
— with an extensive hierarchy of its own. But the
difference, in most cases, between the lords and the
warriors of the Buké was a difference of rank based
upon income and title : all alike were samurai, and
nearly all were of Kōbétsu or Shinbétsu descent.
In early times the head of the military class was
appointed by the Emperor, only as a temporary
commander-in-chief : afterwards, these commanders-
in-chief, by usurpation of power, made their office
hereditary, and became veritable *imperatores*, in the
Roman sense. Their title of *shōgun* is well known
to Western readers. The shōgun ruled over between two and three hundred lords of provinces or
districts, whose powers and privileges varied according to income and grade. Under the Tokugawa

shōgunate there were 292 of these lords, or daimyō.
Before that time each lord exercised supreme rule
over his own domain; and it is not surprising that
the Jesuit missionaries, as well as the early Dutch
and English traders should have called the daimyō
"kings." The despotism of the daimyō was first
checked by the founders of the Tokugawa dynasty,
Iyéyasu, who so restricted their powers that they
became, with some exceptions, liable to lose their
estates if proved guilty of oppression and cruelty.
He ranked them all in four great classes: (1) *Sanké*,
or *Go-Sanké*, the "Three Exalted Families" (those
from whom a successor to the shōgunate might
be chosen in case of need); (2) *Kokushū*, "Lords
of Provinces"; (3) *Tozama*, "Outside-Lords";
(4) *Fudai*, "Successful Families": a name given
to those families promoted to lordship or otherwise
rewarded for fealty to Iyéyasu. Of the Sanké, there
were three clans, or families: of the Kokushū, eigh-
teen; of the Tozama, eighty-six; and of the Fudai,
one hundred and seventy-six. The income of the
least of these daimyō was 10,000 *koku* of rice (we
may say about £10,000, though the value of the
koku differed greatly at different periods); and the
income of the greatest, the Lord of Kaga, was estimated at 1,027,000 *koku*.

The great daimyō had their greater and lesser
vassals; and each of these, again, had his force of
trained samurai, or fighting gentry. There was

also a particular class of soldier-farmers, called *gōshi*, some of whom possessed privileges and powers exceeding those of the lesser *daimyō*. These *gōshi*, who were independent landowners, for the most part, formed a kind of yeomanry; but there were many points of difference between the social position of the *gōshi* and that of the English yeomen.

Besides reorganizing the military class, Iyéyasu created several new subclasses. The more important of these were the *hatamoto* and the *gokénin*. The hatamoto, whose appellation signifies " banner-supporters," numbered about 2000, and the gokénin about 5000. These two bodies of samurai formed the special military force of the shōgun; the hatamoto being greater vassals, with large incomes; and the gokénin lesser vassals, with small incomes, who ranked above other common samurai only because of being directly attached to the shōgun's service. . . . The total number of samurai of all grades was about 2,000,000. They were exempted from taxation, and privileged to wear two swords.

Such, in brief outline, was the general ordination of those noble and military classes by whom the nation was ruled with great severity. The bulk of the common people were divided into three classes (we might even say castes, but for Indian ideas long associated with the term): Farmers, Artizans, and Merchants.

Of these three classes, the farmers (*hyakushō*) were the highest ; ranking immediately after the samurai. Indeed, it is hard to draw a line between the samurai-class and the farming-class,— because many samurai were farmers also, and because some farmers held a rank considerably above that of ordinary samurai. Perhaps we should limit the term *hyakushō* (farmers, or peasantry) to those tillers of the soil who lived only by agriculture, and were neither of *Kōbétsu* nor *Shimbétsu* descent. . . .   At all events, the occupation of the peasant was considered honourable : a farmer's daughter might become a servant in the imperial household itself — though she could occupy only an humble position in the service.   Certain farmers were privileged to wear swords.   It appears that in the early ages of Japanese society there was no distinction between farmers and warriors : all able-bodied farmers were then trained fighting-men, ready for war at any moment, — a condition paralleled in old Scandinavian society.   After a special military class had been evolved, the distinction between farmer and samurai still remained vague in certain parts of the country.   In Satsuma and in Tosa, for example, the samurai continued to farm down to the present era : the best of the Kyūshū samurai were nearly all farmers ; and their superior stature and strength were commonly attributed to their rustic occupations.   In other parts of the country, as in Izumo, farming was forbidden to samurai :

they were not even allowed to hold rice-land, though they might own forest-land. But in various provinces they were permitted to farm, even while strictly forbidden to follow any other occupation,— any trade or craft. . . . At no time did any degradation attach to the pursuit of agriculture. Some of the early emperors took a personal interest in farming; and in the grounds of the Imperial Palace at Akasaka may even now be seen a little rice-field. By religious tradition, immemorially old, the first sheaf of rice grown within the imperial grounds should be reaped and offered by the imperial hand to the divine ancestors as a harvest offering, on the occasion of the Ninth Festival, — *Shin-Shō-Sai*.[1]

Below the peasantry ranked the artizan-class (*Shō-kunin*), including smiths, carpenters, weavers, potters, — all crafts, in short. Highest among these were reckoned, as we might expect, the sword-smiths. Sword-smiths not infrequently rose to dignities far beyond their class : some had conferred upon them the high title of *Kami*, written with the same character used in the title of a daimyō, who was usually termed the *Kami* of his province or district. Naturally they enjoyed the patronage of the highest, — emperors and Kugé. The Emperor Go-Toba is known to have worked at sword-making in a smithy

[1] At this festival the first new silk of the year, as well as the first of the new rice-crop, is still offered to the Sun-goddess by the Emperor in person.

of his own.   Religious rites were practised during
the forging of a blade down to modern times. . . .

All the principal crafts had guilds; and, as a
general rule, trades were hereditary.   There are
good historical grounds for supposing that the ancestors of the Shōkunin were mostly Koreans and
Chinese.

The commercial class (*Akindō*), including bankers, merchants, shopkeepers, and traders of all kinds,
was the lowest officially recognized.   The business
of money-making was held in contempt by the superior classes; and all methods of profiting by the
purchase and re-sale of the produce of labour were
regarded as dishonourable.   A military aristocracy
would naturally look down upon the trading-
classes; and there is generally, in militant societies, small respect for the common forms of
labour.   But in Old Japan the occupations of the
farmer and the artizan were not despised : trade
alone appears to have been considered degrading, —
and the discrimination may have been partly a
moral one.   The relegation of the mercantile class
to the lowest place in the social scale must have
produced some curious results.   However rich, for
example, a rice-dealer might be, he ranked below
the carpenters or potters or boat-builders whom he
might employ, — unless it happened that his family
originally belonged to another class.   In later times

the Akindō included many persons of other than Akindō descent; and the class thus virtually retrieved itself.

Of the four great classes of the nation — Samurai, Farmers, Artizans, and Merchants (the *Shi-No-Ko-Shō*, as they were briefly called, after the initial characters of the Chinese terms used to designate them) — the last three were counted together under the general appellation of *Heimin*, " common folk." All heimin were subject to the samurai; any samurai being privileged to kill the heimin showing him disrespect.   But the heimin were actually the nation: they alone created the wealth of the country, produced the revenues, paid the taxes, supported the nobility and military and clergy.   As for the clergy, the Buddhist (like the Shintō) priests, though forming a class apart, ranked with the samurai, not with the heimin.

Outside of the three classes of commoners, and hopelessly below the lowest of them, large classes of persons existed who were not reckoned as Japanese, and scarcely accounted human beings.   Officially they were mentioned generically as *chōri*, and were counted with the peculiar numerals used in counting animals : *ippiki*, *nihiki*, *sambiki*, etc.   Even to-day they are commonly referred to, not as persons (*hito*), but as " things " (*mono*).   To English readers (chiefly through Mr. Mitford's yet unrivalled *Tales of Old*

Japan) they are known as *Éta;* but their appellations varied according to their callings. They were pariah-people : Japanese writers have denied, upon apparently good grounds, that the *chōri* belong to the Japanese race. Various tribes of these outcasts followed occupations in the monopoly of which they were legally confirmed : they were well-diggers, garden-sweepers, straw-workers, sandal-makers, according to local privileges. One class was employed officially in the capacity of torturers and executioners ; another was employed as night-watchmen ; a third as grave-makers. But most of the Éta followed the business of tanners and leather-dressers. They alone had the right to slaughter and flay animals, to prepare various kinds of leather, and to manufacture leather sandals, stirrup-straps, and drumheads, — the making of drumheads being a lucrative occupation in a country where drums were used in a hundred thousand temples. The Eta had their own laws, and their own chiefs, who exercised powers of life and death. They lived always in the suburbs or immediate neighbourhood of towns, but only in separate settlements of their own. They could enter the town to sell their wares, or to make purchases ; but they could not enter any shop, except the shop of a dealer in footgear.[1] As professional singers they were tolerated ; but they were forbidden to enter any house — so they could perform their music or sing

[1] This is still the rule in certain parts of the country.

their songs only in the street, or in a garden. Any occupations other than their hereditary callings were strictly forbidden to them. Between the lowest of the commercial classes and the Éta, the barrier was impassable as any created by caste-tradition in India ; and never was Ghetto more separated from the rest of a European city by walls and gates, than an Éta settlement from the rest of a Japanese town by social prejudice. No Japanese would dream of entering an Éta settlement unless obliged to do so in some official capacity. . . . At the pretty little seaport of Mionoséki, I saw an Éta settlement, forming one termination of the crescent of streets extending round the bay. Mionoséki is certainly one of the most ancient towns in Japan ; and the Éta village attached to it must be very old. Even to-day, no Japanese habitant of Mionoséki would think of walking through that settlement, though its streets are continuations of the other streets : children never pass the unmarked boundary ; and the very dogs will not cross the prejudice-line. For all that the settlement is clean, well built, — with gardens, baths, and temples of its own. It looks like any well-kept Japanese village. But for perhaps a thousand years there has been no fellowship between the people of those contiguous communities. . . . Nobody can now tell the history of these outcast folk : the cause of their social excommunication has long been forgotten.

Besides the Éta proper, there were pariahs called *hinin*, — a name signifying " not-human-beings." Under this appellation were included professional mendicants, wandering minstrels, actors, certain classes of prostitutes, and persons outlawed by society. The *hinin* had their own chiefs, and their own laws. Any person expelled from a Japanese community might join the *hinin ;* but that signified good-by to the rest of humanity. The Government was too shrewd to persecute the *hinin*. Their gipsy-existence saved a world of trouble. It was unnecessary to keep petty offenders in jail, or to provide for people incapable of earning an honest living, so long as these could be driven into the *hinin* class. There the incorrigible, the vagrant, the beggar, would be kept under discipline of a sort, and would practically disappear from official cognizance. The killing of a *hinin* was not considered murder, and was punished only by a fine.

The reader should now be able to form an approximately correct idea of the character of the old Japanese society. But the ordination of that society was much more complex than I have been able to indicate, — so complex that volumes would be required to treat the subject in detail. Once fully evolved, what we may still call Feudal Japan, for want of a better name, presented most of the features of a doubly-compound society of the militant type, with certain marked approaches toward the trebly-compound type. A striking peculiarity, of course, is the absence of a true ecclesiastical hierarchy, — due to the fact that Government never became dissociated from religion. There was at one time a tendency on the part of Buddhism to establish a religious hierarchy independent of central authority; but there were two fatal obstacles in the way of such a development. The first was the condition of Buddhism itself,—divided into a number of sects, some bitterly opposed to others. The second obstacle was the implacable hostility of the military clans, jealous of any religious power capable of interfering, either directly or indirectly, with their policy. So soon as the foreign religion began to prove itself formidable in the world of action, ruthless measures were decided; and the frightful massacres of priests by Nobunaga, in the sixteenth century, ended the political aspirations of Buddhism in Japan.

Otherwise the regimentation of society resembled that of all antique civilizations of the militant type, — all action being both positively and negatively regulated. The household ruled the person; the five-family group, the household; the community, the group; the lord of the soil, the community; the Shōgun, the lord. Over the whole body of the producing classes, two million samurai had power of life and death; over these samurai the daimyō held a like power; and the daimyō were subject to the Shōgun.

Nominally the Shōgun was subject to the Emperor, but not in fact : military usurpation disturbed and shifted the natural order of the higher responsibility. However, from the nobility downwards, the regulative discipline was much reinforced by this change in government. Among the producing classes there were countless combinations — guilds of all sorts ; but these were only despotisms within despotisms — despotisms of the communistic order; each member being governed by the will of the rest ; and enterprise, whether commercial or industrial, being impossible outside of some corporation. . . . We have already seen that the individual was bound to the commune — could not leave it without a permit, could not marry out of it. We have seen also that the stranger was a stranger in the old Greek and Roman sense, — that is to say an enemy, a *hostis*, — and could enter another community only by being religiously adopted into it. As regards exclusiveness, therefore, the social conditions were like those of the early European communities; but the militant conditions resembled rather those of the great Asiatic empires.

Of course such a society had nothing in common with any modern form of Occidental civilization. It was a huge mass of clan-groups, loosely united under a duarchy, in which the military head was omnipotent, and the religious head only an object of

worship, — the living symbol of a cult.   However
this organization might outwardly resemble what we
are accustomed to call feudalism, its structure was
rather like that of ancient Egyptian or Peruvian
society, — minus the priestly hierarchy.   The supreme figure is not an Emperor in our meaning of
the word, — not a king of kings and vicegerent of
heaven, — but a God incarnate, a race-divinity, an
Inca descended from the Sun.   About his sacred
person, we see the tribes ranged in obeisance, —
each tribe, nevertheless, maintaining its own ancestral cult; and the clans forming these tribes, and
the communities forming these clans, and the households forming these communities, have all their separate cults; and out of the mass of these cults have
been derived the customs and the laws.   Yet everywhere the customs and the laws differ more or less,
because of the variety of their origins : they have
this only in common, — that they exact the most
humble and implicit obedience, and regulate every
detail of private and public life.   Personality is
wholly suppressed by coercion ; and the coercion
is chiefly from within, not from without, — the life
of every individual being so ordered by the will of
the rest as to render free action, free speaking, or
free thinking, out of the question.   This means
something incomparably harsher than the socialistic
tyranny of early Greek society : it means religious
communism doubled with a military despotism of

the most terrible kind. The individual did not legally exist, — except for punishment; and from the whole of the producing-classes, whether serfs or freemen, the most servile submission was ruthlessly exacted.

It is difficult to believe that any intelligent man of modern times could endure such conditions and live (except under the protection of some powerful ruler, as in the case of the English pilot Will Adams, created a samurai by Iyéyasu): the incessant and multiform constraint upon mental and moral life would of itself be enough to kill. . . . Those who write to-day about the extraordinary capacity of the Japanese for organization, and about the "democratic spirit" of the people as natural proof of their fitness for representative government in the Western sense, mistake appearances for realities. The truth is that the extraordinary capacity of the Japanese for communal organization, is the strongest possible evidence of their unfitness for any modern democratic form of government. Superficially the difference between Japanese social organization, and local self-government in the modern American, or the English colonial meaning of the term, appears slight; and we may justly admire the perfect self-discipline of a Japanese community. But the real difference between the two is fundamental, prodigious, — measurable only by thousands of years. It is the difference between compulsory and free coöperation, — the difference between the most despotic form of communism, founded upon the most ancient form of religion, and the most highly evolved form of industrial union, with unlimited individual right of competition.

There exists a popular error to the effect that what we call communism and socialism in Western civilization are modern growths, representing aspiration toward some perfect form of democracy. As a matter of fact these movements represent reversion, — reversion toward the primitive conditions of human society. Under every form of ancient despotism we find exactly the same capacity of self-government among the people: it was manifested by the old Egyptians and Peruvians as well as by the early Greeks and Romans; it is exhibited to-day by Hindoo and Chinese communities; it may be studied in Siamese or Annamese villages quite as well as in Japan. It means a religious communistic despotism, — a supreme social tyranny suppressing personality, forbidding enterprise, and making competition a public offence. Such self-government also has its advantages: it was perfectly adapted to the requirements of Japanese life so long as the nation could remain isolated from the rest of the world. Yet it must be obvious that any society whose ethical traditions forbid the individual to profit at the cost of his fellow-men will be placed at an enormous disadvantage when forced into the industrial struggle for existence against communities whose self-government permits of the greatest possible personal freedom, and the widest range of competitive enterprise.

We might suppose that perpetual and universal coercion, moral and physical, would have brought about a state of universal sameness, — a dismal uniformity and monotony in all life's manifestations. But such monotony existed only as to the life of the commune, not as to that of the race. The most wonderful variety characterized this quaint civilization, as it also characterized the old Greek civilization, and for precisely the same reasons. In every patriarchal civilization ruled by ancestor-worship, all tendency to absolute sameness, to general uniformity, is prevented by the character of the aggregate itself, which never becomes homogeneous and plastic. Every unit of that aggregate, each one of the multitude of petty despotisms composing it, most jealously guards its own particular traditions and customs, and remains self-sufficing. Hence results, sooner or later, incomparable variety of detail, small detail, artistic, industrial, architectural, mechanical. In Japan such differentiation and specialization was thus maintained, that you will hardly find in the whole country even two villages where the customs, industries, and methods of production are exactly the same. . . . The customs of the fishing-villages will, perhaps, best illustrate what I mean. In every coast district the various fishing-settlements have their own traditional ways of constructing nets and boats, and their own particular methods of handling them. Now, in the time of the great tidal-wave of 1896, when thirty thousand people perished, and scores of coast-villages were wrecked, large sums of money were collected in Kobé and elsewhere for the benefit of the survivors; and well-meaning foreigners attempted to supply the want of boats and fishing implements by purchasing quantities of locally made nets and boats, and sending them to the afflicted districts. But it was found that these presents were of no use to the men of the northern provinces, who had been accustomed to boats and nets of a totally different kind; and it was further discovered that every fishing-hamlet had special requirements of its own in this regard. . . . Now the differentiations of habit and custom, thus exhibited in the life of the fishing-communities, is paralleled in many crafts and callings. The way of building houses, and of roofing them, differs in almost every province: also the methods of agriculture and of horticulture, the manner of making wells, the methods of weaving and lacquering and pottery-making and tile-baking. Nearly every town and village of importance boasts of some special production, bearing the name of the place, and unlike anything made elsewhere. . . .

No doubt the ancestral cults helped to conserve and to develop such local specialization of industries: the craft-ancestors, the patron-gods of the guild, were supposed to desire that the work of their descendants and worshippers should maintain a particular character of its own. Though individual enterprise was checked by communal regulation, the specialization of local production was encouraged by difference of cults. Family-conservatism or guild-conservatism would tolerate small improvements or modifications suggested by local experience, but would be wary, perhaps superstitious likewise, about accepting the results of strange experience.

Still, for the Japanese themselves, not the least pleasure of travel in Japan is the pleasure of study-ing the curious variety in local production, — the pleasure of finding the novel, the unexpected, the unimagined. Even those arts or industries of Old Japan, primarily borrowed from Korea or from China, appear to have developed and conserved innumerable queer forms under the influence of the numberless local cults.

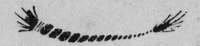

The Rise of the Military Power

ALMOST the whole of authentic Japanese history is comprised in one vast episode: the rise and fall of the military power. . . . It has been customary to speak of Japanese history as beginning with the accession of Jimmu Tennō, alleged to have reigned from 660 to 585 B.C., and to have lived for one hundred and twenty-seven years. Before the time of the Emperor Jimmu was the Age of the Gods, — the period of mythology. But trustworthy history does not begin for a thousand years after the accession of Jimmu Tennō; and the chronicles of those thousand years must be regarded as little better than fairy-tales. They contain records of fact; but fact and myth are so interwoven that it is difficult to distinguish the one from the other. We have legends, for example, of an alleged conquest of Korea in the year 202 A.D., by the Empress Jingō; and it has been tolerably well proved that no such conquest took place.[1] The later records are somewhat less mythical than the earlier. We have traditions apparently founded on

---

[1] See Aston's paper, *Early Japanese History*, in the translations of the Asiatic Society of Japan.

fact, of Korean immigration in the time of the fifteenth ruler, the Emperor Ōjin; then later traditions, also founded on fact, of early Chinese studies in Japan; then some vague accounts of a disturbed state of society, which appears to have continued through the whole of the fifth century. Buddhism was introduced in the middle of the century following; and we have record of the fierce opposition offered to the new creed by a Shintō faction, and of a miraculous victory won by the help of the Four Deva Kings, at the prayer of Shōtoku Taishi, — the great founder of Buddhism, and regent of the Empress Suikō. With the firm establishment of Buddhism in the reign of that Empress (593–628 A.D.), we reach the period of authentic history, and of the thirty-third Japanese sovereign counting from Jimmu Tennō.

But although everything prior to the seventh century remains obscured for us by the mists of fable, much can be inferred, even from the half-mythical records, concerning social conditions during the reigns of the first thirty-three Emperors and Empresses. It appears that the early Mikado lived very simply — scarcely better, indeed, than their subjects. The Shintō scholar Mabuchi tells us that they dwelt in huts with mud walls and roofs of shingle; that they wore hempen clothes; that they carried their swords in simple wooden scabbards, bound round with the tendrils of a wild vine; that they walked about freely among the people; that they carried their own bows and arrows when they went to hunt. But as society developed wealth and power, this early simplicity disappeared; and the gradual introduction of Chinese customs and etiquette effected great changes. The Empress Suikō introduced Chinese court-ceremonies, and first established among the nobility the Chinese grades of rank. Chinese luxury, as well as Chinese learning, soon made its appearance at court; and thereafter the imperial authority appears to have been less and less directly exerted. The new ceremonialism must have rendered the personal exercise of the multiform imperial functions more difficult than before; and it is probable that the temptation to act more or less by deputy would have been strong even in the case of an energetic ruler. At all events we find that the real adminis-tration of government began about this time to pass into the hands of deputies, — all of whom were members of the great Kugé clan of the Fujiwara.

This clan, which included the highest hereditary priesthood, represented a majority of the ancient nobility, claiming divine descent. Ninety-five out of the total one hundred and fifty-five families of Kugé belonged to it, — including the five families, *Go-Sekké*, from which alone the Emperor was by tradition allowed to choose his Empress. Its his-toric name dates only from the reign of the Emperor

Kwammu (782–806 A.D.), who bestowed it as an honour upon Nakatomi no Kamatari; but the clan had long previously held the highest positions at Court. By the close of the seventh century most of the executive power had passed into its hands. Later the office of *Kwambaku*, or Regent, was established, and remained hereditary in the house down to modern times — ages after all real power had been taken from the descendants of Nakatomi no Kamatari. But during almost five centuries the Fujiwara remained the veritable regents of the country, and took every possible advantage of their position. All the civil offices were in the hands of Fujiwara men; all the wives and favourites of the Emperors were Fujiwara women. The whole power of government was thus kept in the hands of the clan; and the political authority of the Emperor ceased to exist. Moreover the succession was regulated entirely by the Fujiwara; and even the duration of each reign was made to depend upon their policy. It was deemed advisable to compel Emperors to abdicate at an early age, and after abdicating to become Buddhist monks, — the successor chosen being often a mere child. There is record of an Emperor ascending the throne at the age of two, and abdicating at the age of four; another Mikado was appointed at the age of five; several at the age of ten. Yet the religious dignity of the throne remained undiminished, or, rather, continued to grow. The more the Mikado was withdrawn from public view by policy and by ceremonial, the more did his seclusion and inaccessibility serve to deepen the awe of the divine legend. Like the Lama of Thibet the living deity was made invisible to the multitude; and gradually the belief arose that to look upon his face was death. . . . It is said that the Fujiwara were not satisfied even with these despotic means of assuring their own domination, and that luxurious forms of corruption were maintained within the palace for the purpose of weakening the character of young emperors who might otherwise have found the energy to assert the ancient rights of the throne.

Perhaps this usurpation — which prepared the way for the rise of the military power — has never been rightly interpreted. The history of all the patriarchal societies of ancient Europe will be found to illustrate the same phase of social evolution. At a certain period in the development of each we find the same thing happening, — the withdrawal of all political authority from the Priest-King, who is suffered, nevertheless, to retain the religious dignity. It may be a mistake to judge the policy of the Fujiwara as a policy of mere ambition and usurpation. The Fujiwara were a religious aristocracy, claiming divine origin, — clan-chiefs of a society in which religion and government were identical, and holding to that society much the same relation as that of the

Eupatridæ to the ancient Attic society. The Mikado had originally become supreme magistrate, military commander, and religious head by consent of a majority of the clan-chiefs, — each of whom represented to his own following what the " Heavenly Sovereign " represented to the social aggregate. But as the power of the ruler extended with the growth of the nation, those who had formerly united to maintain that power began to find it dangerous. They decided to deprive the Heavenly Sovereign of all political and legal authority, without disturbing in any way his religious supremacy. At Athens, at Sparta, at Rome, and elsewhere in ancient Europe, the same policy was carried out, for the same reasons, by religious senates. The history of the early kings of Rome, as interpreted by M. de Coulanges, best illustrates the nature of the antagonism developed between the priest-ruler and the religious aristocracy ; but the same thing took place in all the Greek communities, with about the same result. Everywhere political power was taken away from the early kings ; but they were mostly left in possession of their religious dignities and privileges : they remained supreme priests after having ceased to be rulers. This was the case also in Japan ; and I imagine that future Japanese historians will be able to give us an entirely new interpretation of the Fujiwara episode, as reviewed in the light of modern sociology. At all events, there can be little doubt that, in curtailing the powers of the Heavenly Sovereign, the religious aristocracy must have been actuated by conservative precaution as well as by ambition. There had been various Emperors who made changes in the laws and customs — changes which could scarcely have been viewed with favour by many of the ancient nobility; there had been an Emperor whose diversions can to-day be written of only in Latin; there had even been an Emperor — Kōtoku — who, though "God Incarnate," and chief of the ancient faith, "despised the Way of the Gods," and cut down the holy grove of the shrine of Iku-kuni-dama. Kōtoku, for all his Buddhist piety (perhaps, indeed, because of it), was one of the wisest and best of rulers; but the example of a heavenly sovereign "despising the Way of the Gods," must have given the priestly clan matter for serious reflection. . . . Besides, there is another important fact to be noticed. The Imperial household proper had become, in the course of centuries, entirely detached from the Uji; and the omnipotence of this unit, independent of all other units, constituted in itself a grave danger to aristocratic privileges and established institutions. Too much might depend upon the personal character and will of an omnipotent God-King, capable of breaking with all clan-custom, and of abrogating clan-privileges. On the other hand, there was safety for all alike under the patriarchal rule of the clan, which could check every tendency on the part of any of its members to exert predominant influence at the expense of the rest. But for obvious reasons the Imperial cult — traditional source of all authority and privilege — could not be touched : it was only by maintaining and reinforcing it that the religious nobility could expect to keep the real power in their hands. They actually kept it for nearly five centuries.

The history of all the Japanese regencies, however, amply illustrates the general rule that inherited authority is ever and everywhere liable to find itself supplanted by deputed authority. The Fujiwara appear to have eventually become the victims of that luxury which they had themselves, for reasons of policy, introduced and maintained. Degenerating into a mere court-nobility, they made little effort to exert any direct authority in other than civil directions, entrusting military matters almost wholly to the Buké. In the eighth century the distinction between military and civil organization had been made upon the Chinese plan ; the great military class then came into existence, and began to extend its power rapidly. Of the military clans proper, the most powerful were the Minamoto and the Taira. By deputing to these clans the conduct of all important matters relating to war, the Fujiwara eventually lost their high position and influence. As soon as the Buké found themselves strong enough to lay hands upon the reins of government, — which happened about the middle of the eleventh century, — the Fujiwara supremacy became a thing of the past, although members of the clan continued for centuries to occupy positions of importance under various regents.

But the Buké could not realize their ambition without a bitter struggle among themselves, — the longest and the fiercest war in Japanese history. The Minamoto and the Taira were both Kugé; both claimed imperial descent. In the early part of the contest the Taira carried all before them; and it seemed that no power could hinder them from exterminating the rival clan. But fortune turned at last in favour of the Minamoto; and at the famous sea-fight of Dan-no-ura, in 1185, the Taira were themselves exterminated.

Then began the reign of the Minamoto regents, or rather shōgun. I have elsewhere said that the title "shōgun" originally signified, as did the Roman military term *Imperator*, only a commander-in-chief: it now became the title of the supreme ruler *de facto*, in his double capacity of civil and military sovereign, — the King of kings. From the accession of the Minamoto to power the history of the shōgunate — the long history of the military supremacy — really begins; Japan thereafter, down to the present era of Meiji, having really two Em-

perors : the Heavenly Sovereign, or Deity Incarnate, representing the religion of the race ; and the
veritable Imperator, who wielded all the powers of
the administration.　No one sought to occupy by
force the throne of the Sun's Succession, whence all
authority was at least supposed to be derived.　Regent or shōgun bowed down before it : divinity
could not be usurped.

Yet peace did not follow upon the battle of Dan-
no-ura : the clan-wars initiated by the great struggle
of the Minamoto and the Taira, continued, at irregular intervals, for five centuries more ; and the
nation remained disintegrated.　Nor did the Minamoto long keep the supremacy which they had so
dearly won.　Deputing their powers to the Hōjō
family, they were supplanted by the Hōjō, just as the
Fujiwara had been supplanted by the Taira.　Three
only of the Minamoto shōgun really exercised rule.
During the whole of the thirteenth century, and for
some time afterwards, the Hōjō continued to govern
the country ; and it is noteworthy that these regents
never assumed the title of shōgun, but professed to
be merely shōgunal deputies.　Thus a triple-headed
government appeared to exist ; for the Minamoto
kept up a kind of court at Kamakura.　But they
faded into mere shadows, and are yet remembered by
the significant appellation of " Shadow-Shōgun," or
" Puppet Shōgun."　There was nothing shadowy,
however, about the administration of the Hōjō, —

men of immense energy and ability.   By them Emperor or shōgun could be deposed and banished without scruple ; and the helplessness of the shōgunate can be inferred from the fact, that the seventh Hōjō regent, before deposing the seventh shōgun, sent him home in a palanquin, head downwards and heels upwards.   Nevertheless the Hōjō suffered the phantom-shōgunate to linger on, until 1333. Though unscrupulous in their methods, these regents were capable rulers ; and proved themselves able to save the country in a great emergency, — the famous invasion attempted by Kublai Khan in 1281. Aided by a fortunate typhoon, which is said to have destroyed the hostile fleet in answer to prayer offered up at the national shrines, the Hōjō could repel this invasion.   They were less successful in dealing with certain domestic disorders, — especially those fomented by the turbulent Buddhist priesthood.   During the thirteenth century, Buddhism had developed into a great military power, — strangely like that church-militant of the European middle ages : the period of soldier-priests and fighting-bishops.   The Buddhist monasteries had been converted into fortresses filled with men-at-arms ; Buddhist menace had more than once carried terror into the sacred seclusion of the imperial court.   At an early day, Yoritomo, the far-seeing founder of the Minamoto dynasty, had observed a militant tendency in Buddhism, and had attempted to check it by forbidding all priests and monks either to bear arms, or to maintain armed retainers. But his successors had been careless about enforcing these prohibitions; and the Buddhist military power developed in consequence so rapidly that the shrewdest Hōjō were doubtful of their ability to cope with it. Eventually this power proved capable of giving them serious trouble. The ninety-sixth Mikado, Go-Daigo, found courage to revolt against the tyranny of the Hōjō; and the Buddhist soldiery took part with him. He was promptly defeated, and banished to the islands of Oki; but his cause was soon espoused by powerful lords, who had long chafed under the despotism of the regency. These assembled their forces, restored the banished Emperor, and combined in a desperate attack upon the regent's capital, Kamakura. The city was stormed and burned; and the last of the Hōjō rulers, after a brave but vain defence, performed *harakiri*. Thus shōgunate and regency vanished together, in 1333.

For the moment the whole power of administration had been restored to the Mikado. Unfortunately for himself and for the country, Go-Daigo was too feeble of character to avail himself of this great opportunity. He revived the dead shōgunate by appointing his own son shōgun; he weakly ignored the services of those whose loyalty and courage had restored him; and he foolishly strength-

ened the hands of those whom he had every reason
to fear. As a consequence there happened the most
serious political catastrophe in the history of Japan,
a division of the imperial house against itself.

The unscrupulous despotism of the Hōjō regents
had prepared the possibility of such an event.
During the last years of the thirteenth century, there
were living at the same time in Kyōto, besides the
reigning Mikado, no less than three deposed emperors. To bring about a contest for the succession
was, therefore, an easy matter; and this was soon
accomplished by the treacherous general Ashikaga
Takéuji, to whom Go-Daigo had unwisely shown
especial favour. Ashikaga had betrayed the Hōjō
in order to help the restoration of Go-Daigo: he
subsequently would have betrayed the trust of Go-
Daigo in order to seize the administrative power.
The Emperor discovered this treasonable purpose
when too late, and sent against Ashikaga an army
which was defeated. After some further contest
Ashikaga mastered the capital, drove Go-Daigo a
second time into exile, set up a rival Emperor, and
established a new shōgunate. Now for the first
time, two branches of the Imperial family, each
supported by powerful lords, contended for the right
of succession. That of which Go-Daigo remained
the acting representative, is known in history as the
Southern Branch (*Nanchō*), and by Japanese historians is held to be the only legitimate branch.

The other was called the Northern Branch (*Hokuchō*), and was maintained at Kyōto by the power of the Ashikaga clan; while Go-Daigo, finding refuge in a Buddhist monastery, retained the insignia of empire. . . . Thereafter, for a period of fifty-six years Japan continued to have two Mikado; and the resulting disorder was such as to imperil the national integrity. It would have been no easy matter for the people to decide which Emperor possessed the better claim. Hitherto the imperial presence had represented the national divinity; and the imperial palace had been regarded as the temple of the national religion: the division maintained by the Ashikaga usurpers therefore signified nothing less than the breaking up of the whole tradition upon which existing society had been built. The confusion became greater and greater, the danger increased more and more, until the Ashikaga themselves took alarm. They managed then to end the trouble by persuading the fifth Mikado of the Southern Dynasty, Go Kaméyama, to surrender his insignia to the reigning Mikado of the Northern Dynasty, Go-Komatsu. This having been done, in 1392, Go-Kaméyama was honoured with the title of retired Emperor, and Go-Komatsu was nationally acknowledged as legitimate Emperor. But the names of the other four Emperors of the Northern Dynasty are still excluded from the official list.

The Ashikaga shōgunate thus averted the supreme

peril; but the period of this military domination, which endured until 1573, was destined to remain the darkest in Japanese history. The Ashikaga gave the country fifteen rulers, several of whom were men of great ability: they tried to encourage industry; they cultivated literature and the arts; but they could not give peace. Fresh disputes arose; and lords whom the shōgunate could not subdue made war upon each other. To such a condition of terror was the capital reduced that the court nobility fled from it to take refuge with daimyō powerful enough to afford them protection. Robbery became rife throughout the land; and piracy terrorized the seas. The shōgunate itself was reduced to the humiliation of paying tribute to China. Agriculture and industry at last ceased to exist outside of the domains of certain powerful lords. Provinces became waste; and famine, earthquake, and pestilence added their horror to the misery of ceaseless war. The poverty prevailing may be best imagined from the fact that when the Emperor known to history as Go-Tsuchi-mikado — one hundred and second of the Sun's Succession — died in the year 1500, his corpse had to be kept at the gates of the palace forty days, because the expenses of the funeral could not be defrayed. Until 1573 the misery continued; and the shōgunate meanwhile degenerated into insignificance. Then a strong captain arose and ended the house of Ashikaga, and seized the reins of power.

This usurper was Oda Nobunaga; and the usurpation was amply provoked. Had it not occurred, Japan might never have entered upon an era of peace.

For there had been no peace since the fifth century. No emperor or regent or shōgun had ever been able to impose his rule firmly upon the whole country. Somewhere or other, there were always wars of clan with clan. By the time of the sixteenth century personal safety could be found only under the protection of some military leader, able to exact his own terms for the favour of such protection. The question of the imperial succession, — which had almost wrecked the empire during the fourteenth century, — might be raised again at any time by some reckless faction, with the probable result of ruining civilization, and forcing the nation back to its primitive state of barbarism. Never did the future of Japan appear so dark as at the moment when Oda Nobunaga suddenly found himself the strongest man in the empire, and leader of the most formidable Japanese army that had ever obeyed a single head. This man, a descendant of Shintō priests, was above all things a patriot. He did not seek the title of shōgun, and never received it. His hope was to save the country; and he saw that this could be done only by centralizing all feudal power under one control, and strenuously enforcing law. Looking about him for the ways and means of effect-

ing this centralization, he perceived that one of the
very first obstacles to be removed was that created
by the power of Buddhism militant, — the feudal
Buddhism developed under the Hōjō regency, and
especially represented by the great Shin and Tendai
sects. As both had already given aid to his enemies, it was easy to find a cause for quarrel; and he
first proceeded against the Tendai. The campaign
was conducted with ferocious vigour; the monastery-
fortresses of Hiyei-san were stormed and razed, and
all the priests, with all their adherents, put to the
sword — no mercy being shown even to women and
children. By nature Nobunaga was not cruel; but
his policy was ruthless, and he knew when and why
to strike hard. The power of the Tendai sect
before this massacre may be imagined from the fact
that three thousand monastery buildings were burnt
at Hiyei-san. The Shin sect of the Hongwanji,
with headquarters at Ōsaka, was scarcely less powerful; and its monastery, occupying the site of the
present Ōsaka castle, was one of the strongest fortresses in the country. Nobunaga waited several
years, merely to prepare for the attack. The soldier-
priests defended themselves well; upwards of fifty
thousand lives are said to have been lost in the
siege; yet only the personal intervention of the
Emperor prevented the storming of the stronghold,
and the slaughter of every being within its walls.
Through respect for the Emperor, Nobunaga agreed

to spare the lives of the Shin priests: they were only dispossessed and scattered, and their power forever broken. Buddhism having been thus effectually crippled, Nobunaga was able to turn his attention to the warring clans. Supported by the greatest generals that the nation ever produced,— Hidéyoshi and Iyéyasu, — he proceeded to enforce pacification and order; and his grand purpose would probably have been soon accomplished, but for the revengeful treachery of a subordinate, who brought about his death in 1582.

Nobunaga, with Taira blood in his veins, had been essentially an aristocrat, inheriting all the aptitudes of his great race for administration, and versed in all the traditions of diplomacy. His avenger and successor, Hideyoshi, was a totally different type of soldier: a son of peasants, an untrained genius who had won his way to high command by shrewdness and courage, natural skill of arms, and immense inborn capacity for all the chess-play of war. With the great purpose of Nobunaga he had always been in sympathy; and he actually carried it out, — subduing the entire country, from north to south, in the name of the Emperor, by whom he was appointed Regent (*Kwambaku*). Thus universal peace was temporarily established. But the vast military powers which Hidéyoshi had collected and disciplined, threatened to become refractory. He found employment for them by declaring unpro-

voked war against Korea, whence he hoped to effect
the conquest of China. The war with Korea
opened in 1592, and dragged on unsatisfactorily
until 1598, when Hidéyoshi died. He had proved
himself one of the greatest soldiers ever born, but
not one of the best among rulers. Perhaps the
issue of the war in Korea would have been more
fortunate, if he could have ventured to conduct it
himself. As a matter of fact, it merely exhausted
the force of both countries; and Japan had little to
show for her dearly bought victories abroad except
the *Mimidzuka* or "Ear-Monument" at Nara, —
marking the spot where thirty thousand pairs of
foreign ears, cut from the pickled heads of slain,
were buried in the grounds of the temple of
Daibutsu. . . .

Into the vacant place of power then stepped the
most remarkable man that Japan ever produced, —
Tokugawa Iyéyasu. Iyéyasu was of Minamoto
descent, and an aristocrat to the marrow of his bones.
As a soldier he was scarcely inferior to Hidéyoshi,
whom he once defeated, — but he was much more
than a soldier: a far-sighted statesman, an incomparable diplomat, and something of a scholar.
Cool, cautious, secretive, — distrustful, yet generous,
— stern, yet humane, — by the range and the versa-
tility of his genius he might be not unfavourably
contrasted with Julius Cæsar. All that Nobunaga
and Hidéyoshi had wished to do, and failed to

do, Iyéyasu speedily accomplished. After fulfilling Hidéyoshi's dying injunction, not to leave the troops in Korea " to become ghosts haunting a foreign land," — that is to say, in the condition of spirits without a cult, — Iyéyasu had to face a formidable league of lords resolved to dispute his claim to rule. The terrific battle of Sekigahara left him master of the country ; and he at once took measures to consolidate his power, and to perfect, even to the least detail, all the machinery of military government. As shōgun, he reorganized the daimiates, redistributed a majority of fiefs among those whom he could trust, created new military grades, and ordered and so balanced the powers of the greater daimyō as to make it next to impossible for them to dare a revolt. Later on the daimyō were even required to furnish security for their good behaviour: they were obliged to pass a certain time of the year [1] in the shōgun's capital, leaving their families as hostages during the rest of the year. The entire administration was readjusted upon a simple and sagacious plan ; and the Laws of Iyéyasu prove him to have been an excellent legislator. For the first time in Japanese history the nation was integrated, — integrated, at least, in so far as the peculiar nature of the social unit rendered possible. The counsels

---

[1] The period of obligatory residence in Yedo was not the same for all *daimyō*. In some cases the obligation seems to have extended to six months ; in others, the requirement was to pass every alternate year in the capital.

of the founder of Yedo were followed by his successors ; and the Tokugawa shōgunate, which lasted
until 1867, gave the country fifteen military
sovereigns. Under these, Japan enjoyed both peace
and prosperity for the time of two hundred and
fifty years ; and her society was thus enabled to
evolve to the full limit of its peculiar type. Industries and arts developed in new and wonderful ways ;
literature found august patronage. The national
cult was carefully maintained ; and all precautions
were taken to prevent the occurrence of another
such contest for the imperial succession as had nearly
ruined the country in the fourteenth century.

We have seen that the history of military rule in
Japan embraces nearly the whole period of authentic
history, down to modern times, and closes with the
second period of national integration. The first
period had been reached when the clans first accepted the leadership of the chief of the greatest
clan, — thereafter revered as the Heavenly Sovereign, Supreme Pontiff, Supreme Arbiter, Supreme
Commander, and Supreme Magistrate. How long
a time was required for this primal integration, under
a patriarchal monarchy, we cannot know ; but we
have learned that the later integration, under a
duarchy, occupied considerably more than a thousand years. . . . Now the extraordinary fact to
note is that, during all those centuries, the imperial

cult was carefully maintained by even the enemies of the Mikado; the only legitimate ruler being, in national belief, the Tenshi, "Son of Heaven," — the Tennō, "Heavenly King." Through every period of disorder the Offspring of the Sun was the object of national worship, and his palace the temple of the national faith. Great captains might coerce the imperial will; but they styled themselves, none the less, the worshippers and slaves of the incarnate deity; and they would no more have thought of trying to occupy his throne, than they would have thought of trying to abolish all religion by decree. Once only, by the arbitrary folly of the Ashikaga shōgun, the imperial cult had been seriously interfered with; and the social earthquake consequent upon that division of the imperial house, apprised the usurpers of the enormity of their blunder. . . . Only the integrity of the imperial succession, the uninterrupted maintenance of the imperial worship, made it possible even for Iyéyasu to clamp together the indissoluble units of society.

Herbert Spencer has taught the student of sociology to recognize that religious dynasties have extraordinary powers of longevity, because they possess extraordinary power to resist change; whereas military dynasties, depending for their perpetuity upon the individual character of their sovereigns, are particularly liable to disintegration. The immense duration of the Japanese imperial dynasty, as contrasted with the history of the various shōgunates and regencies representing a merely military domination, illustrates this teaching in a most remarkable way. Back through twenty-five hundred years we can follow the line of the imperial succession, till it vanishes out of sight into the mystery of the past. Here we have evidence of that extreme power of resisting all changes which is inherently characteristic of religious conservatism; on the other hand, the history of shōgunates and regencies proves the tendency to disintegration of institutions having no religious foundation, and therefore no religious power of cohesion. The remarkable duration of the Fujiwara rule, as compared with others, may perhaps be accounted for by the fact that the Fujiwara represented a religious, rather than a military, aristocracy. Even the marvellous military structure devised by Iyéyasu had begun to decay before alien aggression precipitated its inevitable collapse.

The Religion of Loyalty

' **M**ILITANT societies," says the author of the *Principles of Sociology*, "must have a patriotism which regards the triumph of their society as the supreme end of action; they must possess the loyalty whence flows obedience to authority, — and, that they may be obedient, they must have abundant faith." The history of the Japanese people strongly exemplifies these truths. Among no other people has loyalty ever assumed more impressive and extraordinary forms; and among no other people has obedience ever been nourished by a more abundant faith, — that faith derived from the cult of the ancestors.

The reader will understand how filial piety — the domestic religion of obedience — widens in range with social evolution, and eventually differentiates both into that political obedience required by the community, and that military obedience exacted by the war-lord, — obedience implying not only submission, but affectionate submission, — not merely the sense of obligation, but the sentiment of duty. In its origin such dutiful obedience is essentially religious; and, as expressed in loyalty, it retains the

religious character, — becomes the constant manifestation of a religion of self-sacrifice. Loyalty is
developed early in the history of a militant people;
and we find touching examples of it in the earliest
Japanese chronicles. We find also terrible ones, —
stories of self-immolation.

To his divinely descended lord, the retainer
owed everything — in fact, not less than in theory:
goods, household, liberty, and life. Any or all of
these he was expected to yield up without a mur-
mur, on demand, for the sake of the lord. And
duty to the lord, like the duty to the family ancestor, did not cease with death. As the ghosts of
parents were to be supplied with food by their
living children, so the spirit of the lord was to be
worshipfully served by those who, during his life-
time, owed him direct obedience. It could not be
permitted that the spirit of the ruler should enter
unattended into the world of shadows: some, at
least, of those who served him living were bound
to follow him in death. Thus in early societies
arose the custom of human sacrifices, — sacrifices
at first obligatory, afterwards voluntary. In Japan,
as stated in a former chapter, they remained an
indispensable feature of great funerals, up to the
first century, when images of baked clay were first
substituted for the official victims. I have already
mentioned how, after this abolition of obligatory

junshi, or following of one's lord in death, the practice of voluntary *junshi* continued up to the sixteenth century, when it actually became a military
fashion. At the death of a daimyō it was then
common for fifteen or twenty of his retainers to
disembowel themselves. Iyéyasu determined to
put an end to this custom of suicide, which is thus
considered in the 76th article of his celebrated
Legacy : —

"Although it is undoubtedly the ancient custom for a
vassal to follow his Lord in death, there is not the slightest
reason in the practice. Confucius has ridiculed the making
of *Yō* [*effigies buried with the dead*]. These practices are
strictly forbidden, more especially to primary retainers, but
to secondary retainers likewise, even of the lowest rank.
He is the reverse of a faithful servant who disregards this
prohibition. His posterity shall be impoverished by the
confiscation of his property, as a warning for those who
disobey the laws."

Iyéyasu's command ended the practice of *junshi*
among his own vassals ; but it continued, or revived
again, after his death. In 1664 the shōgunate issued
an edict proclaiming that the family of any person
performing *junshi* should be punished ; and the
shōgunate was in earnest. When this edict was
disobeyed by one Uyémon no Hyogé, who disem-
bowelled himself at the death of his lord, Okudaira
Tadamasa, the government promptly confiscated the
lands of the family of the suicide, executed two of

his sons, and sent the rest of the household into exile. Though cases of *junshi* have occurred even within this present era of Meiji, the determined attitude of the Tokugawa government so far checked the practice that even the most fervid loyalty latterly made its sacrifices through religion, as a rule. Instead of performing *harakiri*, the retainer shaved his head at the death of his lord, and became a Buddhist monk.

The custom of *junshi* represents but one aspect of Japanese loyalty : there were other customs equally, if not even more, significant, — for example, the custom of military suicide, not as *junshi*, but as a self-inflicted penalty exacted by the traditions of samurai discipline. Against *harakiri*, as punitive suicide, there was no legislative enactment, for obvious reasons. It would seem that this form of self-destruction was not known to the Japanese in early ages ; it may have been introduced from China, with other military customs. The ancient Japanese usually performed suicide by strangulation, as the *Nihongi* bears witness. It was the military class that established the *harakiri* as a custom and privilege. Previously, the chiefs of a routed army, or the defenders of a castle taken by storm, would thus end themselves to avoid falling into the enemy's hands, — a custom which continued into the present era. About the close of the fifteenth century, the military custom of permitting any samurai to perform *harakiri*, instead of subjecting him to the shame of execution, appears to have been generally established. Afterwards it became the recognized duty of a samurai to kill himself at the word of command. All samurai were subject to this disciplinary law, even lords of provinces; and in samurai families, children of both sexes were trained how to perform suicide whenever personal honour or the will of a liege-lord, might require it. . . . Women, I should observe, did not perform *harakiri*, but *jigai*, — that is to say, piercing the throat with a dagger so as to sever the arteries by a single thrust-and-cut movement. . . . The particulars of the *harakiri* ceremony have become so well known through Mitford's translation of Japanese texts on the subject, that I need not touch upon them. The important fact to remember is that honour and loyalty required the samurai man or woman to be ready at any moment to perform self-destruction by the sword. As for the warrior, any breach of trust (voluntary or involuntary), failure to execute a difficult mission, a clumsy mistake, and even a look of displeasure from one's liege, were sufficient reasons for *harakiri*, or, as the aristocrats preferred to call it, by the Chinese term, *seppuku*. Among the highest class of retainers, it was also a duty to make protest against misconduct on the part of their lord by performing *seppuku*, when all other means of bringing him to reason had failed, — which heroic custom has been made the subject of several popular dramas founded upon fact. In the case of married women of the samurai class, — directly responsible to their husbands, not to the lord, — *jigai* was resorted to most often as a means of preserving honour in time of war, though it was sometimes performed merely as a sacrifice of loyalty to the spirit of the husband, after his untimely death.[1] In the case of girls it was not uncommon for other reasons, — samurai maidens often entering into the service of noble households, where the cruelty of intrigue might easily bring about a suicide, or where loyalty to the wife of the lord might exact it. For the samurai maiden in service was bound by loyalty to her mistress not less closely than the warrior to the lord; and the heroines of Japanese feudalism were many.

In the early ages it appears to have been the custom for the wives of officials condemned to death to kill themselves; — the ancient chronicles are full of examples. But this custom is perhaps to be partly accounted for by the ancient law, which held the household of the offender equally responsible with him for the offence, independently of the facts in the case. However, it was certainly also common enough for a bereaved wife to perform suicide, not through despair, but through the wish to follow her

---

[1] The Japanese moralist Yekken wrote : "A woman has no feudal lord : she must reverence and obey her husband."

husband into the other world, and there to wait upon him as in life. Instances of female suicide, representing the old ideal of duty to a dead husband, have occurred in recent times. Such suicides are usually performed according to the feudal rules, — the woman robing herself in white for the occasion. At the time of the late war with China there occurred in Tōkyō one remarkable suicide of this kind; the victim being the wife of Lieutenant Asada, who had fallen in battle. She was only twenty-one. On hearing of her husband's death, she at once began to make preparations for her own, — writing letters of farewell to her relatives, putting her affairs in order, and carefully cleaning the house, according to old-time rule. Thereafter she donned her death-robe; laid mattings down opposite to the alcove in the guest-room; placed her husband's portrait in the alcove, and set offerings before it. When everything had been arranged, she seated herself before the portrait, took up her dagger, and with a single skilful thrust divided the arteries of her throat.

Besides the duty of suicide for the sake of preserving honour, there was also, for the samurai woman, the duty of suicide as a moral protest. I have already said that among the highest class of retainers it was thought a moral duty to perform *harakiri* as a remonstrance against shameless conduct on the part of one's lord, when all other means of persuasion had been tried in vain. Among samurai women — taught to consider their husbands as their lords, in the feudal meaning of the term — it was held a moral obligation to perform *jigai*, by way of protest against disgraceful behaviour upon the part of a husband who would not listen to advice or reproof. The ideal of wifely duty which impelled such sacrifice still survives; and more than one recent example might be cited of a generous life thus laid down in rebuke of some moral wrong. Perhaps the most touching instance occurred in 1892, at the time of the district elections in Nagano prefecture. A rich voter named Ishijima, after having publicly pledged himself to aid in the election of a certain candidate, transferred his support to the rival candidate. On learning of this breach of promise, the wife of Ishijima, robed herself in white, and performed *jigai* after the old samurai manner. The grave of this brave woman is still decorated with flowers by the people of the district; and incense is burned before her tomb.

To kill oneself at command — a duty which no loyal samurai would have dreamed of calling in question — appears to us much less difficult than another duty, also fully accepted : the sacrifice of children, wife, and household for the sake of the lord. Much of Japanese popular tragedy is devoted to incidents of such sacrifice made by retainers or

dependents of daimyō, — men or women who gave
their children to death in order to save the children
of their masters.[1]   Nor have we any reason to suppose that the facts have been exaggerated in these
dramatic compositions, most of which are based
upon feudal history.   The incidents, of course, have
been rearranged and expanded to meet theatrical requirements ; but the general pictures thus given of
the ancient society are probably even less grim than
the vanished reality.   The people still love these
tragedies ; and the foreign critic of their dramatic
literature is wont to point out only the blood-spots,
and to comment upon them as evidence of a public
taste for gory spectacles, — as proof of some innate
ferocity in the race.   Rather, I think, is this love of
the old tragedy proof of what foreign critics try
always to ignore as much as possible, — the deeply
religious character of the people.   These plays continue to give delight, — not because of their horror,
but because of their moral teaching, — because of
their exposition of the duty of sacrifice and courage,
the religion of loyalty.   They represent the martyrdoms of feudal society for its noblest ideals.

All down through that society, in varying forms,
the same spirit of loyalty had its manifestations.
As the samurai to his liege-lord, so the apprentice
was bound to the patron, and the clerk to the mer-

[1] See, for a good example, the translation of the drama *Terakoya*, published,
with admirable illustrations, by T. Haségawa (Tōkyō).

chant. Everywhere there was trust, because everywhere there existed the like sentiment of mutual
duty between servant and master. Each industry
and occupation had its religion of loyalty, — requiring, on the one side, absolute obedience and sacrifice
at need; and on the other, kindliness and aid.
And the rule of the dead was over all.

Not less ancient than the duty of dying for parent
or lord was the social obligation to avenge the killing of either. Even before the beginnings of settled
society, this duty is recognized. The oldest chronicles of Japan teem with instances of obligatory vengeance. Confucian ethics more than affirmed the
obligation, — forbidding a man to live "under the
same heaven" with the slayer of his lord, or parent,
or brother; and fixing all the degrees of kinship, or
other relationship, within which the duty of vengeance was to be considered imperative. Confucian
ethics, it will be remembered, became at an early
date the ethics of the Japanese ruling-classes, and so
remained down to recent times. The whole Confucian system, as I have remarked elsewhere, was
founded upon ancestor-worship, and represented
scarcely more than an amplification and elaboration
of filial piety: it was therefore in complete accord
with Japanese moral experience. As the military
power developed in Japan, the Chinese code of vengeance became universally accepted; and it was sus-

tained by law as well as by custom in later ages. Iyéyasu himself maintained it — exacting only that preliminary notice of an intended vendetta should be given in writing to the district criminal court. The text of his article on the subject is interesting : —

"In respect to avenging injury done to master or father, it is acknowledged by the Wise and Virtuous [*Confucius*] that you and the injurer cannot live together under the canopy of heaven. A person harbouring such vengeance shall give notice in writing to the criminal court; and although no check or hindrance may be offered to the carrying out of his design within the period allowed for that purpose, it is forbidden that the chastisement of an enemy be attended with riot. Fellows who neglect to give notice of their intended revenge are like wolves of pretext :[1] their punishment or pardon should depend upon the circumstances of the case."

Kindred, as well as parents; teachers, as well as lords, were to be revenged. A considerable proportion of popular romance and drama is devoted to the subject of vengeance taken by women; and, as a matter of fact, women, and even children, sometimes became avengers when there were no men of a wronged family left to perform the duty. Apprentices avenged their masters; and even sworn friends were bound to avenge each other.

---

[1] Or "hypocritical wolves," — that is to say, brutal murderers seeking to excuse their crime on the pretext of justifiable vengeance. (The translation is by Lowder.)

Why the duty of vengeance was not confined to the circle of natural kinship is explicable, of course, by the peculiar organization of society. We have seen that the patriarchal family was a religious corporation; and that the family-bond was not the bond of natural affection, but the bond of the cult. We have also seen that the relation of the household to the community, and of the community to the clan, and of the clan to the tribe, was equally a religious relation. As a necessary consequence, the earlier customs of vengeance were regulated by the bond of the family, communal, or tribal cult, as well as by the bond of blood; and with the introduction of Chinese ethics, and the development of militant conditions, the idea of revenge as duty took a wider range. The son or the brother by adoption was in respect of obligation the same as the son or brother by blood; and the teacher stood to his pupil in the relation of father to child. To strike one's natural parent was a crime punishable by death: to strike one's teacher was, before the law, an equal offence. This notion of the teacher's claim to filial reverence was of Chinese importation: an extension of the duty of filial piety to "the father of the mind." There were other such extensions; and the origin of all, Chinese or Japanese, may be traced alike to ancestor-worship.

Now, what has never been properly insisted upon, in any of the books treating of ancient

Japanese customs, is the originally religious significance of the *kataki-uchi*.   That a religious origin
can be found for all customs of vendetta established
in early societies is, of course, well known; but a
peculiar interest attaches to the Japanese vendetta
in view of the fact that it conserved its religious
character unchanged down to the present era.   The
kataki-uchi was essentially an act of propitiation, as
is proved by the rite with which it terminated, —
the placing of the enemy's head upon the tomb of
the person avenged, as an offering of atonement.
And one of the most impressive features of this
rite, as formerly practised, was the delivery of an
address to the ghost of the person avenged.   Sometimes the address was only spoken; sometimes it
was also written, and the manuscript left upon
the tomb.

There is probably none of my readers unacquainted with Mitford's ever-delightful *Tales of
Old Japan*, and his translation of the true story of
the " Forty-Seven Rōnins."   But I doubt whether
many persons have noticed the significance of the
washing of Kira Kōtsuké-no-Suké's severed head,
or the significance of the address inscribed to their
dead lord by the brave men who had so long waited
and watched for the chance to avenge him.   This
address, of which I quote Mitford's translation, was
laid upon the tomb of the Lord Asano.   It is still
preserved at the temple called Sengakuji: —

" *The fifteenth year of Genroku* [*1703*], *the twelfth month,
the fifteenth day.* — We have come this day to do homage
here : forty-seven men in all, from Oishi Kuranosuké
down to the foot-soldier Térasaka Kichiyémon, — all
cheerfully about to lay down our lives on your behalf.
We reverently announce this to the honoured spirit of
our dead master. On the fourteenth day of the third
month of last year, our honoured master was pleased to
attack Kira Kōtsuké-no-Suké, for what reason we know
not. Our honoured master put an end to his own life ;
but Kira Kōtsuké-no-Suké lived. Although we fear that
after the decree issued by the Government, this plot of
ours will be displeasing to our honoured master, still we,
who have eaten of your food, could not without blushing
repeat the verse, " *Thou shalt not live under the same heaven,
nor tread the same earth with the enemy of thy father or lord,*"
nor could we have dared to leave hell [Hades] and present
ourselves before you in Paradise, unless we had carried out
the vengeance which you began. Every day that we waited
seemed as three autumns to us. Verily we have trodden
the snow for one day, nay, for two days, and have tasted food
but once. The old and decrepit, the sick and the ailing,
have come forth gladly to lay down their lives. Men
might laugh at us, as at grasshoppers trusting in the
strength of their arms, and thus shame our honoured lord ;
but we could not halt in our deed of vengeance. Having
taken counsel together last night, we have escorted my
Lord Kōsuké-no-Suké hither to your tomb. This dirk,
by which our honoured lord set great store last year, and
entrusted to our care, we now bring back. If your noble
spirit be now present before this tomb, we pray you, as a

sign, to take the dirk, and, striking the head of your enemy
with it a second time, to dispel your hatred forever. This
is the respectful statement of forty-seven men."

It will be observed that the Lord Asano is addressed as if he were present and visible. The
head of the enemy has been carefully washed, according to the rule concerning the presentation of
heads to a living superior. It is laid upon the tomb
together with the nine-inch sword, or dagger, originally used by the Lord Asano in performing *harakiri*
at Government command, and afterwards used by
Oïshi Kuranosuké in cutting off the head of Kira
Kōtsuké-no-Suké;—and the spirit of the Lord
Asano is requested to take up the weapon and to
strike the head, so that the pain of ghostly anger may
be dissipated forever. Then, having been themselves all sentenced to perform *harakiri*, the forty-
seven retainers join their lord in death, and are buried
in front of his tomb. Before their graves the smoke
of incense, offered by admiring visitors, has been
ascending daily for two hundred years.[1]

One must have lived in Japan, and have been
able to feel the true spirit of the old Japanese life,
in order to comprehend the whole of this romance of
loyalty ; but I think that whoever carefully reads Mr.
Mitford's version of it, and his translation of the

[1] It has been long the custom also for visitors to leave their cards upon the
tombs of the Forty-seven Rōnin. When I last visited Sengakuji, the ground
about the tombs was white with visiting-cards.

authentic documents relating to it, will confess himself moved.   That address especially touches, — because of the affection and the faith to which it testifies, and the sense of duty beyond this life.   However much revenge must be condemned by our modern ethics, there is a noble side to many of the old Japanese stories of loyal vengeance; and these stories affect us by the expression of what has nothing to do with vulgar revenge, — by their exposition of gratitude, self-denial, courage in facing death, and faith in the unseen.   And this means, of course, that we are, consciously or unconsciously, impressed by their religious quality.   Mere individual revenge — the postponed retaliation for some personal injury — repels our moral feeling : we have learned to regard the emotion inspiring such revenge as simply brutal — something shared by man with lower forms of animal life.   But in the story of a homicide exacted by the sentiment of duty or gratitude to a dead master, there may be circumstances which can make appeal to our higher moral sympathies, — to our sense of the force and beauty of unselfishness, unswerving fidelity, unchanging affection.   And the story of the Forty-Seven Rōnin is one of this class. . . .

Yet it must be borne in mind that the old Japanese religion of loyalty, which found its supreme manifestation in those three terrible customs of *junshi, harakiri,* and *kataki-uchi,* was narrow in its range. It was limited by the very constitution of society. Though the nation was ruled, through all its groups, by notions of duty everywhere similar in character, the circle of that duty, for each individual, did not extend beyond the clan-group to which he belonged. For his own lord the retainer was always ready to die; but he did not feel equally bound to sacrifice himself for the military government, unless he happened to belong to the special military following of the Shōgun. His fatherland, his country, his world, extended only to the boundary of his chief's domain. Outside of that domain he could be only a wanderer, — a *rōnin,* or "wave-man," as the masterless samurai was termed. Under such conditions that larger loyalty which identifies itself with love of king and country, — which is patriotism in the modern, not in the narrower antique sense, — could not fully evolve. Some common peril, some danger to the whole race — such as the attempted Tartar conquest of Japan — might temporarily arouse the true sentiment of patriotism; but otherwise that sentiment had little opportunity for development. The Isé cult represented, indeed, the religion of the nation, as distinguished from the clan or tribal worship; but each man had been taught to believe that his first duty was to his lord. One cannot efficiently serve two masters; and feudal government practi-

cally suppressed any tendencies in that direction.
The lordship so completely owned the individual,
body and soul, that the idea of any duty to the
nation, outside of the duty to the chief, had neither
time nor chance to define itself in the mind of the
vassal. To the ordinary samurai, for example, an
imperial order would not have been law: he recognized no law above the law of his daimyō. As for
the daimyō, he might either disobey or obey an
imperial command according to circumstances: his
direct superior was the shōgun; and he was obliged
to make for himself a politic distinction between the
Heavenly Sovereign as deity, and the Heavenly
Sovereign as a human personality. Before the ultimate centralization of the military power, there were
many instances of lords sacrificing themselves for
their emperor; but there were even more cases of
open rebellion by lords against the imperial will.
Under the Tokugawa rule, the question of obeying
or resisting an imperial command would have depended upon the attitude of the shōgun; and no
daimyō would have risked such obedience to the
court at Kyōto as might have signified disobedience
to the court at Yedo. Not at least until the shōgunate had fallen into decay. In Iyémitsu's time
the daimyō were strictly forbidden to approach the
imperial palace on their way to Yedo, — even in
response to an imperial command; and they were
also forbidden to make any direct appeal to the

Mikado.   The policy of the shōgunate was to prevent all direct communication between the Kyōto court and the daimyō.   This policy paralyzed intrigue for two hundred years; but it prevented the development of patriotism.

And for that very reason, when Japan at last found herself face to face with the unexpected peril of Western aggression, the abolition of the daimiates was felt to be a matter of paramount importance. The supreme danger required that the social units should be fused into one coherent mass, capable of uniform action, — that the clan and tribal groupings should be permanently dissolved, — that all authority should immediately be centred in the representative of the national religion, — that the duty of obedience to the Heavenly Sovereign should replace, at once and forever, the feudal duty of obedience to the territorial lord.   The religion of loyalty, evolved by a thousand years of war, could not be cast away : properly utilized, it would prove a national heritage of incalculable worth, — a moral power capable of miracles if directed by one wise will to a single wise end.   Destroyed by reconstruction it could not be ; but it could be diverted and transformed.   Diverted, therefore, to nobler ends — expanded to larger needs, — it became the new national sentiment of trust and duty : the modern sense of patriotism.   What wonders it has wrought, within the space of thirty years, the world is now obliged to confess : what more it may be able to accomplish remains to be seen. One thing at least is certain, — that the future of Japan must depend upon the maintenance of this new religion of loyalty, evolved, through the old, from the ancient religion of the dead.

The Jesuit Peril

THE second half of the sixteenth century is the most interesting period in Japanese history — for three reasons. First, because it witnessed the apparition of those mighty captains, Nobunaga, Hidéyoshi, and Iyéyasu, — types of men that a race seems to evolve for supreme emergencies only, — types requiring for their production not merely the highest aptitudes of numberless generations, but likewise an extraordinary combination of circumstances. Secondly, this period is all-important because it saw the first complete integration of the ancient social system, — the definitive union of all the clan-lordships under a central military government. And lastly, the period is of special interest because the incident of the first attempt to christianize Japan — the story of the rise and fall of the Jesuit power — properly belongs to it.

The sociological significance of this episode is instructive. Excepting, perhaps, the division of the imperial house against itself in the twelfth century, the greatest danger that ever threatened Japanese national integrity was the introduction of Christianity by the Portuguese Jesuits. The nation saved itself only by ruthless measures, at the cost of incalculable suffering and of myriads of lives.

It was during the period of great disorder preceding Nobunaga's effort to centralize authority, that this unfamiliar disturbing factor was introduced by Xavier and his followers. Xavier landed at Kagoshima in 1549; and by 1581 the Jesuits had upwards of two hundred churches in the country. This fact alone sufficiently indicates the rapidity with which the new religion spread; and it seemed destined to extend over the entire empire. In 1585 a Japanese religious embassy was received at Rome; and by that date no less than eleven daimyō, — or "kings," as the Jesuits not inaptly termed them — had become converted. Among these were several very powerful lords. The new creed had made rapid way among the common people also: it was becoming "popular," in the strict meaning of the word.

When Nobunaga rose to power, he favoured the Jesuits in many ways — not because of any sympathy with their creed, for he never dreamed of becoming a Christian, but because he thought that their influence would be of service to him in his campaign against Buddhism. Like the Jesuits themselves, Nobunaga had no scruple about means in his pursuit of ends. More ruthless than William the Conqueror, he did not hesitate to put to death his own brother and his own father-in-law, when they dared to oppose his will. The aid and protection which he extended to the foreign priests, for merely political reasons, enabled them to develop their power to a degree which soon gave him cause for repentance. Mr. Gubbins, in his " Review of the Introduction of Christianity into China and Japan," quotes from a Japanese work, called *Ibuki Mogusa*, an interesting extract on the subject : —

" Nobunaga now began to regret his previous policy in permitting the introduction of Christianity. He accordingly assembled his retainers, and said to them : — ' The conduct of these missionaries in persuading people to join them by giving money, does not please me. How would it be, think you, if we were to demolish Nambanji [*The " Temple of the Southern Savages" — so the Portuguese church was called*] ? ' To this Mayéda Tokuzénin replied. — ' It is now too late to demolish the Temple of the Namban. To endeavour to arrest the power of this religion now is like trying to arrest the current of the ocean. Nobles, both great and small, have become adherents of it. If you would exterminate this religion now, there is fear that disturbance should be created among your own retainers. I am therefore of opinion that you should abandon your intention of destroying Nambanji.' Nobunaga in consequence regretted exceedingly his previous action in regard to the Christian religion, and set about thinking how he could root it out."

The assassination of Nobunaga in 1586 may have prolonged the period of toleration. His suc-

cessor Hidéyoshi, who judged the influence of the
foreign priests dangerous, was for the moment occupied with the great problem of centralizing the
military power, so as to give peace to the country.
But the furious intolerance of the Jesuits in the
southern provinces had already made them many
enemies, eager to avenge the cruelties of the new
creed. We read in the histories of the missions
about converted daimyō burning thousands of
Buddhist temples, destroying countless works of
art, and slaughtering Buddhist priests;—and we
find the Jesuit writers praising these crusades as
evidence of holy zeal. At first the foreign faith had
been only persuasive; afterwards, gathering power
under Nobunaga's encouragement, it became coercive and ferocious. A reaction against it set in
about a year after Nobunaga's death. In 1587
Hidéyoshi destroyed the mission churches in Kyōto,
Ōsaka, and Sakai, and drove the Jesuits from the
capital; and in the following year he ordered them
to assemble at the port of Hirado, and prepare to
leave the country. They felt themselves strong
enough to disobey: instead of leaving Japan, they
scattered through the country, placing themselves
under the protection of various Christian daimyō.
Hidéyoshi probably thought it impolitic to push
matters further: the priests kept quiet, and ceased
to preach publicly; and their self-effacement served
them well until 1591. In that year the advent of

certain Spanish Franciscans changed the state of
affairs. These Franciscans arrived in the train of
an embassy from the Philippines, and obtained leave
to stay in the country on condition that they were
not to preach Christianity. They broke their pledge,
abandoned all prudence, and aroused the wrath of
Hidéyoshi. He resolved to make an example ; and
in 1597 he had six Franciscans, three Jesuits, and
several other Christians taken to Nagasaki and there
crucified. The attitude of the great Taikō toward the
foreign creed had the effect of quickening the reaction against it, — a reaction which had already
begun to show itself in various provinces. But
Hidéyoshi's death in 1598 enabled the Jesuits to
hope for better fortune. His successor, the cold
and cautious Iyéyasu, allowed them to hope, and
even to reëstablish themselves in Kyōto, Ōsaka, and
elsewhere. He was preparing for the great contest
which was to be decided by the battle of Sëkiga-
hara ; — he knew that the Christian element was
divided, — some of its leaders being on his own
side, and some on the side of his enemies ; — and
the time would have been ill chosen for any repressive policy. But in 1606, after having solidly established his power, Iyéyasu for the first time showed
himself decidedly opposed to Christianity by issuing
an edict forbidding further mission work, and proclaiming that those who had adopted the foreign
religion must abandon it. Nevertheless the prop-

aganda went on — conducted no longer by Jesuits only, but also by Dominicans and Franciscans. The number of Christians then in the empire is said, with gross exaggeration, to have been nearly two millions. But Iyéyasu neither took, nor caused to be taken, any severe measures of repression until 1614, — from which date the great persecution may be said to have begun. Previously there had been local persecutions only, conducted by independent daimyō, — not by the central government. The local persecutions in Kyūshū, for example, would seem to have been natural consequences of the intolerance of the Jesuits in the days of their power, when converted daimyō burned Buddhist temples and massacred Buddhist priests; and these persecutions were most pitiless in those very districts — such as Bungo, Ōmura, and Higo — where the native religion had been most fiercely persecuted at Jesuit instigation. But from 1614 — at which date there remained only eight, out of the total sixty-four provinces of Japan, into which Christianity had not been introduced — the suppression of the foreign creed became a government matter; and the persecution was conducted systematically and uninterruptedly until every outward trace of Christianity had disappeared.

The fate of the missions, therefore, was really settled by Iyéyasu and his immediate successors;

and it is the part taken by Iyéyasu that especially demands attention. Of the three great captains, all had, sooner or later, become suspicious of the foreign propaganda ; but only Iyéyasu could find both the time and the ability to deal with the social problem which it had aroused. Even Hidéyoshi had been afraid to complicate existing political troubles by any rigorous measures of an extensive character. Iyéyasu long hesitated. The reasons for his hesitation were doubtless complex, and chiefly diplomatic. He was the last of men to act hastily, or suffer himself to be influenced by prejudice of any sort ; and to suppose him timid would be contrary to all that we know of his character. He must have recognized, of course, that to extirpate a religion which could claim, even in exaggeration, more than a million of adherents, was no light undertaking, and would involve an immense amount of suffering. To cause needless misery was not in his nature : he had always proved himself humane, and a friend of the common people. But he was first of all a states-man and patriot ; and the main question for him must have been the probable relation of the foreign creed to political and social conditions in Japan. This question required long and patient investigation ; and he appears to have given it all possible attention. At last he decided that Roman Christianity constituted a grave political danger and that its extirpation would be an unavoidable necessity.

The fact that the severe measures which he and his successors enforced against Christianity — measures steadily maintained for upwards of two hundred years — failed to completely eradicate the creed, proves how deeply the roots had struck. Superficially, all trace of Christianity vanished to Japanese eyes; but in 1865 there were discovered near Nagasaki some communities which had secretly preserved among themselves traditions of the Roman forms of worship, and still made use of Portuguese and Latin words relating to religious matters.

To rightly estimate the decision of Iyéyasu — one of the shrewdest, and also one of the most humane statesmen that ever lived, — it is necessary to consider, from a Japanese point of view, the nature of the evidence upon which he was impelled to act. Of Jesuit intrigues in Japan he must have had ample knowledge — several of them having been directed against himself; — but he would have been more likely to consider the ultimate object and probable result of such intrigues, than the mere fact of their occurrence. Religious intrigues were common among the Buddhists, and would scarcely attract the notice of the military government except when they interfered with state policy or public order. But religious intrigues having for their object the overthrow of government, and a sectarian domination of the country, would be gravely considered.

Nobunaga had taught Buddhism a severe lesson about the danger of such intriguing. Iyéyasu decided that the Jesuit intrigues had a political object of the most ambitious kind; but he was more patient than Nobunaga. By 1603 he had every district of Japan under his yoke; but he did not issue his final edict until eleven years later. It plainly declared that the foreign priests were plotting to get control of the government, and to obtain possession of the country : —

"The Kirishitan band have come to Japan, not only sending their merchant-vessels to exchange commodities, but also longing to disseminate an evil law, to overthrow right doctrine, so that they may change the government of the country, and obtain possession of the land. This is the germ of great disaster, and must be crushed. . . .

"Japan is the country of the gods and of the Buddha : it honours the gods, and reveres the Buddha. . . . The faction of the Bateren [1] disbelieve in the Way of the Gods, and blaspheme the true Law, — violate right-doing, and injure the good. . . . They truly are the enemies of the gods and of the Buddha. . . . If this be not speedily prohibited, the safety of the state will assuredly hereafter be imperilled; and if those who are charged with ordering its affairs do not put a stop to the evil, they will expose themselves to Heaven's rebuke.

"These [missionaries] must be instantly swept out, so that not an inch of soil remains to them in Japan on which

[1] *Bateren*, a corruption of the Portuguese *padre*, is still the term used for Roman Catholic priests, of any denomination.

to plant their feet; and if they refuse to obey this command, they shall suffer the penalty. . . .   Let Heaven and
the Four Seas hear this.   Obey!"[1]

It will be observed that there are two distinct
charges made against the Bateren in this document,
— that of political conspiracy under the guise of
religion, with a view to getting possession of the
government; and that of intolerance, towards both
the Shintō and the Buddhist forms of native worship.   The intolerance is sufficiently proved by the
writings of the Jesuits themselves.   The charge of
conspiracy was less easy to prove; but who could
reasonably have doubted that, were opportunity
offered, the Roman Catholic orders would attempt
to control the general government precisely as they
had been able to control local government already
in the lordships of converted daimyō.   Besides, we
may be sure that by the time at which the edict was
issued, Iyéyasu must have heard of many matters
likely to give him a most evil opinion of Roman
Catholicism: — the story of the Spanish conquests
in America, and the extermination of the West
Indian races; the story of the persecutions in the
Netherlands, and of the work of the Inquisition
elsewhere; the story of the attempt of Philip II to
conquer England, and of the loss of the two great

[1] The entire proclamation, which is of considerable length, has been translated
by Satow, and may be found in Vol. VI, part I, of the *Transactions of the Asiatic
Society of Japan.*

Armadas. The edict was issued in 1614, and Iyéyasu had found opportunity to inform himself about
some of these matters as early as 1600. In that
year the English pilot Will Adams had arrived at
Japan in charge of a Dutch ship. Adams had
started on this eventful voyage in the year 1598, —
that is to say, just ten years after the defeat of the
first Spanish Armada, and one year after the ruin of
the second. He had seen the spacious times of
great Elizabeth — who was yet alive; — he had very
probably seen Howard and Seymour and Drake
and Hawkins and Frobisher and Sir Richard Gren-
ville, the hero of 1591. For this Will Adams was
a Kentish man, who had "serued for Master and
Pilott in her Majesties ships. . . ." The Dutch
vessel was seized immediately upon her arrival at
Kyūshū; and Adams and his shipmates were taken
into custody by the daimyō of Bungo, who reported
the fact to Iyéyasu. The advent of these Protestant sailors was considered an important event by
the Portuguese Jesuits, who had their own reasons
for dreading the results of an interview between such
heretics and the ruler of Japan. But Iyéyasu also
happened to think the event an important one; and
he ordered that Adams should be sent to him at
Ōsaka. The malevolent anxiety of the Jesuits
about the matter had not escaped Iyéyasu's pene-
trating observation. They endeavoured again and
again to have the sailors killed, according to the

written statement of Adams himself, who was certainly no liar; and they had been able·in Bungo to
frighten two scoundrels of the ship's company into
giving false testimony.[1] "The Iesuites and the
Portingalls," wrote Adams, "gaue many euidences
against me and the rest to the Emperour [*Iyéyasu*],
that we were theeues and robbers of all nations, —
and [that] were we suffered to liue,· it should be
against the profit of his Highnes, and the land."
But Iyéyasu was perhaps all the more favourably
inclined towards Adams by the eagerness of the
Jesuits to have him killed — "crossed [*crucified*],"
as Adams called it, — "the custome of iustice in
Japan, as hanging is in our land." He gave them
answer, says Adams, "that we had as yet not doen
to him nor to none of his lande any harme or dam-
mage : therefore against Reason and Iustice to put
vs to death." . . . And there came to pass precisely what the Jesuits had most feared, — what
they had vainly endeavoured by intimidation, by
slander, by all possible intrigue to prevent, — an
interview between Iyéyasu and the heretic Adams.

---

[1] "Daily more and more the Portugalls incensed the justices and the people
against vs. And two of our men, as traytors, gaue themselves in seruice to the king
[*daimyō*], beeing all in all with the Portugals, hauing by them their liues warranted.
The one was called *Gilbert de Conning*, whose mother dwelleth at Middleborough,
who gaue himself out to be marchant of all the goods in the shippe. The other
was called *Iohn Abelson Van Owater*. These traitours sought all manner of wayes
to get the goods into their hands, and made known vnto them all things that had
passed in our voyage. Nine dayes after our arriuall, the great king of the land
[*Iyéyasu*] sent for me to come vnto him." — Letter of Will Adams to his wife.

"Soe that as soon as I came before him," wrote
Adams, "he demanded of me of what countrey we
were: so I answered him in all points; for there
was nothing that he demanded not, both concerning
warre and peace between countrey and countrey: so
that the particulars here to wryte would be too
tedious. And for that time I was commanded to
prison, being well vsed, with one of our mariners
that cam with me to serue me." From another
letter of Adams it would seem that this interview
lasted far into the night, and that Iyéyasu's questions referred especially to politics and religion.
"He asked," says Adams, "whether our countrey
had warres? I answered him yea, with the Spaniards and Portugals — beeing in peace with all other
nations. Further he asked me in what I did be-
leeue? I said, in God, that made heauen and
earth. He asked me diverse other questions of
things of religion, and many other things: As, what
way we came to the country? Having a chart of
the whole world, I shewed him through the *Straight
of Magellan.* At which he wondred, and thought
me to lie. Thus, from one thing to another, I
abode with him till midnight." . . . The two men
liked each other at sight, it appears. Of Iyéyasu,
Adams significantly observes: "He viewed me
well, and seemed to be wonderful favourable." Two
days later Iyéyasu again sent for Adams, and cross-
questioned him just about those matters which the

Jesuits wanted to remain in the dark. "He de-maunded also as conserning the warres between the Spaniard or Portingall and our countrey, and the reasons: the which I gaue him to vnderstand of all things, which he was glad to heare, as it seemed to me. In the end I was commaunded to prisson agein, but my lodging was bettered." . . . Adams did not see Iyéyasu again for nearly six weeks: then he was sent for, and cross-questioned a third time. The result was liberty and favour. Thereafter, at intervals, Iyéyasu used to send for him; and pres-ently we hear of him teaching the great statesman "some points of jeometry, and understanding of the art of mathematickes, with other things." . . . Iyéyasu gave him many presents, as well as a good living, and commissioned him to build some ships for deep-sea sailing. Eventually, the poor pilot was created a samurai, and given an estate. "Being employed in the Emperour's seruice," he wrote, "he hath given me a liuing, like vnto a lordship in England, with eightie or ninetie husbandmen that be as my slaues or seruents: the which, or the like president [*precedent*], was neuer here before geven to any stranger." . . . Witness to the influence of Adams with Iyéyasu is furnished by the correspond-ence of Captain Cock, of the English factory, who thus wrote home about him in 1614: "The truth is the Emperour esteemeth hym much, and he may goe in and speake with hym at all times, when

kynges and princes are kept ovt." [1]   It was through
this influence that the English were allowed to establish their factory at Hirado.   There is no
stranger seventeenth-century romance than that
of this plain English pilot, — with only his simple
honesty and common-sense to help him, — rising
to such extraordinary favour with the greatest and
shrewdest of all Japanese rulers.   Adams was never
allowed, however, to return to England, — perhaps
because his services were deemed too precious to
lose.   He says himself in his letters that Iyéyasu
never refused him anything that he asked for,[2] except the privilege of revisiting England: when he
asked that, once too often, the "ould Emperour"
remained silent.

The correspondence of Adams proves that Iyéyasu disdained no means of obtaining direct information about foreign affairs in regard to religion and
politics.   As for affairs in Japan, he had at his disposal the most perfect system of espionage ever

[1] "It has plessed God to bring things to pass, so as in ye eyes of ye world
[must seem] strange; for the Spaynnard and Portingall hath bin my bitter enemies
to death; and now theay must seek to me, an unworthy wretch; for the Spayn-
ard as well as the Portingall must haue all their negosshes [*negotiations*] go thorough
my hand," — Letter of Adams dated January 12, 1613.

[2] Even favours for the people who had sought to bring about his death.   "I
pleased him so," wrote Adams, "that what I said he would not contrarie.   At
which my former enemies did wonder; and at this time must entreat me to do them
a friendship, which to both Spaniards and Portingals have I doen: recompencing
them good for eulll.   So, to passe my time to get my liuing, it hath cost mee great
labour and trouble at the first, but God hath blessed my labour."

established; and he knew all that was going on.
Yet he waited, as we have seen, fourteen years
before he issued his edict. Hidéyoshi's edict was,
indeed, renewed by him in 1606; but that referred
particularly to the public preaching of Christianity;
and while the missionaries outwardly conformed to
the law, he continued to suffer them within his own
dominions. Persecutions were being carried on elsewhere; but the secret propaganda was also being
carried on, and the missionaries could still hope.
Yet there was menace in the air, like the heaviness
preceding storms. Captain Saris, writing from Japan
in 1613, records a pathetic incident which is very
suggestive. "I gaue leaue," he says, "to divers
women of the better sort to come into my Cabbin,
where the picture of *Venus*, with her sonne *Cupid*,
did hang somewhat wantonly set out in a large
frame. They, thinking it to bee Our Ladie and
her sonne, fell downe and worshipped it, with shewes
of great deuotion, telling me in a whispering manner (that some of their own companions, which were
not so, might not heare), that they were *Christianos*:
whereby we perceived them to be *Christians*, con-
uerted by the Portugall Iesuits." . . . When Iyéyasu first took strong measures, they were directed,
not against the Jesuits, but against a more imprudent
order, — as we know from Adams's correspondence.
"In the yeer 1612," he says, "is put downe all
the sects of the Franciscannes. The Jesouets hau

what priuiledge . . . theare beinge in Nangasaki, in
which place only may be so manny as will of all
sectes : in other places not so many permitted. . . ."
Roman Catholicism was given two more years' grace
after the Franciscan episode.

Why Iyéyasu should have termed it a " false and
corrupt religion," both in his Legacy and elsewhere,
remains to be considered. From the Far-Eastern
point of view he could scarcely have judged it otherwise, after an impartial investigation. It was essentially opposed to all the beliefs and traditions upon
which Japanese society had been founded. The
Japanese State was an aggregate of religious communities, with a God-King at its head ; — the customs of all these communities had the force of
religious laws, and ethics were identified with obedience to custom ; filial piety was the basis of social
order, and loyalty itself was derived from filial piety.
But this Western creed, which taught that a husband
should leave his parents and cleave to his wife, held
filial piety to be at best an inferior virtue. It proclaimed that duty to parents, lords, and rulers
remained duty only when obedience involved no
action opposed to Roman teaching, and that the
supreme duty of obedience was not to the Heavenly
Sovereign at Kyōto, but to the Pope at Rome.
Had not the Gods and the Buddhas been called
devils by these missionaries from Portugal and
Spain ? Assuredly such doctrines were subversive,

no matter how astutely they might be interpreted
by their apologists.   Besides, the worth of a creed
as a social force might be judged from its fruits.
This creed in Europe had been a ceaseless cause
of disorders, wars, persecutions, atrocious cruelties.
This creed, in Japan, had fomented great disturb-
ances, had instigated political intrigues, had wrought
almost immeasurable mischief.   In the event of
future political trouble, it would justify the disobedience of children to parents, of wives to husbands, of subjects to lords, of lords to shōgun.
The paramount duty of government was now to
compel social order, and to maintain those conditions of peace and security without which the nation
could never recover from the exhaustion of a thousand years of strife.   But so long as this foreign
religion was suffered to attack and to sap the foundations of order, there never could be peace. . . .
Convictions like these must have been well established in the mind of Iyéyasu when he issued his
famous edict. . The only wonder is that he should
have waited so long.

Very possibly Iyéyasu, who never did anything
by halves, was waiting until Christianity should find
itself without one Japanese leader of ability.   In
1611 he had information of a Christian conspiracy
in the island of Sado (a convict mining-district) whose
governor, Ōkubo, had been induced to adopt Christianity, and was to be made ruler of the country if

the plot proved successful.   But still Iyéyasu waited.
By 1614 Christianity had scarcely even an Ōkubo
to lead the forlorn hope.   The daimyō converted in
the sixteenth century were dead or dispossessed or
in banishment;   the great Christian generals had
been executed;   the few remaining converts of importance had been placed under surveillance, and
were practically helpless.

The foreign priests and native catechists were not
cruelly treated immediately after the proclamation
of 1614.   Some three hundred of them were put
into ships and sent out of the country, — together
with various Japanese suspected of religious political
intrigues, such as Takayama, former daimyō of
Akashi, who was called " Justo Ucondono" by the
Jesuit writers, and who had been dispossessed and
degraded by Hidéyoshi for the same reasons.   Iyéyasu set no example of unnecessary severity.   But
harsher measures followed upon an event which
took place in 1615, — the very year after the issuing of the edict.   Hidéyori, the son of Hidéyoshi,
had been supplanted — fortunately for Japan — by
Iyéyasu, to whose tutelage the young man had
been confided.   Iyéyasu took all care of him, but
had no intention of suffering him to direct the government of the country, — a task scarcely within the
capacity of a lad of twenty-three.   In spite of various political intrigues in which Hidéyori was known
to have taken part, Iyéyasu had left him in posses-

sion of large revenues, and of the strongest fortress in
Japan, — that mighty castle of Ōsaka, which Hidéyoshi's genius had rendered almost impregnable.
Hidéyori, unlike his father, favoured the Jesuits:
and he made the castle a refuge for adherents of the
"false and corrupt sect." Informed by government
spies of a dangerous intrigue there preparing, Iyéyasu resolved to strike; and he struck hard. In
spite of a desperate defence, the great fortress was
stormed and burnt — Hidéyori perishing in the conflagration. One hundred thousand lives are said to
have been lost in this siege. Adams wrote thus
quaintly of Hidéyori's fate, and the results of his
conspiracy : —

"Hee mad warres with the Emperour . . . allso
by the Jessvits and Ffriers, which mad belleeue he
should be fauord with mirrackles and wounders;
but in fyne it proued the contrari. For the ould
Emperour against him pressentlly maketh his forces
reddy by sea and land, and compasseth his castell
that hc was in; although with loss of multitudes on
both sides, yet in the end rasseth the castell walles,
setteth it on fyre, and burneth hym in it. Thus
ended the warres. Now the Emperour heering of
thees Jessvets and friers being in the castell with his
ennemis, and still from tym to tym agaynst hym,
coumandeth all romische sorte of men to depart ovt
of his countri — thear churches pulld dooun, and
burned. This folowed in the ould Emperour's

daies. Now this yeear, 1616, the old Emperour he died. His son raigneth in his place, and hee is more hot agaynste the romish relligion then his ffather wass: for he hath forbidden thorough all his domynions, on paine of deth, none of his subjects to be romish christiane; which romish seckt to prevent eueri wayes that he maye, he hath forbidden that no stranger merchant shall abid in any of the great citties." . . .

The son here referred to was Hidétada, who, in 1617, issued an ordinance sentencing to death every Roman priest or friar discovered in Japan, — an ordinance provoked by the fact that many priests expelled from the country had secretly returned, and that others had remained to carry on their propaganda under various disguises. Meanwhile, in every city, town, village, and hamlet throughout the empire, measures had been taken for the extirpation of Roman Christianity. Every community was made responsible for the existence in it of any person belonging to the foreign creed; and special magistrates, or inquisitors, were appointed, called *Kirishitan-bugyō*, to seek out and punish members of the prohibited religion.[1] Christians

---

[1] It should be borne in mind that none of these edicts were directed against Protestant Christianity: the Dutch were not considered Christians in the sense of the ordinances, nor were the English. The following extract from a typical village, *Kumichō*, or code of communal regulations, shows the responsibility imposed upon all communities regarding the presence in their midst of Roman Catholic convercs or believers: —

"Every year, between the first and the third month, we will renew our *Shūmon-*

who freely recanted were not punished, but only
kept under surveillance: those who refused to
recant, even after torture, were degraded to the
condition of slaves, or else put to death. In some
parts of the country, extraordinary cruelty was practised, and every form of torture used to compel
recantation. But it is tolerably certain that the
more atrocious episodes of the persecution were
due to the individual ferocity of local governors
or magistrates — as in the case of Takénaka
Unémé-no-Kami, who was compelled by the government to perform *harakiri* for abusing his powers
at Nagasaki, and making persecution a means of
extorting money. Be that as it may, the persecution at last either provoked, or helped to bring
about a Christian rebellion in the daimiate of
Arima, — historically remembered as the Shimabara Revolt. In 1636 a host of peasants, driven
to desperation by the tyranny of their lords —
the daimyō of Arima and the daimyō of Karatsu
(convert-districts) — rose in arms, burnt all the
Japanese temples in their vicinity, and proclaimed
religious war. Their banner bore a cross; their
leaders were converted samurai. They were soon

chō. If we know of any person who belongs to a prohibited sect, we will immediately inform the *Daikwan*. . . . Servants and labourers shall give to their masters
a certificate declaring that they are not Christians. In regard to persons who have
been Christians, but have recanted, — if such persons come to or leave the village,
we promise to report it." — See Professor Wigmore's *Notes on Land-Ten re
and Local Institutions in Old Japan.*

joined by Christian refugees from every part of the
country, until their numbers swelled to thirty or
forty thousand. On the coast of the Shimabara
peninsula they seized an abandoned castle, at a
place called Hara, and there fortified themselves.
The local authorities could not cope with the uprising; and the rebels more than held their own
until government forces, aggregating over 160,000
men, were despatched against them. After a brave
defence of one hundred and two days, the castle was
stormed in 1638, and its defenders, together with
their women and children, put to the sword.
Officially the occurrence was treated as a peasant
revolt; and the persons considered responsible for
it were severely punished; — the lord of Shimabara (Arima) was further sentenced to perform
harakiri. Japanese historians state that the rising
was first planned and led by Christians, who de-
signed to seize Nagasaki, subdue Kyūshū, invite
foreign military help, and compel a change of
government; — the Jesuit writers would have us
believe there was no plot. One thing certain is
that a revolutionary appeal was made to the Christian element, and was largely responded to with
alarming consequences. A strong castle on the
Kyūshū coast, held by thirty or forty thousand
Christians, constituted a serious danger, — a point
of vantage from which a Spanish invasion of the
country might have been attempted with some

chance of success. The government seems to have recognized this danger, and to have despatched in consequence an overwhelming force to Shimabara. If foreign help could have been sent to the rebels, the result might have been a prolonged civil war. As for the wholesale slaughter, it represented no more than the enforcement of Japanese law: the punishment of the peasant revolting against his lord, under any circumstances whatever, being death. So far as concerns the policy of such massacre, it may be remembered that, with less provocation, Nobunaga exterminated the Tendai Buddhists at Hiyei-san. We have every reason to pity the brave men who perished at Shimabara, and to sympathize with their revolt against the atrocious cruelty of their rulers. But it is necessary, as a simple matter of justice, to consider the whole event from the Japanese political point of view.

The Dutch have been denounced for helping to crush the rebellion with ships and cannon: they fired, by their own acknowledgment, 426 shot into the castle. However, the extant correspondence of the Dutch factory at Hirado proves beyond question that they were forced, under menace, to thus act. In any event, it would be difficult to discover a good reason for the merely religious denunciations of their conduct, — although that conduct would be open to criticism from the humane point of view. Dutchmen could not reasonably have refused to assist the Japanese authorities in suppressing a revolt, merely because a large proportion of the rebels happened to profess the religion which had been burning alive as heretics the men and women of the Netherlands. Very possibly, not a few persons of kin to those very Dutch had suffered in the days of Alva. What would have happened to all the English and Dutch in Japan, if the Portuguese and Spanish clergy could have got full control of government, ought to be obvious.

With the massacre of Shimabara ends the real history of the Portuguese and Spanish missions. After that event, Christianity was slowly, steadily, implacably stamped out of visible existence. It had been tolerated, or half-tolerated, for only sixty-five years : the entire history of its propagation and destruction occupies a period of scarcely ninety years. People of nearly every rank, from prince to pauper, suffered for it ; thousands endured tortures for its sake — tortures so frightful that even three of those Jesuits who sent multitudes to useless martyrdom were forced to deny their faith under the infliction ; [1] — and tender women, sentenced to the stake, car-

---

[1] Francisco Cassola, Pedro Marquez, and Giuseppe Chiara. Two of these — probably under compulsion — married Japanese women. For their after-history, see a paper by Satow in the *Transactions of the Asiatic Society of Japan*, Vol. VI, Part I.

ried their little ones with them into the fire, rather
than utter the words that would have saved both
mother and child.   Yet this religion, for which
thousands vainly died, had brought to Japan nothing but evil : disorders, persecutions, revolts, political troubles, and war.   Even those virtues of the
people which had been evolved at unutterable cost
for the protection and conservation of society, —
their self-denial, their faith, their loyalty, their
constancy and courage, — were by this black creed
distorted, diverted, and transformed into forces
directed to the destruction of that society.   Could
that destruction have been accomplished, and a
new Roman Catholic empire have been founded
upon the ruins, the forces of that empire would
have been used for the further extension of priestly
tyranny, the spread of the Inquisition, the perpetual
Jesuit warfare against freedom of conscience and
human progress.   Well may we pity the victims of
this pitiless faith, and justly admire their useless
courage : yet who can regret that their cause was
lost ? . . .   Viewed from another standpoint than
that of religious bias, and simply judged by its
results, the Jesuit effort to Christianize Japan must
be regarded as a crime against humanity, a labour
of devastation, a calamity comparable only, — by
reason of the misery and destruction which it
wrought, — to an earthquake, a tidal-wave, a
volcanic eruption.

The policy of isolation, — of shutting off Japan from the rest of the world, — as adopted by Hidé-tada and maintained by his successors, sufficiently indicates the fear that religious intrigues had inspired. Not only were all foreigners, excepting the Dutch traders, expelled from the country ; all half-breed children of Portuguese or Spanish blood were also expatriated, Japanese families being forbidden to adopt or conceal any of them, under penalties to be visited upon all the members of the household dis-obeying.   In 1636 two hundred and eighty-seven half-breed children were shipped to Macao.   It is possible that the capacity of half-breed children to act as interpreters was particularly dreaded ; but there can be little doubt that, at the time when this ordinance was issued, race-hatred had been fully aroused by religious antagonism.   After the Shima-bara episode all Western foreigners, without exception, were regarded with unconcealed distrust.[1]   The Portuguese and Spanish traders were replaced by the Dutch (the English factory having been closed some years previously) ; but even in the case of these, extraordinary precautions were taken.   They were compelled to abandon their good quarters at Hirado, and transfer their factory to Deshima, — a tiny island only six hundred feet long, by two hun-dred and forty feet wide.   There they were kept under constant guard, like prisoners ; they were not

[1] The Chinese traders, however, were allowed much more liberty than the Dutch.

permitted to go among the people; no man could
visit them without permission, and no woman, except
a prostitute, was allowed to enter their reservation
under any circumstances.   But they had a monopoly
of the trade of the country; and Dutch patience
endured these conditions, for the profit's sake, during more than two hundred years.   Other commerce
with foreign countries than that maintained by the
Dutch factory, and by the Chinese, was entirely suppressed.   For any Japanese to leave Japan was a
capital offence; and any one who might succeed in
leaving the country by stealth, was to be put to
death upon his return.   The purpose of this law
was to prevent Japanese, sent abroad by the Jesuits
for missionary training, from returning to Japan in the
disguise of laymen.   It was forbidden also to construct ships capable of long voyages; and all ships
exceeding a dimension fixed by the government
were broken up.   Lookouts were established along
the coast to watch for strange vessels; and any
European ships entering a Japanese port, excepting
the ships of the Dutch company, were to be attacked
and destroyed.

The great success at first achieved by the Portuguese missions remains to be considered.   In our
present comparative ignorance of Japanese social
history, it is not easy to understand the whole of the
Christian episode.   There are plenty of Jesuit-

missionary records ; but the Japanese contemporary
chronicles yield us scanty information about the missions — probably for the reason that an edict was
issued in the seventeenth century interdicting, not
only all books on the subject of Christianity, but
any book containing the words *Christian* or *Foreign*.
What the Jesuit books do not explain, and what we
should rather have expected Japanese historians to explain, had they been allowed, is how a society founded
on ancestor-worship, and apparently possessing immense capacity for resistance to outward assault,
could have been so quickly penetrated and partly
dissolved by Jesuit energy. The question of all
questions that I should like to see answered, by
Japanese evidence, is this : To what extent did the
missionaries interfere with the ancestor-cult ? It is an
important question. In China, the Jesuits were quick
to perceive that the power of resistance to proselytism
lay in ancestor-worship ; and they shrewdly endeavoured to tolerate it, somewhat as Buddhism before
them had been obliged to do. Had the Papacy
supported their policy, the Jesuits might have
changed the history of China ; but other religious
orders fiercely opposed the compromise, and the
chance was lost. How far the ancestor-cult was tolerated by the Portuguese missionaries in Japan is a
matter of much sociological interest for investigation.
The supreme cult was, of course, left alone, for
obvious reasons. It is difficult to suppose that the

domestic cult was attacked then as implacably as it is attacked now by Protestant and Roman Catholic missionaries alike ; — it is difficult to suppose, for example, that converts were compelled to cast away or to destroy their ancestral tablets. On the other hand, we are yet in doubt as to whether many of the poorer converts — servants and other common folk — possessed a domestic ancestor-cult. The out-cast classes, among whom many converts were made, need not be considered, of course, in this relation. Before the matter can be fairly judged, much remains to be learned about the religious con-dition of the *heimin* during the sixteenth century. Anyhow, whatever methods were followed, the early success of the missions was astonishing. Their work, owing to the particular character of the social organization, necessarily began from the top : the subject could change his creed only by permission of his lord. From the outset this permission was freely granted. In some cases the people were offi-cially notified that they were at liberty to adopt the new religion ; in other cases, converted lords ordered them to do so. It would seem that the foreign faith was at first mistaken for a new kind of Buddh-ism ; and in the extant official grant of land at Ya-maguchi to the Portuguese mission, in 1552, the Japanese text plainly states that the grant (which ap-pears to have included a temple called Daidōji) was made to the strangers that they might preach "the Law of Buddha"—*Buppō shōryō no tamé*. The original document is thus translated by Sir Ernest Satow, who reproduced it in facsimile:—

"With respect to Daidōji in Yamaguchi Agata, Yoshiki department, province of Suwō. This deed witnesses that I have given permission to the priests who have come to this country from the Western regions, in accordance with their request and desire, that they may found and erect a monastery and house in order to develope the Law of Buddha.

"The 28th day of the 8th month of the 21st year of Tembun.

"SUWŌ NO SUKÉ.

"[August Seal]" [1]

If this error [or deception?] could have occurred at Yamaguchi, it is reasonable to suppose that it also occurred in other places. Exteriorly the Roman rites resembled those of popular Buddhism: the people would have observed but little that was unfamiliar to them in the forms of the service, the vestments, the beads, the prostrations, the images, the bells, and the incense. The virgins and the saints would have been found to resemble the aureoled Boddhisattvas and Buddhas; the angels and the demons would have been at once identified with the *Ten-*

[1] In the Latin and Portuguese translations, or rather pretended translations of this document, there is nothing about preaching the Law of Buddha; and there are many things added which do not exist in the Japanese text at all. See *Transactions of the Asiatic Society of Japan* (Vol. VIII, Part II) for Satow's comment on this document and the false translations made of it.

nin and the *Oni*. All that pleased popular imagination in the Buddhist ceremonial could be witnessed, under slightly different form, in those temples which had been handed over to the Jesuits, and consecrated by them as churches or chapels. The fathomless abyss really separating the two faiths could not have been perceived by the common mind; but the outward resemblances were immediately observable. There were furthermore some attractive novelties. It appears, for example, that the Jesuits used to have miracle-plays performed in their churches for the purpose of attracting popular attention. . . . But outward attractions of whatever sort, or outward resemblances to Buddhism, could only assist the spread of the new religion; they could not explain the rapid progress of the propaganda.

Coercion might partly explain it, — coercion exercised by converted daimyō upon their subjects. Populations of provinces are known to have followed, under strong compulsion, the religion of their converted lords; and hundreds — perhaps thousands — of persons must have done the same thing through mere habit of loyalty. In these cases it is worth while to consider what sort of persuasion was used upon the daimyō. We know that one great help to the missionary work was found in Portuguese commerce, — especially the trade in firearms and ammunition. In the disturbed state of the country preceding the advent to power of Hidéyoshi, this trade was a powerful bribe in religious negotiation with provincial lords. The daimyō able to use fire-arms would necessarily possess some advantage over a rival lord having no such weapons; and those lords able to monopolize the trade could increase their power at the expense of their neighbours. Now this trade was actually offered for the privilege of preaching; and sometimes much more than that privilege was demanded and obtained. In 1572 the Portuguese presumed to ask for the whole town of Nagasaki, as a gift to their church, — with power of jurisdiction over the same; threatening, in case of refusal, to establish themselves elsewhere. The daimyō, Ōmura, at first demurred, but eventually yielded; and Nagasaki then became Christian terri-tory, directly governed by the Church. Very soon the fathers began to prove the character of their creed by furious attacks upon the local religion. They set fire to the great Buddhist temple, Jinguji, and attributed the fire to the "wrath of God," — after which act, by the zeal of their converts, some eighty other temples, in or about Nagasaki, were burnt. Within Nagasaki territory Buddhism was totally suppressed, — its priests being persecuted and driven away. In the province of Bungo the Jesuit persecution of Buddhism was far more violent, and conducted upon an extensive scale. Ōtomo Sōrin Munéchika, the reigning daimyō, not

only destroyed all the Buddhist temples in his dominion (to the number, it is said, of three thousand),
but had many of the Buddhist priests put to death.
For the destruction of the great temple of Hikōzan,
whose priests were reported to have prayed for the
tyrant's death, he is said to have maliciously chosen
the sixth day of the fifth month (1576), — the
festival of the Birthday of the Buddha!

Coercion, exercised by their lords upon a docile
people trained to implicit obedience, would explain
something of the initial success of the missions ; but
it would leave many other matters unexplained :
the later success of the secret propaganda, the fer-
vour and courage of the converts under persecution,
the long-continued indifference of the chiefs of the
ancestor-cult to the progress of the hostile faith. . . .
When Christianity first began to spread through
the Roman empire, the ancestral religion had fallen
into decay, the structure of society had lost its original form, and there was no religious conservatism
really capable of successful resistance. But in the
Japan of the sixteenth and seventeenth centuries,
the religion of the ancestors was very much alive ;
and society was only entering upon the second
period of its yet imperfect integration. The Jesuit
conversions were not made among a people already
losing their ancient faith, but in one of the most
intensely religious and conservative societies that
ever existed. Christianity of any sort could not

have been introduced into such a society without
effecting structural disintegrations, — disintegrations,
at least, of a local character.   How far these disintegrations extended and penetrated we do not know;
and we have yet no adequate explanation of the
long inertia of the native religious instinct in the
face of danger.

But there are certain historical facts which appear
to throw at least a side-light upon the subject.   The
early Jesuit policy in China, as established by Ricci,
had been to leave converts free to practise the ancestral rites.   So long as this policy was followed,
the missions prospered.   When, in consequence of
this compromise, dissensions arose, the matter was
referred to Rome.   Pope Innocent X decided for
intolerance by a bull issued in 1645; and the Jesuit
missions were thereby practically ruined in China.
Pope Innocent's decision was indeed reversed the
very next year by a bull of Pope Alexander VIII;
but again and again contests were raised by the
religious bodies over this question of ancestor-
worship, until in 1693 Pope Clement XI definitively
prohibited converts from practising the ancestral rites
under any form whatsoever. . . .   All the efforts
of all the missions in the Far East have ever since
then failed to advance the cause of Christianity.
The sociological reason is plain.

We have seen, then, that up to the year 1645
the ancestor-cult had been tolerated by the Jesuits

in China, with promising results; and it is probable
that an identical policy of tolerance was maintained
in Japan during the second half of the sixteenth
century. The Japanese missions began in 1549,
and their history ends with the Shimabara slaughter
in 1638, — about seven years before the first Papal
decision against the tolerance of ancestor-worship.
The Jesuit mission-work seems to have prospered
steadily, in spite of all opposition, until it was
interfered with by less cautious and more uncompromising zealots. By a bull issued in 1585 by Greg-
ory XIII, and confirmed in 1600 by Clement III,
the Jesuits alone were authorized to do missionary-
work in Japan; and it was not until after their
privileges had been ignored by Franciscan zeal that
trouble with the government began. We have seen
that in 1593 Hidéyoshi had six Franciscans executed.
Then the issue of a new Papal bull in 1608, by Paul
V, allowing Roman Catholic missionaries of all
orders to work in Japan, probably ruined the Jesuit
interests. It will be remembered that Iyéyasu suppressed the Franciscans in 1612, — a proof that
their experience with Hidéyoshi had profited them
little. On the whole, it appears more than likely
that both Dominicans and Franciscans recklessly
meddled with matters which the Jesuits (whom they
accused of timidity) had been wise enough to leave
alone, and that this interference hastened the inevitable ruin of the missions.

We may reasonably doubt whether there were a million Christians in Japan at the beginning of the seventeenth century : the more probable claim of six hundred thousand can be accepted. In this era of toleration the efforts of all the foreign missionary bodies combined, and the yearly expenditure of immense sums in support of their work, have enabled them to achieve barely one-fifth of the success attributed to their Portuguese predecessors, upon a not incredible estimate.   The sixteenth-century Jesuits were indeed able to exercise, through various lords, the most forcible sort of coercion upon whole populations of provinces ; but the modern missions certainly enjoy advantages educational, financial, and legislative, much outweighing the doubtful value of the power to coerce; and the smallness of the results which they have achieved seems to require explanation. The explanation is not difficult. Needless attacks upon the ancestor-cult are necessarily attacks upon the constitution of society; and Japanese society instinctively resists these assaults upon its ethical basis.   For it is an error to suppose that this Japanese society has yet arrived even at such a condition as Roman society presented in the second or third century of our era. Rather it remains at a stage resembling that of a Greek or Latin society many centuries before Christ. The introduction of railroads, telegraphs, modern arms of precision, modern applied science of all kinds, has not yet

sufficed to change the fundamental order of things.
Superficial disintegrations are rapidly proceeding; new
structures are forming; but the social condition still
remains much like that which, in southern Europe,
long preceded the introduction of Christianity.

Though every form of religion holds something
of undying truth, the evolutionist must classify religions. He must regard a monotheistic faith as representing, in the progress of human thought, a very
considerable advance upon any polytheistic creed;
monotheism signifying the fusion and expansion of
countless ghostly beliefs into one vast concept of
unseen omnipotent power. And, from the standpoint of psychological evolution, he must of course
consider pantheism as an advance upon monotheism,
and must further regard agnosticism as an advance
upon both. But the value of a creed is necessarily
relative.; and the question of its worth is to be
decided, not by its adaptability to the intellectual
developments of a single cultured class, but by its
larger emotional relation to the whole society of
which it embodies the moral experience. Its value
to any other society must depend upon its power of
self-adaptation to the ethical experience of that
society. We may grant that Roman Catholicism
was, by sole virtue of its monotheistic conception, a
stage in advance of the primitive ancestor-worship.
But it was adapted only to a form of society at

which neither Chinese nor Japanese civilization had arrived, — a form of society in which the ancient family had been dissolved, and the religion of filial piety forgotten. Unlike that subtler and incomparably more humane creed of India, which had learned the secret of missionary-success a thousand years before Loyola, the religion of the Jesuits could never have adapted itself to the social conditions of Japan; and by the fact of this incapacity the fate of the missions was really decided in advance. The intolerance, the intrigues, the savage persecutions carried on, — all the treacheries and cruelties of the Jesuits, — may simply be considered as the manifestations of such incapacity; while the repressive measures taken by Iyéyasu and his successors signify sociologically no more than the national perception of supreme danger. It was recognized that the triumph of the foreign religion would involve the total disintegration of society, and the subjection of the empire to foreign domination.

Neither the artist nor the sociologist, at least, can regret the failure of the missions. Their extirpation, which enabled Japanese society to evolve to its type-limit, preserved for modern eyes the marvellous world of Japanese art, and the yet more marvellous world of its traditions, beliefs, and customs. Roman Catholicism, triumphant, would have swept all this out of existence. The natural antago-

nism of the artist to the missionary may be found in
the fact that the latter is always, and must be, an
unsparing destroyer.   Everywhere the developments of art are associated in some sort with religion ; and by so much as the art of a people reflects
their beliefs, that art will be hateful to the enemies
of those beliefs.   Japanese art, of Buddhist origin,
is especially an art of religious suggestion, — not
merely as regards painting and sculpture, but likewise as regards decoration, and almost every product
of æsthetic taste.   There is something of religious
feeling associated even with the Japanese delight in
trees and flowers, the charm of gardens, the love of
nature and of nature's voices, — with all the poetry
of existence, in short.   Most assuredly the Jesuits
and their allies would have ended all this, every
detail of it, without the slightest qualm.   Even
could they have understood and felt the meaning
of that world of strange beauty, — result of a race-
experience never to be repeated or replaced, — they
would not have hesitated a moment in the work of
obliteration and effacement.   To-day, indeed, that
wonderful art-world is being surely and irretrievably
destroyed by Western industrialism.   But industrial
influence, though pitiless, is not fanatic ; and the
destruction is not being carried on with such ferocious rapidity but that the fading story of beauty
can be recorded for the future benefit of human
civilization.

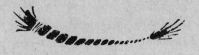

Feudal Integration

IT was under the later Tokugawa Shōgun — during the period immediately preceding the modern régime — that Japanese civilization reached the limit of its development. No further evolution was possible, except through social reconstruction. The conditions of this integration chiefly represented the reinforcement and definition of conditions preexisting, — scarcely anything in the way of fundamental change. More than ever before the old compulsory systems of coöperation were strengthened; more than ever before all details of ceremonial convention were insisted upon with merciless exactitude. In preceding ages there had been more harshness; but at no previous period had there been less liberty. Nevertheless, the results of this increased restriction were not without ethical value: the time was yet far off at which personal liberty could prove a personal advantage; and the paternal coercion of the Tokugawa rule helped to develop and to accentuate much of what is most attractive in the national character. Centuries of warfare had previously allowed small opportunity for the cultivation of the more delicate qualities of that character: the refinements, the

343

ingenuous kindliness, ,the joy in life that afterward lent so rare a charm to Japanese existence.
But during two hundred years of peace, prosperity,
and national isolation, the graceful and winning side
of this human nature found chance to bloom; and
the multiform restraints of law and custom then
quickened and curiously shaped the blossoming, —
as the gardener's untiring art evolves the flowers of
the chrysanthemum into a hundred forms of fantastic
beauty. . . .   Though the general social tendency
under pressure was toward rigidity, constraint left
room, in special directions, for moral and æsthetic
cultivation.

In order to understand the social condition, it
will be necessary to consider the nature of the
paternal rule in its legal aspects.   To modern
imagination the old Japanese laws may well seem
intolerable; but their administration was really less
uncompromising than that of our Western laws.
Besides, although weighing heavily upon all classes,
from the highest to the lowest, the legal burden
was proportioned to the respective strength of the
bearers; the application of law being made less
and less rigid as the social scale descended.   In
theory at least, from the earliest times, the poor
and unfortunate had been considered as entitled
to pity; and the duty of showing them all possible mercy was insisted upon in the oldest extant
moral code of Japan, — the Laws of Shōtoku Tai-

shi. But the most striking example of such discrimination appears in the Legacy of Iyéyasu,
which represents the conception of justice in a
time when society had become much more developed, its institutions more firmly fixed, and all its
bonds tightened. This stern and wise ruler, who
declared that " the people are the foundation of
the Empire," commanded leniency in dealing with
the humble. He ordained that any lord, no matter what his rank, convicted of breaking laws " to
the injury of the people," should be punished by
the confiscation of his estates. Perhaps the humane
spirit of the legislator is most strongly shown in his
enactments regarding crime, as, for example, where
he deals with the question of adultery — necessarily
a crime of the first magnitude in any society based
on ancestor-worship. By the 50th article of the
Legacy, the injured husband is confirmed in his
ancient right to kill, — but with this important
provision, that should he kill but one of the guilty
parties, he must himself be held as guilty as either
of them. Should the offenders be brought up for
trial, Iyéyasu advises that, in the case of common
people, particular deliberation be given to the
matter : he remarks upon the weakness of human
nature, and suggests that, among the young and
simple-minded, some momentary impulse of passion may lead to folly even when the parties are
not naturally depraved. But in the next article,

No. 51, he orders that no mercy whatever be shown to men and women of the upper classes when convicted of the same crime. "These," he declares, "are expected to know better than to occasion disturbance by violating existing regulations; and such persons, breaking the laws by lewd trifling or illicit intercourse, shall at once be punished without deliberation or consultation.[1]   It is not the same in this case as in the case of farmers, artizans, and traders." . . . Throughout the entire code, this tendency to tighten the bonds of law in the case of the military classes, and to loosen them mercifully for the lower classes, is equally visible. Iyéyasu strongly disapproved of unnecessary punishments; and held that the frequency of punishments was proof, not of the ill-conduct of subjects, but of the ill-conduct of officials. The 91st article of his code puts the matter thus plainly, even as regarded the Shōgunate: "When punishments and executions abound in the Empire, it is a proof that the military ruler is without virtue and degenerate." . . . He devised particular enactments to protect the peasantry and the poor from the cruelty or the rapacity of powerful lords. The great daimyō were strictly forbidden, when making their obligatory journeys to Yedo, "to disturb or harass the people at the post-houses," or suffer themselves "to be puffed up with military pride."

[1] That is to say, immediately put to death.

The private, not less than the public conduct of
these great lords, was under Government surveillance; and they were actually liable to punishment
for immorality! Concerning debauchery among
them, the legislator remarked that "even though
this can hardly be pronounced insubordination,"
it should be judged and punished *according to the
degree in which it constitutes a bad example for the
lower classes* (Art. 88).[1] As to veritable insubordination there was no pardon: the severity of the law
on this subject allowed of no exception or mitiga-
tion. The 53d section of the Legacy proves this
to have been regarded as the supreme crime:
"The guilt of a vassal murdering his suzerain is
in principle the same as that of an arch-traitor to
the Emperor. His immediate companions, his
relations,—all even to his most distant connexions,—shall be cut off, hewn to atoms, root
and fibre. The guilt of a vassal only lifting his
hand against his master, even though he does not

---

[1] Though even daimyō were liable to suffer for debauchery, Iyéyasu did not
believe in the expediency of attempting to suppress all vice by law. There is a
strangely modern ring in his remarks upon this subject, in the 73d section of the
Legacy: "Virtuous men have said, both in poetry and in classic works, that
houses of debauch, for women of pleasure and for street-walkers, are the worm-
eaten spots of cities and towns. But these are necessary evils, and if they be
forcibly abolished, men of unrighteous principles will become like ravelled thread,
and there will be no end to daily punishments and floggings." In many castle-
towns, however, such houses were never allowed—probably in view of the large
military force, assembled in such towns, which had to be maintained under iron
discipline.

assassinate him, is the same." In strong contrast
to this grim ordinance is the spirit of all the regulations touching the administration of law among
the lower classes. Forgery, incendiarism, and poi-
soning were indeed crimes justifying the penalty of
burning or crucifixion; but judges were instructed
to act with as much leniency as circumstances permitted in the case of ordinary offences. "With
regard to minute details affecting individuals of
the inferior classes," says the 73d article of the
code, "learn the wide benevolence of Kōso of
the Han [Chinese] dynasty." It was further ordered that magistrates of the criminal and civil
courts should be chosen only from "a class of
men who are upright and pure, distinguished for
charity and benevolence." All magistrates were
kept under close supervision, and their conduct
regularly reported by government spies.

Another humane aspect of Tokugawa legislation
is furnished by its dictates in regard to the relations
of the sexes. Although concubinage was tolerated
in the Samurai class, for reasons relating to the continuance of the family-cult, Iyéyasu denounces the
indulgence of the privilege for merely selfish reasons: "Silly and ignorant men neglect their true
wives for the sake of a loved mistress, and thus disturb the most important relation. . . . Men so far
sunk as this may always be known as Samurai without
fidelity or sincerity." Celibacy, condemned by pub-

lic opinion,—except in the case of Buddhist priests,—
was equally condemned by the code. "One should
not live alone after sixteen years of age," declares the
legislator; "all mankind recognize marriage as the
first law of nature." The childless man was obliged
to adopt a son; and the 47th article of the Legacy
ordained that the family estate of a person dying
without male issue, and without having adopted a
son, should be "forfeited without any regard to
his relatives or connexions." This law, of course,
was made in support of the ancestor-cult, the continuance of which it was deemed the paramount duty
of each man to provide for; but the government
regulations concerning adoption enabled everybody
to fulfil the legal requirement without difficulty.

Considering that this code which inculcated humanity, repressed moral laxity, prohibited celibacy,
and rigorously maintained the family-cult, was drawn
up in the time of the extirpation of the Jesuit missions, the position assumed in regard to religious
freedom appears to us one of singular liberality.
"High and low alike," proclaims the 31st article,
"may follow their own inclinations with respect to
religious tenets which have obtained down to the
present time, except as regards the false and corrupt
school [*Roman Catholicism*]. Religious disputes have
ever proved the bane and misfortune of this Empire,
and must be firmly suppressed." . . . But the
seeming liberality of this article must not be mis-

interpreted: the legislator who made so rigid an enactment in regard to the religion of the family was not the man to proclaim that any Japanese was free to abandon the faith of his race for an alien creed. One must carefully read the entire Legacy in order to understand Iyéyasu's real position, — which was simply this: that any man was free to adopt any religion tolerated by the State, *in addition to his ancestor-cult*. Iyéyasu was himself a member of the Jōdo sect of Buddhism, and a friend of Buddhism in general. But he was first of all a Shintōist; and the third article of his code commands devotion to the Kami as the first of duties: — "Keep your heart pure; and so long as your body shall exist, be diligent in paying honour and veneration to the Gods." That he placed the ancient cult above Buddhism should be evident from the text of the 52d article of the Legacy, in which he declares that no one should suffer himself to neglect the national faith because of a belief in any other form of religion. This text is of particular interest: —

"My body, and the bodies of others, being born in the Empire of the Gods, to accept unreservedly the teachings of other countries, — such as Confucian, Buddhist, or Taoïst doctrines, — and to apply one's whole and undivided attention to them, would be, in short, to desert one's own master, and transfer one's loyalty to another. Is not this to forget the origin of one's being?"

Of course the Shōgun, professing to derive his authority from the descendant of the elder gods, could not with consistency have proclaimed the right of freedom to doubt those gods : his official religious duty permitted of no compromise. But the interest attaching to his opinions, as expressed in the Legacy, rests upon the fact that the Legacy was not a public, but a strictly private document, intended for the perusal and guidance of his successors only. Altogether his religious position was much like that of the liberal Japanese statesman of to-day, — respect for whatever is good in Buddhism, qualified by the patriotic conviction that the first religious duty is to the cult of the ancestors, the ancient creed of the race. . . . Iyéyasu had preferences regarding Buddhism; but even in this he showed no narrowness. Though he wrote in his Legacy, " Let my posterity ever be of the honoured sect of Jōdo," he greatly reverenced the high-priest of the Tendai temple, Yeizan, who had been one of his instructors, and obtained for him the highest court-office possible for a Buddhist priest to obtain, as well as the headship of the Tendai sect. Moreover the Shōgun visited Yeizan to make there official prayer for the prosperity of the country.

There is every reason to believe that within the territories of the Shōgunate proper, comprising the greater part of the Empire, the administration of

ordinary criminal law was humane, and that the
infliction of punishment was made, in the case of
the common people, to depend largely upon circumstances. Needless severity was a crime before the
higher military law, which, in such cases, made no
distinctions of rank. Although the ring-leaders of
a peasant-revolt, for example, would be sentenced
to death, the lord through whose oppression the
uprising was provoked, would be deprived of a part
or the whole of his estates, or degraded in rank, or
perhaps even sentenced to perform *harakiri*. Professor Wigmore, whose studies of Japanese law first
shed light upon the subject, has given us an excellent review of the spirit of the ancient legal methods. He points out that the administration of law
was never made impersonal in the modern sense;
that unbending law did not, for the people at least,
exist in relation to minor offences. The Anglo-
Saxon idea of inflexible law is the idea of a justice
impartial and pitiless as fire : whoever breaks the
law must suffer the consequence, just as surely as
the person who puts his hand into fire must experience pain. But in the administration of the old
Japanese law, everything was taken into consideration : the condition of the offender, his intelligence,
his degree of education, his previous conduct, his
motives, suffering endured, provocation received,
and so forth ; and final judgment was decided by
moral common sense rather than by legal enactment

or precedent. Friends and relatives were allowed
to make plea for the offender, and to help him in
whatever honest way they could. If a man were
falsely accused, and proved innocent upon trial, he
would not only be consoled by kind words, but
would probably receive substantial compensation;
and it appears that judges were accustomed, at the
end of important trials, to reward good conduct as
well as to punish crime.[1] . . . On the other hand,
litigation was officially discouraged. Everything possible was done to prevent any cases from being taken
into court, which could be settled or compromised by
communal arbitration; and the people were taught
to consider the court only as the last possible
resort.

The general character of the Tokugawa rule can
be to some degree inferred from the foregoing facts.
It was in no sense a reign of terror that compelled
peace and encouraged industry for two hundred and

---

[1] The following extracts from a sentence said to have been passed by the famous
judge, Ōoka Tadasuké, at the close of a celebrated criminal trial, are illustrative:
"Musashiya Chōbei and Gotō Hanshirō, these actions of yours are worthy of
the highest praise: as a remuneration I award ten silver *ryō* to each of you. . . .
Tami, you, for maintaining your brother, are to be commended: for this you are to
receive the amount of five *kwammon*. Kō, daughter of Chohachi, you are obedient
to your parents: in consideration of this, the sum of five silver *ryō* is awarded to
you." — (See Dening's *Japan in Days of Yore*.) The good old custom of re-
warding notable cases of filial piety, courage, generosity, etc., though not now
practised in the courts, is still maintained by the local governments. The rewards
are small; but the public honour which they confer upon the recipient is very great.

fifty years. Though the national civilization was restrained, pruned, clipped in a thousand ways, it was at the same time cultivated, refined, and strengthened. The long peace established throughout the Empire what had never before existed, — a universal feeling of security. The individual was bound more than ever by law and custom; but he was also protected: he could move without anxiety to the length of his chains. Though coerced by his fellows, they helped him to bear the coercion cheerfully: everybody aided everybody else to fulfil the obligations and to support the burdens of communal life. Conditions tended, therefore, toward the general happiness as well as toward the general prosperity. There was not, in those years, any struggle for existence, — not at least in our modern meaning of the phrase. The requirements of life were easily satisfied; every man had a master to provide for him or to protect him; competition was repressed or discouraged; there was no need for supreme effort of any sort, — no need for the straining of any faculty. Moreover, there was little or nothing to strive after: for the vast majority of the people, there were no prizes to win. Ranks and incomes were fixed; occupations were hereditary; and the desire to accumulate wealth must have been checked or numbed by those regulations which limited the rich man's right to use his money as he might please. Even a great lord -- even the Shōgun himself —

could not do what he pleased. As for any common
person, — farmer, craftsman, or shopkeeper, — he
could not build a house as he liked, or furnish it
as he liked, or procure for himself such articles of
luxury as his taste might incline him to buy. The
richest *heimin*, who attempted to indulge himself in
any of these ways, would at once have been forcibly
reminded that he must not attempt to imitate the
habits, or to assume the privileges, of his betters.
He could not even order certain kinds of things to
be made for him. The artizans or artists who
created objects of luxury, to gratify æsthetic taste,
were little disposed to accept commissions from
people of low rank : they worked for princes, or
great lords, and could scarcely afford to take the
risk of displeasing their patrons. Every man's
pleasures were more or less regulated by his place
in society, and to pass from a lower into a higher
rank was no easy matter. Extraordinary men were
sometimes able to do this, by attracting the favour
of the great. But many perils attended upon such
distinction ; and the wisest policy for the *heimin* was
to remain satisfied with his position, and try to find
as much happiness in life as the law allowed.

Personal ambition being thus restrained, and the
cost of existence reduced to a minimum much below
our Western ideas of the necessary, there were really
established conditions highly favourable to certain
forms of culture, in despite of sumptuary regula-

tions.   The national mind was obliged to seek
solace for the monotony of existence, either in
amusement or study. Tokugawa policy had left
imagination partly free in the directions of literature
and art — the cheaper art ; and within those two
directions repressed personality found means to
utter itself, and fancy became creative.   There was
a certain amount of danger attendant upon even
such intellectual indulgences ; and much was dared.
Æsthetic taste, however, mostly followed the line
of least resistance.   Observation concentrated itself
upon the interest of everyday life, — upon incidents
which might be watched from a window, or studied
in a garden, — upon familiar aspects of nature in
various seasons, — upon trees, flowers, birds, fishes,
or reptiles, — upon insects and the ways of them, —
upon all kinds of small details, delicate trifles, amusing curiosities.   Then it was that the race-genius
produced most of that queer bric-à-brac which still
forms the delight of Western collectors.   The painter,
the ivory-carver, the decorator, were left almost un-
troubled in their production of fairy-pictures, exquisite grotesqueries, miracles of liliputian art in metal
and enamel and lacquer-of-gold.   In all such small
matters they could feel free ; and the results of that
freedom are now treasured in the museums of Europe
and America.   It is true that most of the arts (nearly
all of Chinese origin) were considerably developed
before the Tokugawa era ; but it was then that they

began to assume those inexpensive forms which placed æsthetic gratification within reach of the common people. Sumptuary legislation or rule might yet apply to the use and possession of costly production, but not to the enjoyment of form; and the beautiful, whether shaped in paper or in ivory, in clay or gold, is always a power for culture. It has been said that in a Greek city of the fourth century before Christ, every household utensil, even the most trifling object, was in respect of design an object of art; and the same fact is true, though in another and a stranger way, of all things in a Japanese home: even such articles of common use as a bronze candlestick, a brass lamp, an iron kettle, a paper lantern, a bamboo curtain, a wooden pillow, a wooden tray, will reveal to educated eyes a sense of beauty and fitness entirely unknown to Western cheap production. And it was especially during the Tokugawa period that this sense of beauty began to inform everything in common life. Then also was developed the art of illustration; then came into existence those wonderful colour-prints (the most beautiful made in any age or country) which are now so eagerly collected by wealthy dilettanti. Literature also ceased, like art, to be the enjoyment of the upper classes only: it developed a multitude of popular forms. This was the age of popular fiction, of cheap books, of popular drama, of story-telling for young and old. . . . We may certainly call the Tokugawa period the happiest in the long life of the nation. The mere increase of population and of wealth would prove the fact, irrespective of the general interest awakened in matters literary and æsthetic. It was an age of popular enjoyment, also of general culture and social refinement.

Customs spread downward from the top of society. During the Tokugawa period, various diversions or accomplishments, formerly fashionable in upper circles only, became common property. Three of these were of a sort indicating a high degree of refinement: poetical contests, tea-ceremonies, and the complex art of flower-arrangement. All were introduced into Japanese society long before the Tokugawa régime; — the fashion of poetical competitions must be as old as Japanese authentic history. But it was under the Tokugawa Shōgunate that such amusements and accomplishments became national. Then the tea-ceremonies were made a feature of female education throughout the country. Their elaborate character could be explained only by the help of many pictures; and it requires years of training and practice to graduate in the art of them. Yet the whole of this art, as to detail, signifies no more than the making and serving of a cup of tea. However, it is a real art — a most exquisite art. The actual making of the infusion is a matter of no consequence in itself: the supremely important matter is that the act be performed in the most perfect,

most polite, most graceful, most charming manner
possible. Everything done — from the kindling of
the charcoal fire to the presentation of the tea —
must be done according to rules of supreme etiquette : rules requiring natural grace as well as great
patience to fully master. Therefore a training in
the tea-ceremonies is still held to be a training in
politeness, in self-control, in delicacy, — a discipline
in deportment. . . . Quite as elaborate is the art of
arranging flowers. There are many different schools ;
but the object of each system is simply to display
sprays of leaves and flowers in the most beautiful
manner possible, and according to the irregular
graces of Nature herself. This art also requires
years to learn ; and the teaching of it has a moral as
well as an æsthetic value.

It was in this period also that etiquette was cultivated to its uttermost, — that politeness became dif-
fused throughout all ranks, not merely as a fashion,
but as an art. In all civilized societies of the militant type politeness becomes a national characteristic
at an early period ; and it must have been a common
obligation among the Japanese, as their archaic
tongue bears witness, before the historical epoch.
Public enactments on the subject were made as early
as the seventh century by the founder of Japanese Buddhism, the prince-regent, Shōtoku Taishi.
" Ministers and functionaries," he proclaimed,

" should make decorous behaviour[1] their leading principle ; for their leading principle of the government
of the people consists in decorous behaviour. If the
superiors do not behave with decorum, the inferiors
are disorderly : if inferiors are wanting in proper behaviour, there must necessarily be offences. Therefore it is that when lord and vassal behave with
propriety, the distinctions of rank are not confused :
when the people behave with propriety, the government of the Commonwealth proceeds of itself."
Something of the same old Chinese teaching we find
reëchoed, a thousand years later, in the Legacy of
Iyéyasu : " The art of governing a country consists
in the manifestation of due deference on the part of
a suzerain to his vassals. Know that if you turn
your back upon this, you will be assassinated ; and
the Empire will be lost." We have already seen
that etiquette was rigidly enforced upon all classes
by the military rule : for at least ten centuries
before Iyéyasu, the nation had been disciplined in
politeness, under the edge of the sword. But under
the Tokugawa Shōgunate politeness became particularly a popular characteristic, — a rule of conduct
maintained by even the lowest classes in their daily
relations. Among the higher classes it became the
art of beauty in life. All the taste, the grace, the

[1] Or, " ceremony " : the Chinese term used signifying everything relating to
gentlemanly and upright conduct. The translation is Mr. Aston's (see Vol. II,
p. 130, of his translation of the *Nihongi*).

nicety which then informed artistic production in precious material, equally informed every detail of speech and action. Courtesy was a moral and æsthetic study, carried to such incomparable perfection that every trace of the artificial disappeared. Grace and charm seemed to have become habit, — inherent qualities of the human fibre, — and doubtless, in the case of one sex at least, did so become.

For it has well been said that the most wonderful æsthetic products of Japan are not its ivories, nor its bronzes, nor its porcelains, nor its swords, nor any of its marvels in metal or lacquer — but its women. Accepting as partly true the statement that woman everywhere is what man has made her, we might say that this statement is more true of the Japanese woman than of any other. Of course it required thousands and thousands of years to make her; but the period of which I am speaking beheld the work completed and perfected. Before this ethical creation, criticism should hold its breath; for there is here no single fault save the fault of a moral charm unsuited to any world of selfishness and struggle. It is the moral artist that now commands our praise, — the realizer of an ideal beyond Occidental reach. How frequently has it been asserted that, as a moral being, the Japanese woman does not seem to belong to the same race as the Japanese man! Considering that heredity is limited by sex, there is reason in the assertion: the Japanese woman *is* an ethically different being from the Japanese man. Perhaps no such type of woman will appear again in this world for a hundred thousand years: the conditions of industrial civilization will not admit of her existence. The type could not have been created in any society shaped on modern lines, nor in any society where the competitive struggle takes those unmoral forms with which we have become too familiar. Only a society under extraordinary regulation and regimentation, — a society in which all self-assertion was repressed, and self-sacrifice made a universal obligation, — a society in which personality was clipped like a hedge, permitted to bud and bloom from within, never from without, — in short, only a society founded upon ancestor-worship, could have produced it. It has no more in common with the humanity of this twentieth century of ours — perhaps very much less — than has the life depicted upon old Greek vases. Its charm is the charm of a vanished world — a charm strange, alluring, indescribable as the perfume of some flower of which the species became extinct in our Occident before the modern languages were born. Transplanted successfully it cannot be: under a foreign sun its forms revert to something altogether different, its colours fade, its perfume passes away. The Japanese woman can be known only in her own country, — the Japanese woman as prepared and perfected by the old-time education for that strange society in which the charm

of her moral being, — her delicacy, her supreme unselfishness, her child-like piety and trust, her exquisite
tactful perception of all ways and means to make happiness about her, — can be comprehended and valued.

I have spoken only of her moral charm: it requires time for the unaccustomed foreign eye to
discern the physical charm. Beauty, according to
our Western standards, can scarcely be said to exist
in this race, — or, shall we say that it has never yet
been developed? One seeks in vain for a facial
angle satisfying Western æsthetic canons. It is
seldom that one meets even with a fine example
of that physical elegance, — that manifestation of
the economy of force, — which we call grace, in
the Greek meaning of the word. Yet there is
charm — great charm — both of face and form:
the charm of childhood — childhood with its every
feature yet softly and vaguely outlined (*effacé*, as a
French artist would call it), — childhood before
the limbs have fully lengthened, — slight and
dainty, with admirable little hands and feet. The
eyes at first surprise us, by the strangeness of
their lids, so unlike Aryan eyelids, and folding
upon another plan. Yet they are often very
charming; and a Western artist would not fail
to appreciate the graceful terms, invented by
Japanese or Chinese art, to designate particular
beauties in the lines of the eyelids. Even if she
cannot be called handsome, according to Western

standards, the Japanese woman must be confessed pretty, — pretty like a comely child; and if she be seldom graceful in the Occidental sense, she is at least in all her ways incomparably graceful: her every motion, gesture, or expression being, in its own Oriental manner, a perfect thing, — an act performed, or a look conferred, in the most easy, the most graceful, the most modest way possible. By ancient custom, she is not permitted to display her grace in the street: she must walk in a particular shrinking manner, turning her feet inward as she patters along upon her wooden sandals. But to watch her at home, where she is free to be comely, — merely to see her performing any household duty, or waiting upon guests, or arranging flowers, or playing with her children, — is an education in Far Eastern æsthetics for whoever has the head and the heart to learn. . . . But is she not, then, one may ask, an artificial product, — a forced growth of Oriental civilization? I would answer both "Yes" and "No." She is an artificial product in only the same evolutional sense that all character is an artificial product; and it required tens of centuries to mould her. She is not, on the other hand, an artificial type, because she has been particularly trained to be her true self at all times when circumstances allow, — or, in other words, to be delightfully natural. The old-fashioned education of her sex was directed to the development of every quality essentially feminine, and to the suppression of the opposite quality. Kindliness, docility, sympathy, tenderness, daintiness — these and other attributes were cultivated into incomparable blossoming. " Be good, sweet maid, and let who will be clever : do noble things, not dream them, all day long " —— those words of Kingsley really embody the central idea in her training. Of course the being, formed by such training only, must be protected by society ; and by the old Japanese society she was protected. Exceptions did not affect the rule. What I mean is that she was able to be purely herself, within certain limits of emotional etiquette, in all security. Her success in life was made to depend on her power to win affection by gentleness, obedience, kindliness ; — not the affection merely of a husband, but of the husband's parents and grandparents, and brothers-in-law and sisters-in-law, — in short of all the members of a strange household. Thus to succeed required angelic goodness and patience ; and the Japanese woman realized at least the ideal of a Buddhist angel. A being working only for others, thinking only for others, happy only in making pleasure for others, — a being incapable of unkindness, incapable of selfishness, incapable of acting contrary to her own inherited sense of right, — and in spite of this softness and gentleness ready, at any moment, to lay down her life, to sacrifice everything at the call of duty: such was the character of the Japanese woman. Most strange may seem the combination, in this child-soul, of gentleness and force, tenderness and courage, — yet the explanation is not far to seek. Stronger within her than wifely affection or parental affection or even maternal affection,— stronger than any womanly emotion, was the moral conviction born of her great faith. This religious quality of character can be found among ourselves only within the shadow of cloisters, where it is cultivated at the expense of all else; and the Japanese woman has been therefore compared to a Sister of Charity. But she had to be very much more than a Sister of Charity, — daughter-in-law and wife and mother, and to fulfil without reproach the multiform duties of her triple part. Rather might she be compared to the Greek type of noble woman, — to Antigoné, to Alcestis. With the Japanese woman, as formed by the ancient training, each act of life was an act of faith: her existence was a religion, her home a temple, her every word and thought ordered by the law of the cult of the dead. . . . This wonderful type is not extinct — though surely doomed to disappear. A human creature so shaped for the service of gods and men that every beat of her heart is duty, that every drop of her blood is moral feeling, were not less out of place in the future world of competitive selfishness, than an angel in hell.

The Shintō Revival

THE slow weakening of the Tokugawa Shōgunate was due to causes not unlike those
which had brought about the decline of previous regencies: the race degenerated during that
long period of peace which its rule had inaugurated;
the strong builders were succeeded by feebler and
feebler men. Nevertheless the machinery of administration, astutely devised by Iyéyasu, and further
perfected by Iyémitsu, worked so well that the
enemies of the Shōgunate could find no opportunity
for a successful attack until foreign aggression un-
expectedly came to their aid. The most dangerous
enemies of the government were the great clans of
Satsuma and Chōshū. Iyéyasu had not ventured
to weaken them beyond a certain point: the risks
of the undertaking would have been great; and, on
the other hand, the alliance of those clans was for
the time being a matter of vast political importance.
He only took measures to preserve a safe balance
of power, placing between those formidable allies
new lordships in whose rulers he could put trust, —
a trust based first upon interest, secondly upon kinship. But he always felt that danger to the Shō-

gunate might come from Satsuma and Chōshū ; and he left to his successors careful instructions about the policy to be followed in dealing with such possible enemies. He felt that his work was not perfect, — that certain outlying blocks of the structure had not been properly clamped to the rest. He could not do more in the direction of consolidation, simply because the material of society had not yet sufficiently evolved, had not yet become plastic enough, to permit of perfect and permanent cohesion. In order to effect that, it would have been necessary to dissolve the clans. But Iyéyasu did all that human foresight could have safely attempted under the circumstances ; and no one was more keenly conscious than himself of the weak points in his wonderful organization.

For more than two hundred years the Satsuma and Chōshū clans, and several others ready to league with them, submitted to the discipline of the Tokugawa rule. But they chafed under it, and watched for a chance to break the yoke. All the while this chance was being slowly created for them — not by any political changes, but by the patient toil of Japanese men of letters. Three among these — the greatest scholars that Japan ever produced — especially prepared the way, by their intellectual labours, for the abolition of the Shōgunate. They were Shintō scholars ; and they represented the not unnatural reaction of native conservatism against the long tyranny of alien ideas and alien beliefs, — against the literature and philosophy and bureaucracy of China, — against the preponderant influence upon education of the foreign religion of Buddhism. To all this they opposed the old native literature of Japan, the ancient poetry, the ancient cult, the early traditions and rites of Shintō. The names of these three remarkable men were Mabuchi (1697–1769), Motowori (1730–1801), and Hirata (1776–1843). Their efforts actually resulted in the disestablishment of Buddhism, and in the great Shintō revival of 1871.

The intellectual revolution made by these scholars could have been prepared only during a long era of peace, and by men enjoying the protection and patronage of members of the ruling class. By a strange chance, it was the house of Tokugawa itself which first gave to literature such encouragement and aid as made possible the labours of the Shintō scholars. Iyéyasu had been a lover of learning; and had devoted the later years of his life — passed in retirement at Shidzuoka — to the collection of ancient books and manuscripts. He bequeathed his Japanese books to his eighth son, the Prince of Ōwari; and his Chinese books to another son, the Prince of Kishū. The Prince of Ōwari himself composed several works upon Japanese early literature. Other descendants of Iyéyasu inherited the great

Shōgun's love of letters: one of his grandsons, Mitsukuni, the second Prince of Mito (1622–1700), compiled, with the aid of various scholars, the first important history of Japan, — the *Dai-Nihon-Shi*, in 240 books. Also he compiled a work of 500 volumes upon the ceremonies and the etiquette of the Imperial Court, and set aside from his revenues a sum equal to about £30,000 per annum, to cover the cost of publishing the splendid productions. . . . Under the patronage of great lords like these — collectors of libraries — there gradually developed a new school of men-of-letters : men who turned away from Chinese literature to the study of the Japanese classics. They reëdited the ancient poetry and chronicles ; they republished the sacred records, with ample commentaries. They produced whole libraries of works upon religious, historical, and philological subjects ; they made grammars and dictionaries ; they wrote treatises on the art of poetry, on popular errors, on the nature of the gods, on government, on the manners and customs of ancient days. . . . The foundations of this new scholarship were laid by two Shintō priests, — Kada and Mabuchi.

The high patrons of learning never suspected the possible results of those researches which they had encouraged and aided. The study of the ancient records, the study of Japanese literature, the study of the early political and religious conditions,

naturally led men to consider the history of those
foreign literary influences which had well-nigh
stifled native learning, and to consider also the history of the foreign creed which had overwhelmed
the religion of the ancestral gods. Chinese ethics,
Chinese ceremonial, and Chinese Buddhism had
reduced the ancient faith to the state of a minor
belief — almost to the state of a superstition. "The
Shintō gods," exclaimed one of the scholars of the
new school, "have become the servants of the Buddhas!" But those Shintō gods were the ancestors
of the race, — the fathers of its emperors and princes,
— and their degradation could not but involve the
degradation of the imperial tradition. Already, indeed, the emperors had been deprived not only of
their immemorial rights and privileges, but of their
revenues: many had been deposed and banished and
insulted. Just as the gods had been admitted only
as inferior personages to the Buddhist pantheon, so
their living descendants were now permitted to reign
only as the dependants of military usurpers. By
sacred law the whole soil of the empire belonged to
the Heavenly Sovereign: yet there had been great
poverty at times in the imperial palace; and the
revenues, allotted for the maintenance of the
Mikado, had often been insufficient to relieve his
family from want. Assuredly all this was wrong.
The Shōgunate had indeed established peace and
inaugurated prosperity; but who could forget that

it had originated in a military usurpation of imperial rights? Only by the restoration of the Son of Heaven to his ancient position of power, and by the relegation of the military chiefs to their proper state of subordination, could the best interests of the nation be really served. . . .

All this was thought and felt and strongly suggested; but not all of it was openly proclaimed. To have publicly preached against the military government as a usurpation would have been to invite destruction. The Shintō scholars dared only so much as the politics and the temper of their time seemed to permit, — though they closely approached the danger-line. By the end of the eighteenth century, however, their teaching had created a strong party in favour of the official revival of the ancient religion, the restoration of the Mikado to supreme power, and the repression, if not suppression, of the military power. Yet it was not until the year 1841 that the Shōgunate took alarm, and proclaimed its disquiet by banishing from the capital the great scholar Hirata, and forbidding him to write anything more. Not long afterwards he died. But he had been able to teach for forty years; he had written and published several hundred volumes; and the school of which he was the last and greatest theologian already exerted far-reaching influence. The restive lords of Chōshū, Satsuma, Tosa, and Hizen were watching and waiting. They perceived

the worth of the new ideas to their own policy; they
encouraged the new Shintōism; they felt that a time
was coming when they could hope to shake off the
domination of the Tokugawa. And their opportunity came at last with the advent to Japan of
Commodore Perry's fleet.

The events of that time are well known, and need
not here be dwelt upon at any length. Suffice to
say that after the Shōgunate had been terrified into
making commercial treaties with the United States
and other powers, and practically compelled to open
sundry ports to foreign trade, great discontent arose
and was fomented as much as possible by the enemies of the military government. Meanwhile the
Shōgunate had ascertained for itself the impossibility
of resisting foreign aggression: it was fairly well
informed as to the strength of Western countries.
The imperial court was nowise informed; and the
Shōgunate naturally dreaded to furnish the information. To acknowledge incapacity to resist Occidental aggression would be to invite the ruin of the
Tokugawa house; to resist, on the other hand,
would be to invite the destruction of the Empire.
The enemies of the Shōgunate then persuaded the
imperial court to order the expulsion of the foreigners; and this order — which, it must be remembered, was essentially a religious order, emanating
from the source of all acknowledged authority —
placed the military government in a serious dilemma.

It tried to effect by diplomacy what it could not accomplish by force; but while it was negotiating for the withdrawal of the foreign settlers, matters were suddenly forced to a crisis by the Prince of Chōshū, who fired upon various ships belonging to the foreign powers.   This action provoked the bombardment of Shimonoséki, and the demand of an indemnity of three million dollars.   The Shōgun Iyémochi attempted to chastise the daimyō of Chōshū for this act of hostility; but the attempt only proved the weakness of the military government.   Iyémochi died soon after this defeat; and his successor Hitotsubashi had no chance to do anything, — for the now evident feebleness of the Shōgunate gave its enemies courage to strike a fatal blow.   Pressure was brought upon the imperial court to proclaim the abolition of the Shōgunate; and the Shōgunate was abolished by decree.   Hitotsubashi submitted; and the Tokugawa régime thus came to an end, — although its more devoted followers warred for two years afterwards, against hopeless odds, to reëstablish it.   In 1867 the entire administration was reorganized; the supreme power, both military and civil, being restored to the Mikado.   Soon afterward the Shintō cult, officially revived in its primal simplicity, was declared the Religion of State; and Buddhism was disendowed. Thus the Empire was reëstablished upon the ancient lines; and all that the literary party had hoped for seemed to be realized — except one thing. . . .

Be it here observed that the adherents of the literary party wanted to go much further than the great founders of the new Shintōism had dreamed of going. These later enthusiasts were not satisfied with the abolition of the Shōgunate, the restoration of imperial power, and the revival of the ancient cult: they wanted a return of all society to the simplicity of primitive times; they desired that all foreign influence should be got rid of, and that the official ceremonies, the future education, the future literature, the ethics, the laws, should be purely Japanese. They were not even satisfied with the disendowment of Buddhism: there was a vigorous proposal made for its total suppression! And all this would have signified, in more ways than one, a social retrogression towards barbarism. The great scholars had never proposed to cast away Buddhism and all Chinese learning; they had only insisted that the native religion and culture should have precedence. But the new literary party desired what would have been equivalent to the destruction of a thousand years' experience. Happily the clansmen who had broken down the Shōgunate saw both past and future in another light. They understood that the national existence was in peril, and that resistance to foreign pressure would be hopeless. Satsuma had witnessed the bombardment of Kagoshima in

1863; Chōshū, the bombardment of Shimonoséki in 1864. Evidently the only chance of being able to face Western power would be through the patient study of Western science; and the survival of the Empire depended upon the Europeanization of society. By 1871 the daimiates were abolished; in 1873 the edicts against Christianity were withdrawn; in 1876 the wearing of swords was prohibited. The samurai, as a military body, were suppressed; and all classes were declared thenceforward equal before the law. New codes were compiled; a new army and navy organized; a new police system established; a new system of education introduced at Government expense; and a new constitution promised. Finally, in 1891, the first Japanese parliament (strictly speaking) was convoked. By that time the entire framework of society had been remodelled, so far as laws could remodel it, upon a European pattern. The nation had fairly entered upon its third period of integration. The clan had been legally dissolved; the family was no longer the legal unit of society: by the new constitution the individual had been recognized.

When we consider the history of some vast and sudden political change in its details only, — the factors of the movement, the combinations of immediate cause and effect, the influences of strong personality, the conditions impelling individual action,

— then the transformation is apt to appear to us the work and the triumph of a few superior minds. We forget, perhaps, that those minds themselves were the product of their epoch, and that every such rapid change must represent the working of a national or race-instinct quite as much as the operation of individual intelligence. The events of the Meiji reconstruction strangely illustrate the action of such instinct in the face of peril, — the readjustment of internal relations to sudden changes of environment. The nation had found its old political system powerless before the new conditions; and it transformed that system. It had found its military organization incapable of defending it; and it reconstructed that organization. It had found its educational system useless in the presence of unforeseen necessities; and it replaced that system, — simultaneously crippling the power of Buddhism, which might otherwise have offered serious opposition to the new developments required. And in that hour of greatest danger the national instinct turned back at once to the moral experience upon which it could best rely, — the experience embodied in its ancient cult, the religion of unquestioning obedience. Relying upon Shintō tradition, the people rallied about their ruler, descendant of the ancient gods, and awaited his will with unconquerable zeal of faith. By strict obedience to his commands the peril might be averted, — never otherwise: this was

the national conviction. And the imperial order
was simply that the nation should strive by study
to make itself, as far as possible, the intellectual
equal of its enemies. How faithfully that command
was obeyed, — how well the old moral discipline of
the race served it in the period of that supreme
emergency, — I need scarcely say. Japan, by right
of self-acquired strength, has entered into the circle
of the modern civilized powers, — formidable by
her new military organization, respectable through
her achievements in the domain of practical science.
And the force to effect this astonishing self-
improvement, within the time of thirty years,
she owes assuredly to the moral habit derived
from her ancient cult, — the religion of the
ancestors. To fairly measure the feat, we should
remember that Japan was evolutionally younger
than any modern European nation, by at least
twenty-seven hundred years, when she went to
school! . . .

Herbert Spencer has shown that the great value
to society of ecclesiastical institutions lies in their
power to give cohesion to the mass, — to strengthen
rule by enforcing obedience to custom, and by op-
posing innovations likely to supply any element
of disintegration. In other words, the value of a
religion, from the sociological standpoint, lies in its
conservatism. Various writers have alleged that the

Japanese national religion proved itself weak by incapacity to resist the overwhelming influence of Buddhism. I cannot help thinking that the entire social history of Japan yields proof to the contrary. Though Buddhism did for a long period appear to have almost entirely absorbed Shintō, by the acknowledgment of the Shintō scholars themselves; though Buddhist emperors reigned who neglected or despised the cult of their ancestors; though Buddhism directed, during ten centuries, the education of the nation, Shintō remained all the while so very much alive that it was able not only to dispossess its rival at last, but to save the country from foreign domination. To assert that the Shintō revival signified no more than a stroke of policy imagined by a group of statesmen, is to ignore all the antecedents of the event. No such change could have been wrought by mere decree had not the national sentiment welcomed it. . . . Moreover, there are three important facts to be remembered in regard to the former Buddhist predomination : (1) Buddhism conserved the family-cult, modifying the forms of the rite; (2) Buddhism never really supplanted the Ujigami cults, but maintained them ; (3) Buddhism never interfered with the imperial cult. Now these three forms of ancestor-worship, — the domestic, the communal, and the national, — constitute all that is vital in Shintō. No single essential of the ancient faith had ever been weakened, much less abolished, under the long pressure of Buddhism.

The Supreme Cult is not now the State Religion ; by request of the chiefs of Shintō, it is not even officially classed as a religion. Obvious reasons of state policy decided this course. Having fulfilled its grand task, Shintō abdicated. But as representing all those traditions which appeal to race-feeling, to the sentiment of duty, to the passion of loyalty, and the love of country, it yet remains an immense force, a power to which appeal will not be vainly made in another hour of national peril.

Survivals

IN the gardens of certain Buddhist temples there
are trees which have been famous for centuries,
— trees trained and clipped into extraordinary
shapes. Some have the form of dragons; others have
the form of pagodas, ships, umbrellas. Supposing that
one of these trees were abandoned to its own natural
tendencies, it would eventually lose the queer shape
so long imposed upon it; but the outline would
not be altered for a considerable time, as the new
leafage would at first unfold only in the direction of
least resistance : that is to say, within limits originally established by the shears and the pruning-knife.
By sword and law the old Japanese society had been
pruned and clipped, bent and bound, just like such
a tree; and after the reconstructions of the Meiji
period, — after the abolition of the daimiates, and
the suppression of the military class, — it still maintained its former shape, just as the tree would continue to do when first abandoned by the gardener.
Though delivered from the bonds of feudal law,
released from the shears of military rule, the great
bulk of the social structure preserved its ancient

aspect; and the rare spectacle bewildered and delighted and deluded the Western observer. Here
indeed was Elf-land, — the strange, the beautiful,
the grotesque, the very mysterious, — totally unlike
aught of strange and attractive ever beheld elsewhere. It was not a world of the nineteenth century after Christ, but a world of many centuries
before Christ: yet this fact — the wonder of wonders — remained unrecognized; and it remains unrecognized by most people even to this day.

Fortunate indeed were those privileged to enter
this astonishing fairyland thirty odd years ago, before the period of superficial change, and to observe
the unfamiliar aspects of its life: the universal urbanity, the smiling silence of crowds, the patient deliberation of toil, the absence of misery and struggle.
Even yet, in those remoter districts where alien
influence has wrought but little change, the charm
of the old existence lingers and amazes; and the
ordinary traveller can little understand what it
means. That all are polite, that nobody quarrels,
that everybody smiles, that pain and sorrow remain
invisible, that the new police have nothing to do,
would seem to prove a morally superior humanity.
But for the trained sociologist it would prove something different, and suggest something very terrible.
It would prove to him that this society had been
moulded under immense coercion, and that the
coercion must have been exerted uninterruptedly

for thousands of years. He would immediately
perceive that ethics and custom had not yet become dissociated, and that the conduct of each
person was regulated by the will of the rest. He
would know that personality could not develop in
such a social medium, — that no individual superiority dare assert itself, that no competition would
be tolerated. He would understand that the outward charm of this life — its softness, its smiling
silence as of dreams — signified the rule of the
dead. He would recognize that between those
minds and the minds of his own epoch no kin
ship of thought, no community of sentiment, no
sympathy whatever could exist, — that the separating
gulf was not to be measured by thousands of leagues,
but only by thousands of years, — that the psychological interval was hopeless as the distance from
planet to planet. Yet this knowledge probably
would not — certainly should not — blind him to
the intrinsic charm of things. Not to feel the
beauty of this archaic life is to prove oneself insensible to all beauty. Even that Greek world,
for which our scholars and poets profess such loving admiration, must have been in many ways a
world of the same kind, whose daily mental existence no modern mind could share.

Now that the great social tree, so wonderfully
clipped and cared for during many centuries,

is losing its fantastic shape, let us try to see how much of the original design can still be traced.

Under all the outward aspects of individual activity that modern Japan presents to the visitor's gaze, the ancient conditions really persist to an extent that no observation could reveal. Still the immemorial cult rules all the land. Still the family-law, the communal law, and (though in a more irregular manner) the clan-law, control every action of existence. I do not refer to any written law, but only to the old unwritten religious law, with its host of obligations deriving from ancestor-worship. It is true that many changes — and, in the opinion of the wise, too many changes — have been made in civil legislation; but the ancient proverb, "Government-laws are only seven-day laws," still represents popular sentiment in regard to hasty reforms. The old law, the law of the dead, is that by which the millions prefer to act and think. Though ancient social groupings have been officially abolished, re-groupings of a corresponding sort have been formed, instinctively, throughout the country districts. In theory the individual is free; in practice he is scarcely more free than were his forefathers. Old penalties for breach of custom have been abrogated; yet communal opinion is able to compel the ancient obedience. Legal enactments can nowhere effect immediate change of sentiment and long-established usage, — least of all among a people of such fixity of character as the Japanese. Young persons are no more at liberty now, than were their fathers and mothers under the Shōgunate, to marry at will, to invest their means and efforts in undertakings not sanctioned by family approval, to consider themselves in any way enfranchised from family authority; and it is probably better for the present that they are not. No man is yet complete master of his activities, his time, or his means.

Though the individual is now registered, and made directly accountable to the law, while the household has been relieved from its ancient responsibility for the acts of its members, still the family practically remains the social unit, retaining its patriarchal organization and its particular cult. Not unwisely, the modern legislators have protected this domestic religion: to weaken its bond at this time were to weaken the foundations of the national moral life, — to introduce disintegrations into the most deeply seated structures of the social organism. The new codes forbid the man who becomes by succession the head of a house to abolish that house: he is not permitted to suppress a cult. No legal presumptive heir to the headship of a family can enter into another family as adopted son or husband; nor can he abandon the paternal house to establish an independent

family of his own.[1]   Provision has been made to
meet extraordinary cases; but no individual is allowed, without good and sufficient reason, to free
himself from those traditional obligations which the
family-cult imposes.   As regards adoption, the new
law maintains the spirit of the old, with fresh provision for the conservation of the family religion, —
permitting any person of legal age to adopt a son,
on the simple condition that the person adopted
shall be younger than the adopter.   The new
divorce-laws do not permit the dismissal of a wife
for sterility alone (and divorce for such cause had
long been condemned by Japanese sentiment); but,
in view of the facilities given for adoption, this reform does not endanger the continuance of the cult.
An interesting example of the manner in which the
law still protects ancestor-worship is furnished by
the fact that an aged and childless widow, last representative of her family, is not permitted to remain
without an heir.   She must adopt a son if she can:
if she cannot, because of poverty, or for other rea-

---

[1] That is to say, he cannot separate himself from the family in law; but he is
free to live in a separate house.   The tendency to further disintegration of the family
is shown by a custom which has been growing of late years, — especially in Tōkyō:
the custom of demanding, as a condition of marriage, that the bride shall not be
obliged to live in the same house with the parents of the bridegroom   This custom
is yet confined to certain classes, and has been adversely criticised.   Many young
men, on marrying, leave the parental home to begin independent housekeeping, —
though remaining legally attached to their parents' families, of course. . . .   It
will perhaps be asked, What becomes of the cult in such cases?   The cult remains
in the parental home.   When the parents die, then the ancestral tablets are transferred to the home of the married son.

sons, the local authorities will provide a son for her,
— that is to say, a male heir to maintain the family-
worship. Such official interference would seem to
us tyrannical: it is simply paternal, and represents
the continuance of an ancient regulation intended to
protect the bereaved against what Eastern faith still
deems the supreme misfortune, — the extinction of
the home-cult. . . . In other respects the later
codes allow of individual liberty unknown in previous generations. But the ordinary person would
not dream of attempting to claim a legal right opposed
to common opinion. Family and public sentiment
are still more potent than law. The Japanese news-
papers frequently record tragedies resulting from the
prevention or dissolution of unions; and these tragedies afford strong proof that most young people
would prefer even suicide to the probable consequence of a successful appeal to law against family
decision.

The communal form of coercion is less apparent
in the large cities; but everywhere it endures to
some extent, and in the agricultural districts it remains supreme. Between the new conditions and
the old there is this difference, that the man who
finds the yoke of his district hard to bear can flee
from it: he could not do so fifty years ago. But
he can flee from it only to enter into another state
of subordination of nearly the same kind. Full

advantage, nevertheless, has been taken of this
modern liberty of movement: thousands yearly
throng to the cities; other thousands travel over the
country, from province to province; working for a
year or a season in one place, then going to another,
with little more to hope for than experience of
change. Emigration also has been taking place
upon an extensive scale; but for the common class
of emigrants, at least, the advantage of emigration
is chiefly represented by the chance of earning larger
wages. A Japanese emigrant community abroad
organizes itself upon the home-plan;[1] and the individual emigrant probably finds himself as much
under communal coercion in Canada, Hawaii, or the
Philippine Islands, as he could ever have been in
his native province. Needless to say that in foreign
countries such coercion is more than compensated
by the aid and protection which the communal organization insures. But with the constantly increasing number of restless spirits at home, and the
ever widening experience of Japanese emigrants

[1] Except as regards the communal cult, perhaps. The domestic cult is transplanted; emigrants who go abroad, accompanied by their families, take the ancestral tablets with them. To what extent the communal cult may have been
established in emigrant communities, I have not yet been able to learn. It would
appear, however, that the absence of Ujigami in certain emigrant settlements is to
be accounted for solely by the pecuniary difficulty of constructing such temples and
maintaining competent officials. In Formosa, for example, though the domestic
ancestor-cult is maintained in the homes of the Japanese settlers, Ujigami have not
yet been established. The government, however, has erected several important
Shintō temples; and I am told that some of these will probably be converted into
Ujigami when the Japanese population has increased enough to justify the measure.

abroad, it would seem likely that the power of the commune for compulsory coöperation must become considerably weakened in the near future.

As for the tribal or clan law, it survives to the degree of remaining almost omnipotent in administrative circles, and in all politics. Voters, officials, legislators, do not follow principles in our sense of the word: they follow men, and obey commands. In these spheres of action the penalties of disobedience to orders are endless as well as serious: by a single such offence one may array against oneself powers that will continue their hostile operation for years and years, — unreasoningly, implacably, blindly, with the weight and persistence of natural forces, — of winds or tides. Any comprehension of the history of Japanese politics during the last fifteen years is not possible without some know ledge of clan-history. A political leader, fully acquainted with the history of clan-parties, and their offshoots, can accomplish marvellous things; and even foreign residents, with long experience of Japanese life, have been able, by pressing upon clan-interests, to exercise a very real power in government circles. But to the ordinary foreigner, Japanese contemporary politics must appear a chaos, a disintegration, a hopeless flux. The truth is that most things remain, under varying outward forms, " as all were ordered, ages since," — though the shiftings have become more rapid, and the results less obvious, in the haste of an era of steam and electricity.

The greatest of living Japanese statesmen, the Marquis Ito, long ago perceived that the tendency of political life to agglomerations, to clan-groupings, presented the most serious obstacle to the successful working of constitutional government. He understood that this tendency could be opposed only by considerations weightier than clan-interests, considerations worthy of supreme sacrifice. He therefore formed a party of which every member was pledged to pass over clan-interests, clique-interests, personal and every other kind of interests, for the sake of national interests. Brought into collision with a hostile cabinet in 1903, this party achieved the feat of controlling its animosities even to the extent of maintaining its foes in power; but large fragments broke off in the process. So profoundly is the grouping-tendency, the clan-sentiment, identified with national character, that the ultimate success of Marquis Ito's policy must still be considered doubtful. Only a national danger — the danger of war, — has yet been able to weld all parties together, to make all wills work as one.

Not only politics, but nearly all phases of modern life, yield evidence that the disintegration of the old society has been superficial rather than fundamental. Structures dissolved have recrystallized, taking forms dissimilar in aspect to the original forms, but inwardly built upon the same plan. For the dissolutions really effected represented only a separation of masses, not a breaking up of substance into independent units; and these masses, again cohering, continue to act only as masses. Independence of personal action, in the Western sense, is still almost inconceivable. The individual of every class above the lowest must continue to be at once coercer and coerced. Like an atom within a solid body, he can vibrate; but the orbit of his vibration is fixed. He must act and be acted upon in ways differing little from those of ancient time.

As for being acted upon, the average man is under three kinds of pressure: pressure from above, exemplified in the will of his superiors; pressure about him, represented by the common will of his fellows and equals; pressure from below, represented by the general sentiment of his inferiors. And this last sort of coercion is not the least formidable.

Individual resistance to the first kind of pressure — that represented by authority — is not even to be thought of; because the superior represents a clan, a class, an exceedingly multiple power of some description; and no solitary individual, in the present order of things, can strive against a combination. To resist injustice he must find ample support, in which case his resistance does not represent individual action.

Resistance to the second kind of pressure — communal coercion — signifies ruin, loss of the right to form a part of the social body.

Resistance to the third sort of pressure, embodied in the common sentiment of inferiors, may result in almost anything, — from momentary annoyance to sudden death, — according to circumstances.

In all forms of society these three kinds of pressure are exerted to some degree; but in Japanese society, owing to inherited tendency, and traditional sentiment, their power is tremendous.

Thus, in every direction, the individual finds himself confronted by the despotism of collective opinion : it is impossible for him to act with safety except as one unit of a combination. The first kind of pressure deprives him of moral freedom, exacting unlimited obedience to orders; the second kind of pressure denies him the right to use his best faculties in the best way for his own advantage (that is to say, denies him the right of free competition); the third kind of pressure compels him, in directing the actions of others, to follow tradition, to forbear innovations, to avoid making any changes, however beneficial, which do not find willing acceptance on the part of his inferiors.

These are the social conditions which, under

normal circumstances, make for stability, for conservation; and they represent the will of the dead.
They are inevitable to a militant state; they make
the strength of that state; they render facile the
creation and maintenance of formidable armies.
But they are not conditions favourable to success in
the future international competition, — in the industrial struggle for existence against societies incom-
parabiy more plastic, and of higher mental energy.

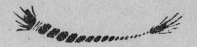

Modern Restraints

FOR even a vague understanding of modern Japan, it will be necessary to consider the effect of the three forms of social coercion, mentioned in the preceding chapter, as restraints upon individual energy and capacity. All three represent survivals of the ancient religious responsibility. I shall treat of them in order inverse, beginning with the under-pressure.

It has often been asserted by foreign observers that the real power in Japan is exercised not from above, but from below. There is some truth in this assertion, but not all the truth : the conditions are much too complex to be covered by any general statement. What cannot be gainsaid is that superior authority has always been more or less restrained by tendencies to resistance from below. . . . At no time in Japanese history, for example, do the peasants appear to have been left without recourse against excessive oppression, — notwithstanding all the humiliating regulations imposed on their existence. They were suffered to frame their own village-laws, to estimate the possible amount of their tax payments, and to make protest — through official channels — against unmerciful exaction. They were made to pay as much as they could; but they were not reduced to bankruptcy or starvation; and their holdings were mostly secured to them by laws forbidding the sale or alienation of family property. Such was at least the general rule. There were, however, wicked daimyō, who treated their farmers with extreme cruelty, and found ways to prevent complaints or protests from reaching the higher authorities. The almost invariable result of such tyranny was revolt; and the tyrant was then made responsible for the disorder, and punished. Though denied in theory, the right of the peasant to rebel against oppression was respected in practice; the revolt was punished, but the oppressor was like-wise punished. Daimyō were obliged to reckon with their farmers in regard to any fresh imposition of taxes or forced labour. We also find that al-though *heimin* were made subject to the military class, it was possible for artizans and commercial folk to form, in the great cities, strong associations by which military tyranny was kept in check. Everywhere the reverential deference of the com-mon people to authority, as exercised in usual direc-tions, seems to have been accompanied by an extraordinary readiness to defy authority exercised in other directions.

It may seem strange that a society in which reli-

gion and government, ethics and custom, were practically identical, should furnish striking examples of
resistance to authority. But the religious fact itself
supplies the explanation. From the earliest period
there was firmly established, in the popular mind,
the conviction that implicit obedience to authority
was the universal duty under all ordinary circumstances. But with this conviction there was united
another, — that resistance to authority (excepting
the sacred authority of the Supreme Ruler) was
equally a duty under extraordinary circumstances.
And these seemingly opposed convictions were not
really inconsistent. So long as rule followed precedent, — so long as its commands, however harsh,
did not conflict with sentiment and tradition, — that
rule was regarded as religious, and there was absolute submission. But when rulers presumed to
break with ethical usage, — in a spirit of reckless
cruelty or greed, — then the people might feel it a
religious obligation to resist with all the zeal of voluntary martyrdom. The danger-line for every form
of local tyranny was departure from precedent. Even
the conduct of regents and princes was much restrained by the common opinion of their retainers,
and by the knowledge that certain kinds of arbitrary
conduct were likely to provoke assassination.

Deference to the sentiment of vassals and retainers
was from ancient time a necessary policy with Japanese rulers, — not merely because of the peril involved

by needless oppression, but much more because of
the recognition that duties are well performed only
when subordinates feel assured that their efforts will
be fairly considered, and that sudden needless changes
will not be made to their disadvantage. This old
policy still characterizes Japanese administration;
and the deference of high authority to collective
opinion astonishes and puzzles the foreign observer.
He perceives only that the conservative power of
sentiment, as exercised by groups of subordinates,
remains successfully opposed to those conditions of
discipline which we think indispensable to social
progress. Just as in Old Japan the ruler of a district was held responsible for the behaviour of his
subjects, so to-day, in New Japan, every official in
charge of a department is held responsible for the
smooth working of its routine. But this does not
mean that he is responsible only for the efficiency
of a service: it means that he is held responsible
likewise for failure to satisfy the wishes of his subordinates, or at least the majority of his subordinates. If this majority be displeased with their
minister, governor, president, manager, chief, or
director, the fact is considered proof of administrative incompetency. . . . Perhaps educational circles
afford the most curious examples of this old idea of
responsibility. A student-revolt is commonly supposed to mean, not that the students are intractable,
but that the superintendent or teacher does not know

his business. Thus the principal of a college, the director of a school, holds his office only on the condition that his rule gives satisfaction to a majority of the students. In the higher government institutions, each professor or lecturer is made responsible for the success of his lectures. No matter how great may be his ability in other directions, the official instructor, unable to make himself liked by his pupils, will be got rid of in short order — unless some powerful protectors interfere on his behalf. The efforts of the man will never be judged (officially) by any accepted standard of excellence, — never estimated by their intrinsic worth; they will be considered only according to their direct effect upon the average of minds.[1] Almost everywhere this antique system of responsibility is maintained. A minister of state is by public sentiment made responsible not only for the results of his administration, but likewise for any scandals or troubles that may occur in his department, independently of the question whether he could or could not have prevented them. To a considerable degree, therefore, it is true that the ulti-

---

[1] Unjust as this policy must appear to the Western reader (a policy which certainly presupposes ethical conditions very different from our own), it was probably at one time the best possible under the new order. Considering the extraordinary changes suddenly made in the educational system, it will be obvious that a teacher's immediate value was likely — twenty years ago — to depend on his ability to make his teaching attractive. If he attempted to teach either above or below the average capacity of his pupils, or if he made his instruction unpalatable to minds greedy for new knowledge, but innocent as to method, his inexperience could be corrected by the will of his class.

mate power is below. The highest official is not able with impunity to impose his personal will in certain directions; and, for the time being, it is probably better that his powers are thus restrained.

From above downwards through all the grades of society, the same system of responsibility, and the same restraints upon individual exercise of will, persist under varying forms. The conditions within the household differ but little in this regard from the conditions in a government department: no householder, for example, can impose his will, beyond certain fixed limits, even upon his own servants or dependents. Neither for love nor money can a good servant be induced to break with traditional custom; and the old opinion, that the value of a servant is proved by such inflexibility, has been justified by the experience of centuries. Popular sentiment remains conservative; and the apparent zeal for superficial innovation affords no indication of the real order of existence. Fashions and formalities, house-interiors and street-vistas, habits and methods, and all the outer aspects of life are changed; but the old regimentation of society persists under all these surface-shiftings; and the national character remains little affected by all the transformations of Meiji.

The second kind of coercion to which the individual is subjected — the communal, or communistic —

seems likely to prove mischievous in the near future, as it signifies practical suppression of the right to compete. . . . The everyday life of any Japanese city offers numberless suggestions of the manner in which the masses continue to think and to act by groups. But no more familiar and forcible illustration of the fact can be cited than that which is furnished by the code of the *kurumaya* or jinrikisha-men. According to its terms, one runner must not attempt to pass by another going in the same direction. Exceptions have been made, grudgingly, in favour of runners in private employ, — men selected for strength and speed, who are expected to use their physical powers to the utmost. But among the tens of thousands of public *kurumaya*, it is the rule that a young and active man must not pass by an old and feeble man, nor even by a needlessly slow and lazy man. To take advantage of one's own superior energy, so as to force competition, is an offence against the calling, and certain to be resented. You engage a good runner, whom you order to make all speed: he springs away splendidly, and keeps up the pace until he happens to overtake some weak or lazy puller, who seems to be moving as slowly as the gait permits. Therewith, instead of bounding by, your man drops immediately behind the slow-going vehicle, and slackens his pace almost to a walk. For half an hour, or more, you may be thus delayed by the regulation which obliges the strong and

swift to wait for the weak and slow. An angry
appeal is made to the runner who dares to pass
another; and the idea behind the words might be
thus expressed: "You know that you are breaking the rule, — that you are acting to the disadvantage of your comrades! This is a hard calling; and
our lives would be made harder than hey are, if
there were no rules to prevent selfish competition!"
Of course there is no thought of the consequences
of such rules to business interests at large. . . .
Now it is not unjust to say that this moral code of
the *kurumaya* exemplifies an unwritten law which
has been always imposed, in varying forms, upon
every class of workers in Japan: "You must not
try, without special authorization, to pass your fellows." . . . *La carrière est ouverte aux talents —
mais la concurrence est defendue!*

Of course the modern communal restraint upon
free competition represents the survival and extension of that altruistic spirit which ruled the ancient
society, — not the mere continuance of any fixed
custom. In feudal times there were no *kurumaya*;
but all craftsmen and all labourers formed guilds or
companies; and the discipline maintained by those
guilds or companies prohibited competition as under-
taken for merely personal advantage. Similar or
nearly similar forms of organization are maintained
by artizans and labourers to-day; and the relation

of any outside employer to skilled labour is regulated, by the guild or company, in the old communistic manner. . . . Let us suppose, for instance, that you wish to have a good house built. For that undertaking, you will have to deal with a very intelligent class of skilled labour; for the Japanese house-carpenter may be ranked with the artist almost as much as with the artizan. You may apply to a building-company; but, as a general rule, you will do better by applying to a master-carpenter, who combines in himself the functions of architect, contractor, and builder. In any event you cannot select and hire workmen: guild-regulations forbid. You can only make your contract; and the master-carpenter, when his plans have been approved, will undertake all the rest,— purchase and transport of material,— hire of carpenters, plasterers, tilers, mat-makers, screen-fitters, brass-workers, stone-cutters, locksmiths, and glaziers. For each master-carpenter represents much more than his own craft-guild: he has his clients in every trade related to house-building and house-furnishing; and you must not dream of trying to interfere with his claims and privileges. . . . He builds your house according to contract; but that is only the beginning of the relation. You have really made with him an agreement which you must not break, without good and sufficient reason, for the rest of your life. Whatever afterwards may happen to any part of your house, — walls, floor, ceiling, roof, foundation, — you must arrange for repairs with him, never with anybody else. Should the roof leak, for instance, you must not send for the nearest tiler or tinsmith; if the plaster cracks, you must not send for a plasterer. The man who built your house holds himself responsible for its condition; and he is jealous of that responsibility: none but he has the right to send for the plasterer, the roofer, the tinsmith. If you interfere with that right, you may have some unpleasant surprises. If you make appeal to the law against that right, you will find that you can get no carpenter, tiler, or plasterer to work for you at any terms. Compromise is always possible; but the guilds will resent a needless appeal to the law. And after all, these craft-guilds are usually faithful performers, and well worth conciliating.

Or take the occupation of landscape-gardening. You want a pretty garden; and you hire a professional gardener who comes to you well recommended. He makes the garden; and you pay his price. But your gardener really represents a company; and by engaging him it is understood that either he, or some other member of the gardeners' corporation to which he belongs, will continue to take care of your garden as long as you own it. At each season he will pay your garden a visit, and put everything to rights: he will clip the hedges, prune the fruit trees, repair the fences, train the climbing-plants, look after the flowers, — putting up paper awnings to protect delicate shrubs from the sun during the hot season, or making little tents of straw to shelter them in time of frost; — he will do a hundred useful and ingenious things for a very small remuneration. You cannot dismiss him, however, without good reason, and hire another gardener to take his place. No other gardener would serve you at any price, unless assured that the original relation had been dissolved by mutual consent. If you have just cause for complaint, the matter can be settled through arbitration; and the guild will see that you have no further trouble. But you cannot dismiss your gardener without cause, merely to engage another.

The above examples will suffice to show the character of the old communistic organization which is yet maintained in a hundred forms. This communism suppressed competition, except as between groups; but it insured good work, and secured easy conditions for the workman. It was the best system possible in those ages of isolation when there was no such thing as want, and when the population, for yet undetermined causes, appears to have remained always below the numerical level at which serious pressure begins. . . . Another interesting survival is represented by existing conditions of ap-

prenticeship and service, — conditions which also
originated in the patriarchal organization, and imposed other kinds of restraint upon competition.
Under the old régime service was, for the most
part, unsalaried.   Boys taken into a commercial
house to learn the business, or apprentices bound
to a master-workman, were boarded, lodged, clothed,
and even educated by their patron, with whom they
might hope to pass the rest of their lives.   But they
were not paid wages until they had learned the business or the trade of their employer, and were fully
capable of managing a business or a workshop of
their own.   To a considerable degree these conditions still prevail in commercial centres, — though
the merchant or patron seldom now finds it necessary to send his clerk or apprentice to school.
Many of the great commercial houses pay salaries
only to men of great experience : other employés
are only trained and cared for until their term of
service ends, when the most clever among them will
be reëngaged as experts, and the others helped to
start in business for themselves.   In like manner
the apprentice to a trade, when his term expires,
may be reëngaged by his master as a hired journey-
man, or helped to find permanent employ elsewhere.
These paternal and filial relations between employer
and employed have helped to make life pleasant and
labour cheerful ; and the quality of all industrial production must suffer much when they disappear.

Even in private domestic service the patriaichal system still prevails to a degree that is little imagined ; and this subject deserves more than a passing mention. I refer especially to female service. The maid-servant, according to the old custom, is not primarily responsible to her employers, but to her own family ; and the terms of her service must be arranged with her family, who pledge themselves for their daughter's good behaviour. As a general rule, a nice girl does not seek domestic service for the sake of the wages (which it is now the custom to pay), nor for the sake of a living, but chiefly to prepare herself for marriage ; and this preparation is desired as much in the hope of doing credit to her own family, as in the hope of better fitting herself for membership in the family of her future husband. The best servants are country girls ; and they are sometimes put out to service very young. Parents are careful about choosing the family into which their daughter thus enters : they particularly desire that the house be one in which a girl can learn nice ways, — therefore a house in which things are ordered according to the old etiquette. A good girl expects to be treated rather as a helper than as a hireling, — to be kindly considered, and trusted, and liked. In an old-fashioned household the maid is indeed so treated ; and the relation is not a brief one — from three to five years being the term of service usually agreed upon. But when a girl is taken into service at the age of eleven or twelve, she will probably remain for eight or ten years. Besides wages, she is entitled to receive from her employers the gift of a dress, twice every year, besides other necessary articles of clothing; and she is entitled also to a certain number of holidays. Such wages, or presents in money, as she receives, should enable her to provide herself, by degrees, with a good wardrobe. Except in the event of some extraordinary misfortune, her parents will make no claim upon her wages; but she remains subject to them; and when she is called home to be married, she must go. During the period of her service, the services of her family are also at the disposal of her employers. Even if the mistress or master desire no recognition of the interest taken in the girl, some recognition will certainly be made. If the servant be a farmer's daughter, it is probable that gifts of vegetables, fruits, or fruit trees, garden-plants or other country products, will be sent to the house at intervals fixed by custom;—if the parents belong to the artizan-class, it is likely that some creditable example of handicraft will be presented as a token of gratitude. The gratitude of the parents is not for the wages or the dresses given to their daughter, but for the practical education she receives, and for the moral and material care taken of her, as a temporarily adopted child of the house. The employers may reciprocate such attentions on the part of the parents by contributing to the girl's wedding outfit.   The relation, it will be observed, is entirely between families, not between individuals ; and it is a permanent relation.   Such a relation, in feudal ages, might continue through many generations.

The patriarchal conditions which these survivals exemplify helped to make existence easy and happy. Only from a modern point of view is it possible to criticise them.   The worst that can be said about them is that their moral value was chiefly conservative, and that they tended to repress effort in new directions.   But where they still endure, Japanese life keeps something of its ancient charm ; and where they have disappeared, that charm has vanished forever.

There remains to be considered a third form of restraint, — that exercised upon the individual by official authority.   This also presents us with various survivals, which have their bright as well as their dark aspects.

We have seen that the individual has been legally freed from most of the obligations imposed by the ancient law.   He is no longer obliged to follow a particular occupation ; he is able to travel ; he is at liberty to marry into a higher or a lower class than his own ; he is not even forbidden to change his religion ; he can do a great many things — at his own risk. But where the law leaves him free, the family and the community do not; and the persistence of old sentiment and custom nullifies many of the rights legally conferred. Precisely in the same way, his relations to higher authority are still controlled by traditions which maintain, in despite of constitutional law, many of the ancient restraints, and not a little of the ancient coercion. In theory any man of great talent and energy may rise, from rank to rank, up to the highest positions. But as private life is still controlled to no small degree by the old communism, so public life is yet controlled by survivals of class or clan despotism. The chances for ability to rise without assistance, to win its way to rank and power, are extraordinarily small; since to contend alone against an opposition that thinks by groups, and acts by masses, must be almost hopeless. Only commercial or industrial life now offers really fair opportunities to capable men. The few talented persons of humble origin who do succeed in official directions owe their success chiefly to party-help or clan-patronage : in order to force any recognition of personal ability, group must be opposed to group. Alone, no man is likely to accomplish anything by mere force of competition, outside of trade or commerce. . . . It is true, of course, that individual talent must in every country encounter many forms of opposition. It is likewise true that the malevolence of envy and the brutalities of class-prejudice

have their sociological worth : they help to make it
impossible for any but the most gifted to win and
to keep success. But in Japan the peculiar constitution of society lends excessive power to social
intrigues directed against obscure ability, and makes
them highly injurious to the interests of the nation ;
— for at no previous time in her history has Japan
needed, so much as now, the best capacities of her
best men, irrespective of class or condition.

But all this was inevitable in the period of reconstruction. More significant is the fact that in no
single department of its multitudinous service does
the Government yet offer substantial reward to rising merit. No matter how well a man may strive
to win Government approbation, he must strive for
little more than honour and the bare means of existence. The costliest efforts are no more highly paid
in proportion to their worth than the cheapest; the
most invaluable services are scarcely better recognized than those most easily dispensed with or
replaced. (There have been some remarkable
exceptions : I am stating only the general rule.)
By extraordinary energy, patience, and cleverness,
one may reach, with class-help, some position which
in Europe would assure comfort as well as honour ;
but the emoluments of such a position in Japan will
scarcely cover the actual cost of living. Whether
in the army or in the navy, in the departments of
justice, of education, of communications, or of

home affairs, — the differences in remuneration nowhere represent the differences in capacity and
responsibility. To rise from grade to grade signifies pecuniarily almost nothing, — for the expenses
of each higher position augment out of all proportion to the salaries fixed by law. The general rule
has been to exact everywhere the greatest possible
amount of service for the least possible amount of
pay.[1] Any one unacquainted with the social his-

[1] Salaries of judges range from £70 to £500 per annum, — the latter figure
representing the highest possible emolument. The highest salary allowed to a Japanese professor in the imperial universities has been fixed at £120. The wages of
employés in the postal departments is barely sufficient to meet the cost of living.
The police are paid from £1 to £1 10s. per month, according to locality; and
the average pay of school-teachers is yet lower (being 9 yen 50 sen, or about 19s.
per month), — many receiving less than 7s. a month.

Readers may be interested in the following table of army-payments (1904) : —

	MONTHLY PAY	ALLOWANCE FOR HOUSE-RENT	TOTA
	yen	yen	yen
General	500 (£50)	25 : 00	525 : 00
Lieutenant-General	333	18 : 75	351 : 75
Major-General	263	12 : 50	275 : 50
Colonel	179	10 : 00	189 : 00
Lieutenant-Colonel	146	8 : 75	154 : 75
Major	102	7 : 50	109 : 50
Captain (1st grade)	70	4 : 75	74 : 75
" (2d grade)	60	4 : 75	64 : 75
Lieutenant (1st grade) . . .	45	4 : 00	49 : 00
" (2d grade) . . .	34	4 : 00	40 : 00
Second Lieutenant	30	3 : 50	33 : 50

When these rates of pay were fixed, about twenty years ago, house-rent was
cheap : a good house could be rented anywhere at 3 yen or 4 yen per month. To-

tory of the country might suppose that the policy
of the Government toward its employés consisted
in substituting empty honours for material advantages. But the truth is that the Government has
simply maintained, under modern forms, the ancient
feudal condition of service, — service in exchange
for the means of simple but honourable living. In
feudal times the farmer was expected to pay all that
he could pay for the right to exist; the artist or
artizan was expected to content himself with the
good fortune of having a distinguished patron ;
even the ordinary samurai were supplied with barely
more than the necessary by their liege-lords. To
receive considerably more than the necessary signified extraordinary favour; and the gift was usually
accompanied by promotion. But although the same
policy is yet successfully maintained by Government,
under the modern system of money-payments, the
conditions everywhere, outside of commercial life,
are incomparably harder than in feudal times. Then
the poorest samurai was secured against want, and
not liable to be dismissed from his post without
fault. Then the teacher received no salary; but
the respect of the community and the gratitude
of his pupils assured him of the means to live re-

day in Tōkyō an officer can scarcely rent even a very small house at less than
18 *yen* or 20 *yen* ; and prices of food-stuffs have tripled. Yet there have been very
few complaints. Officers whose pay will not allow them to rent houses hire rooms
wherever they can. Many suffer hardship ; but all are proud of the privilege of
serving, and no one dreams of resigning.

spectably.   Then the artizans were patronized by
great lords who vied with each other in the encouragement of humble genius.   They might expect the
genius to be satisfied with merely nominal payment,
so far as money was concerned; but they secured
him against want or discomfort, allowed him ample
leisure to perfect his work, made him happy in the
certainty that his best would be prized and praised.
But now that the cost of living has tripled or quadrupled, even the artist and the artizan have small
encouragement to do their best: cheap rapid work
is replacing the beautiful leisurely work of the old
days; and the best traditions of the crafts are doomed
to perish.   It cannot even be said that the state of
the agricultural classes to-day is happier or better
than in the time when a farmer's land could not
legally be taken from him.   And as the cost of life
continues always to increase, it is evident that at no
distant time, the present patient order of things will
become impossible.

To many it would seem that a wise government
must recognize the impracticability of indefinitely
maintaining its present demand for self-sacrifice, —
must perceive the necessity of encouraging talent,
inviting fair competition, and making the prizes of
life large enough to stimulate healthy egoism.   But
it is possible that the Government has been acting
more wisely than outward appearances would indicate.   Several years ago a Japanese official made in

my presence this curious observation: "Our Government does not wish to encourage competition beyond the necessary. The people are not prepared for it; and if it were strongly encouraged, the worst side of character would came to the surface." How far this statement really expressed any policy I do not know. But every one is aware that free competition can be made as cruel and as pitiless as war, — though we are apt to forget what experience must have been undergone before Occidental free competition could become as comparatively merciful as it is. Among a people trained for centuries to regard all selfish competition as criminal, and all profit-seeking despicable, any sudden stimulation of effort for purely personal advantage might well be impolitic. Evidence as to how little the nation was prepared, twelve or thirteen years ago, for Western forms of free government, has been furnished by the history of the earlier district-elections and of the first parliamentary sessions. There was really no personal enmity in those furious election-contests, which cost so many lives; there was scarcely any personal antagonism in those parliamentary debates of which the violence astonished strangers. The political struggles were not really between individuals, but between clan-interests, or party-interests; and the devoted followers of each clan or party understood the new politics only as a new kind of war, — a war of loyalty to be fought for the leader's sake, —

a war not to be interfered with by any abstract notions of right or justice. Suppose that a people have been always accustomed to think of loyalty in relation to persons rather than to principles, — loyalty as involving the duty of self-sacrifice regardless of consequence, — it is obvious that the first experiments of such a people with parliamentary government will not reveal any comprehension of fair play in the Western sense. Eventually that comprehension may come; but it will not come quickly. And if you can persuade such a people that in other matters every man has a right to act according to his own convictions, and for his own advantage, independently of any group to which he may belong, the immediate result will not be fortunate, — because the sense of individual moral responsibility has not yet been sufficiently cultivated outside of the group-relation.

The probable truth is that the strength of the government up to the present time has been chiefly due to the conservation of ancient methods, and to the survival of the ancient spirit of reverential submission. Later on, no doubt, great changes will have to be made; meanwhile, much must be bravely endured. Perhaps the future history of modern civilization will hold record of nothing more touching than the patient heroism of those myriads of Japanese patriots, content to accept, under legal conditions of freedom, the official servitude of feudal days, — satisfied to give their talent, their strength, their utmost effort, their lives, for the simple privilege of obeying a government that still accepts all sacrifices in the feudal spirit — as a matter of course, — as a national duty.   And as a national duty, indeed, the sacrifices are made.   All know that Japan is in danger, between the terrible friendship of England and the terrible enmity of Russia, — that she is poor, — that the cost of maintaining her armaments is straining her resources, — that it is everybody's duty to be content with as little as possible. So the complaints are not many. . . .   Nor has the simple obedience of the nation at large been less touching, — especially, perhaps, as regards the imperial order to acquire Western knowledge, to learn Western languages, to imitate Western ways.   Only those who have lived in Japan during or before the early nineties are qualified to speak of the loyal eagerness that made self-destruction by over-study a common form of death, — the passionate obedience that impelled even children to ruin their health in the effort to master tasks too difficult for their little minds (tasks devised by well-meaning advisers with no knowledge of Far-Eastern psychology), — and the strange courage of persistence in periods of earthquake and conflagration, when boys and girls used the tiles of their ruined homes for school-slates, and bits of fallen plaster for pencils.   What trage-

dies I migh relate even of the higher educational
life of universities ! — of fine brains giving way
under pressure of work beyond the capacity of the
average European student, — of triumphs won in
the teeth of death, — of strange farewells from
pupils in the time of the dreaded examinations, as
when one said to me: "Sir, I am very much afraid
that my paper is bad, because I came out of the
hospital to make it — there is something the matter
with my heart." (His diploma was placed in his
hands scarcely an hour before he died.) . . . And
all this striving — striving not only against difficulties of study, but in most cases against difficulties
of poverty, and underfeeding, and discomfort —
has been only for duty, and the means to live. To
estimate the Japanese student by his errors, his failures, his incapacity to comprehend sentiments and
ideas alien to the experience of his race, is the mistake of the shallow: to judge him rightly one must
have learned to know the silent moral heroism of
which he is capable.

Official Education

THE extent to which national character has been fixed by the discipline of centuries, and the extent of its extraordinary capacity to resist change, is perhaps most strikingly indicated by certain results of State education. The whole nation is being educated, with Government help, upon a European plan; and the full programme includes the chief subjects of Western study, excepting Greek and Latin classics. From Kindergarten to University the entire system is modern in outward seeming; yet the effect of the new education is much less marked in thought and sentiment than might be supposed. This fact is not to be explained merely by the large place which old Chinese study still occupies in the obligatory programme, nor by differences of belief: it is much more due to the fundamental difference in the Japanese and the European conceptions of education as means to an end. In spite of new system and programme the whole of Japanese education is still conducted upon a traditional plan almost the exact opposite of the Western plan. With us, the repressive part of moral training begins in early childhood: the European or American teacher is strict with the little ones; we think that it is important to inculcate the duties of behaviour, — the "must" and the "must not" of individual obligation, — as soon as possible. Later on, more liberty is allowed. The well-grown boy is made to understand that his future will depend upon his personal effort and capacity; and he is thereafter left, in a great measure, to take care of himself, being occasionally admonished or warned, as seems needful. Finally, the adult student of promise and character may become the intimate, or, under happy circumstances, even the friend of his tutor, to whom he can look for counsel in all difficult situations. And throughout the whole course of mental and moral training competition is not only expected, but required. But it is more and more required as discipline is more and more relaxed, with the passing of boyhood into manhood. The aim of Western education is the cultivation of individual ability and personal character, — the creation of an independent and forceful being.

Now Japanese education has always been conducted, and, in spite of superficial appearances, is still being conducted, mostly upon the reverse pla. . Its object never has been to train the individual for independent action, but to train him for coöperative action, — to fit him to occupy an exact place in the mechanism of a rigid society. Constraint among ourselves begins with childhood, and gradually relaxes; constraint in Far-Eastern training begins later, and thereafter gradually tightens; and it is not a constraint imposed directly by parents or teachers — which fact, as we shall presently see, makes an enormous difference in results. Not merely up to the age of school-life, — supposed to begin at six years, — but considerably beyond it, a Japanese child enjoys a degree of liberty far greater than is allowed to Occidental children. Exceptional cases are common, of course; but the general rule is that the child be permitted to do as he pleases, providing that his conduct can cause no injury to himself or to others. He is guarded, but not constrained; admonished, but rarely compelled. In short, he is allowed to be so mischievous that, as a Japanese proverb says, "even the holes by the roadside hate a boy of seven or eight years old"[1] (*Nanatsu, yatsu — michibata no ana desaimon nikumu*). Punishment is administered only when absolutely necessary; and on such occasions, by ancient custom, the entire household — servants and all — intercede for the offender; the little brothers and sisters, if any there be, begging in turn to bear the penalty instead. Whipping is not a common punishment, except among the roughest classes; the moxa is preferred as a deterrent; and it is a severe one. To frighten a child by loud harsh words, or angry looks, is condemned by general opinion: all punishment ought

[1] By former custom a newly-born child was said to be one year old; and in this case the words "seven or eight years old" mean "six or seven years old."

to be inflicted as quietly as possible, the punisher
calmly admonishing the while. To slap a child
about the head, for any reason, is a proof of vulgarity
and ignorance. It is not customary to punish by
restraining from play, or by a change of diet, or by
any denial of accustomed pleasures. To be perfectly
patient with children is the ethical law. At school
the discipline begins; but it is at first so very light
that it can hardly be called discipline: the teacher
does not act as a master, but rather as an elder
brother; and there is no punishment beyond a public admonition. Whatever restraint exists is chiefly
exerted on the child by the common opinion of his
class; and a skilful teacher is able to direct that
opinion. Also each class is nominally governed by
one or two little captains, selected for character and
intelligence; and when a disagreeable order has to
be given, it is the child-captain, the *kyūchō*, who is
commissioned with the duty of giving it. (These
little details are worthy of note: I cite them only
to show how early in school-life begins the discipline
of opinion, the pressure of the common will, and
how perfectly this policy accords with the ethical
traditions of the race.) In higher classes the pressure slightly increases; and in higher schools it is
very much stronger; the ruling power always being
class-sentiment, not the individual will of the teacher.
In middle schools the pupils become serious: class-
opinion there attains a force to which the teacher

himself must bend, as it is quite capable of expelling him for any attempt to override it. Each middle-school class has its elected officers, who represent and enforce the moral code of the majority, — the traditional standard of conduct. (This moral standard is deteriorating; but it survives everywhere to some degree.) Fighting or bullying are yet unknown in Japanese schools of this grade for obvious reasons: there can be little indulgence of personal anger, and no attempt at personal domination, under a discipline enforcing a uniform manner of behaviour. It is never the domination of the one over the many that regulates class-life: it is always the rule of the many over the one, — and the power is formidable. The student who consciously or unconsciously offends class-sentiment will suddenly find himself isolated, — condemned to absolute solitude. No one will speak to him or notice him even outside of the school, until such time as he decides to make a public apology, when his pardon will depend upon a majority-vote.

Such temporary ostracism is not unreasonably feared, because it is regarded even outside of student-circles as a disgrace; and the memory of it will cling to the offender during the rest of his career. However high he may rise in official or professional life in after years, the fact that he was once condemned by the general opinion of his schoolmates will not be forgotten, — though circumstances may occur which will turn the fact to his credit. . . . In the great Government schools — to one of which the student may proceed after graduating from a middle-school — class-discipline is still more severe. The instructors are mostly officials looking for promotion: the students are grown men, preparing for the University, and destined, with few exceptions, for public office. In this quietly and coldly ordered world there is little place for the joy of youth, and small opportunity for sympathetic expansion. There are gatherings and societies; but these are arranged or established for practical purposes — chiefly in relation to particular branches of study; there is little time for merry-making, and less inclination. Under all circumstances, a certain formal demeanour is exacted by tradition, — a tradition older by far than any public school. Everybody watches everybody: eccentricities or singularities are quickly marked and quietly suppressed. The results of this class-discipline, as maintained in some institutions, must seem to the foreign observer discomforting. What most impressed me about these higher official schools was the sinister silence of them. In one where I taught for several years — the most conservative school in the country — there were more than a thousand young men, full of life and energy; yet during the intervals between classes, or during recreation-hours in the playground, the garden, and the gymnastic hall, the general hush gave one a strange sense of oppression. One might watch a game of foot-ball being played, and hear nothing but the thud of the kicking; or one might watch wrestling-contests in the *jiujutsu*-room, and hear no word spoken for half an hour at a time. (The rules of *jiujutsu*, it is true, require not only silence, but the total suppression of all visible emotional interest on the part of the spectators.) All this repression at first seemed to me very strange — though I knew that thirty years previously, the training at samurai-schools compelled the same impassiveness and reticence.

At last the University is reached, — the great gate of ceremony to public office. Here the student finds himself released from the restraints previously imposed upon his private life,[1] though the class-will continues to rule him in certain directions. As a rule, the student passes into official life after having graduated, marries, and becomes the head, or the

[1] This release is of recent date; and the results, by the acknowledgment of the students themselves, have not been good. Twenty-five years ago, University study was so seriously thought about that a scholar who failed, through his own fault, would have been considered a criminal. There was then a Chinese poem in vogue, which used to be sung at the departure of youths for the University of that time (*Daigaku Nankō*) by their friends and relations: —

Danji kokorozashi wo tatété, kyōkwan wo idzu;
Gaku moshi narazunba, shisudomo kaëradzu.

[*The young man, having made a firm resolve, leaves his native home.*
If he fail to acquire learning, then, even though he die, he must never return.]

In those years also it was obligatory upon students to live and dress simply, and to abstain from all self-indulgence.

prospective head, of a household. How sudden the transformation of the man at this epoch of his career, only those who have observed the transformation can imagine. It is then that the full significance of Japanese education reveals itself.

Few incidents of Japanese life are more surprising than the metamorphosis of the gawky student into the dignified, impassive, easy-mannered official. But a little time ago he was respectfully asking, cap in hand, the explanation of some text, the meaning of some foreign idiom; to-day, perhaps, he is judging cases in some court, or managing diplomatic correspondence under ministerial supervision, or directing the management of some public school. Whatever you may have thought of his particular capacity as a student, you will scarcely doubt his particular fitness for the position to which he has been called. Success in study was at best a secondary consideration in the matter of his appointment, — though he *had* to succeed. He was put through some special course, under high protection, after having been selected for certain qualities of character, — or at least for the promise of such qualities. There may have been favouritism in his case; but, generally speaking, capable men are appointed to positions of trust: the Government seldom makes serious mistakes. This man has value beyond what mere study could make for him, — some capacity in the direction of management or of organization, —

some natural force or talent which his training has
served to cultivate. According to the quality of his
worth, his position was chosen for him in advance.
His long, hard schooling has taught him more than
books can teach, and more than a stupid person can
ever learn : how to read minds and motives, — how
to remain impassive under all circumstances, — how
to reach a truth quickly by simple questioning, —
how to live upon his guard (even against the most
intimate of old acquaintances), — how to remain,
even when most amiable, secretive and inscrutable.
He has graduated in the art of worldly wisdom.
He is really a wonderful person, a highly developed
type of his race ; and no inexperienced Occidental
is capable of judging him, because his visible acquirements count for very little in the measure of his
relative value. His University study — his English or French or German knowledge — serves him
only as so much oil to make easy the working of
certain official machinery : he esteems this learning
only as means to some administrative end ; his
real learning, considerably deeper, represents the
development of the Japanese soul of him. Between
that mind and any Western mind the distance has
become immeasurable. And now, less than ever
before, does he belong to himself. He belongs to
a family, to a party, to a government : privately he
is bound by custom ; publicly he must act according to order only, and never dream of yielding to

any impulses at variance with order, however generous or sensible such impulses may be. A word
might ruin him: he has learned to use no words
unnecessarily. By silent submission and tireless
observance of duty he may rise, and rise quickly:
he may become Governor, Chief Justice, Minister
of State, Minister Plenipotentiary; but the higher
he rises, the heavier will his bonds become.

Long training in caution and self-control is indeed
an indispensable preparation for official existence;
the ability either to keep a position won, or to resign
it with honour, depending much upon such training.
The most sinister circumstance of official life is the
absence of moral freedom, — the absence of the
right to act according to one's own convictions of
justice. The subordinate, who desires above all
things to keep his place, is not supposed to have
personal convictions or sympathies — save by permission. He is not the slave of a man, but of a
system — a system as old as China. Were human
nature perfect, that system would be perfect; but so
long as human nature remains what it is now, the
system leaves much to be desired. Everything may
depend upon the personal character of those temporarily intrusted with higher power; and the only
choice left for the most capable servant under a bad
master may be to resign or to do wrong. The
strong man faces the problem bravely and resigns;
but for one strong man there are fifty timid ones.

Probably the prospect of a broken career is much less terrifying than the ancient idea of crime attaching to any form of insubordination. As the forms of a religion survive after the faith in doctrine has passed away, so the power of Government to coerce even conscience still remains, though religion is no longer identified with Government. The system of secrecy, implacably enforced, helps to maintain the vague awe that has always attached to the idea of administrative authority; and such authority is practically omnipotent within those limits which I have already indicated. To be favoured by authority means to experience all the illusive pleasure of a suddenly created popularity: an entire community, a whole city, is made by a word to turn all the amiable side of its human nature toward the favourite, — to charm him into the belief that he is worthy of the best that the world can give him. But suppose that the moving powers happen, latter on, to find the favoured man in the way of some policy — lo! at another whispered word he finds himself, without knowing why, the public enemy. None speak to him or salute him or smile upon him — save ironically: long-esteemed friends pass him by without recognition, or, if pursued, reply to his most earnest questions with all possible brevity and caution. Most likely they do not know the "why" of the matter: they only know that orders have been given, and that into the reason of orders it is not good to enquire. Even the street-children know this much, and mock the despondent victim of fortune; even the dogs seem instinctively to divine the change and bark at him as he passes by. . . . Such is the power of official displeasure; and the penalty of a blunder or a breach of discipline may extend considerably further —— but in feudal times the offender would have been simply told to perform *harakiri*. Sometimes, when the wrong men get into power, the force of authority may be used for malevolent ends; and in such event it requires not a little courage to disobey an order to act against conscience. What saved Japanese society in former ages from the worst results of this form of tyranny, was the moral sentiment of the mass, — the common feeling that underlay all submission to authority, and remained always capable, if pressed upon too brutally, of compelling a reaction. Conditions to-day are more favourable to justice; but it requires much tact, steadiness, and resolution on the part of a rising official to steer himself safely among the reefs and the whirlpools of the new political life.

*   *   *   *   *

The reader will now be able to understand the general character, aim, and results of official education as a system. It will be also worth while to consider in detail certain phases of student-life which **equally prove** the survival of old conditions and old traditions. I can speak about these matters from personal experience as a teacher, — an experience extending over nearly thirteen years.

Readers of Goethe will remember the trustful docility of the student received by Doctor Mephistopheles in the First Part of *Faust*, and the very different demeanour of the same student when he reappears, in the Second Part, as Baccalaureus. More than one foreign professor in Japan must have been reminded of that contrast by personal experience, and must have wondered whether some one of the early educational advisers to the Japanese Government did not play, without malice prepense, the very rôle of Mephistopheles. . . . The gentle boy who, with innocent reverence, makes his visit of courtesy to the foreign teacher, bringing for gift a cluster of iris-flowers or odorous spray of plum-blossoms, — the boy who does whatever he is told, and charms by an earnestness, a trustfulness, a grace of manner rarely met with among Western lads of the same age, — is destined to undergo the strangest of transformations long before becoming a baccalaureus. You may meet with him a few years later, in the uniform of some Higher School, and find it difficult to recognize your former pupil, — now graceless, taciturn, secretive, and inclined to demand as a right what could scarcely, with propriety, be requested as a favour. You may find

him patronizing,—possibly something worse. Later
on, at the University, he becomes more formally correct, but also more far away,—so very far away from
his boyhood that the remoteness is a pain to one
who remembers that boyhood. The Pacific is less
wide and deep than the invisible gulf now extending between the mind of the stranger and the mind
of the student. The foreign professor is now regarded merely as a teaching-machine; and he is
more than likely to regret any effort made to maintain an intimate relation with his pupils. Indeed
the whole formal system of official education is
opposed to the development of any such relation.
I am speaking of general facts in this connexion,
not of merely personal experiences. No matter
what the foreigner may do in the hope of finding
his way into touch with the emotional life of his
students, or in the hope of evoking that interest in
certain studies which renders possible an intellectual
tie, he must toil in vain. Perhaps in two or three
cases out of a thousand he may obtain something
precious, —a lasting and kindly esteem, based upon
moral comprehension; but should he wish for more
he must remain in the state of the Antarctic ex-
plorer, seeking, month after month, to no purpose,
some inlet through endless cliffs of everlasting ice.
Now the case of the Japanese professor proves the
barrier natural, to a large extent. The Japanese
professor can ask for extraordinary efforts and

obtain them; he can afford to be easily familiar
with his students outside of class; and he can get
what no stranger can obtain,—their devotion. The
difference has been attributed to race-feeling; but it
cannot be so easily and vaguely explained.

Something of race-sentiment there certainly is;
it were impossible that there should not be. No
inexperienced foreigner can converse for one half
hour with any Japanese — at least with any Japanese
who has not sojourned abroad — and avoid saying
something that jars upon Japanese good taste or
sentiment; and few — perhaps none — among un-
travelled Japanese can maintain a brief conversation
in any European tongue without making some
startling impression upon the foreign listener.
Sympathethic understanding, between minds so
differently constructed, is next to impossible. But
the foreign professor who looks for the impossible
— who expects from his Japanese students the same
quality of intelligent comprehension that he might
reasonably expect from Western students — is naturally disturbed. "Why must there always remain
the width of a world between us?" is a question
often asked and rarely answered.

Some of the reasons should by this time be obvious to my reader; but one among them — and the
most curious — will not. Before stating it, I must
observe that while the relation between the foreign

instructor and the Japanese student is artificial, that
between the Japanese teacher and the student is
traditionally one of sacrifice and obligation. The
inertia encountered by the stranger, the indifference
which chills him at all times, are due in great part
to the misapprehension arising from totally opposite
conceptions of duty. Old sentiment lingers long
after old forms have passed away; and how much
of feudal Japan survives in modern Japan, no
stranger can readily divine. Probably the bulk of
existing sentiment is hereditary sentiment: the
ancient ideals have not yet been replaced by fresh
ones. . . . In feudal times the teacher taught
without salary: he was expected to devote all his
time, thought, and strength to his profession.
High honour was attached to that profession; and
the matter of remuneration was not discussed, — the
instructor trusting wholly to the gratitude of parents
and pupils. Public sentiment bound them to him
with a bond that could not be broken. Therefore
a general, upon the eve of an assault, would take
care that his former teacher should have an opportunity to escape from the place beleaguered. The
tie between teacher and pupil was in force second
only to the tie between parent and child. The
teacher sacrificed everything for his pupil: the
pupil was ready at all times to die for his teacher.
Now, indeed, the hard and selfish aspects of Japanese character are coming to the surface. But a

single fact will sufficiently indicate how much of the old ethical sentiment persists under the new and rougher surface: *Nearly all the higher educational work accomplished in Japan represents, though aided by Government, the results of personal sacrifice.*

From the summit of society to the base, this sacrificial spirit rules. That a large part of the private income of their Imperial Majesties has, for many years, been devoted to public education is well known; but that every person of rank or wealth or high position educates students at his private expense, is not generally known. In the majority of cases this help is entirely gratuitous; in a minority of cases, the expenses of the student are advanced only, to be repaid by instalments at some future time. The reader is doubtless aware that the daimyō in former times used to dispose of the bulk of their incomes in supporting and helping their retainers; supplying hundreds, in some cases thousands, and in some few cases, even tens of thousands, of persons with the necessaries of life; and exacting in return military service, loyalty, and obedience. Those former daimyō or their successors — particularly those who are still large landholders — now vie with each other in assisting education. All who can afford it are educating sons or grandsons or descendants of former retainers; the subjects of this patronage being annually selected from among the students of schools established in the former daimiates. It is only the rich noble who can now support a number of students gratuitously, year after year; the poorer men of rank cannot care for many. But all, or very nearly all, maintain some,—and this even in cases where the patron's income is so small that the expense could not be borne unless the student were pledged to repay it after graduation. In some instances, half of the cost is borne by the patron; the student being required to repay the rest.

Now these aristocratic examples are extensively followed through other grades of society. Merchants, bankers, and manufacturers—all rich men of the commercial and industrial classes—are educating students. Military officers, civil service officials, physicians, lawyers, men of every profession, in short, are doing the same thing. Persons whose incomes are too small to permit of much generosity are able to help students by employing them as door-keepers, messengers, tutors,—giving them board and lodging, and a little pocket-money at times, in return for light services. In Tōkyō, and in most of the large cities, almost every large house is guarded by students who are being thus assisted. As for what the teachers do—that requires special mention.

The majority of teachers in the public schools do not receive salaries enabling them to help students with money; but all teachers earning more than the bare necessary give aid of some sort. Among the instructors and professors of the higher educational establishments, the helping of students seems to be thought of as a matter of course, — so much a matter of course that we might suspect a new " tyranny of custom," especially in view of the smallness of official salaries. But no tyranny of custom would explain the pleasure of sacrifice and the strange persistence of feudal idealism which are revealed by some extraordinary facts. For example : A certain University professor is known to have supported and educated a large number of students by dividing among them, during many years, nearly the whole of his salary. He lodged, clothed, boarded, and educated them, bought their books, and paid their fees, — reserving for himself only the cost of his living, and reducing even that cost by living upon hot sweet potatoes. (Fancy a foreign professor in Japan putting himself upon a diet of bread and water for the purpose of educating gratuitously a number of poor young men !) I know of two other cases nearly as remarkable ; the helper, in one instance, being an old man of more than seventy, who still devotes all his means, time, and knowledge to his ancient ideal of duty. How much obscure sacrifice of this kind has been performed by those least able to afford it never will be known : indeed, the publication of the facts would only give pain. I am guilty of some indiscretion in mentioning even the cases brought to my attention — though human nature is honoured by the mention. . . . Now it should be evident that while Japanese students are accustomed to witness self-denial of this sort on the part of native professors, they cannot be much impressed by any manifestation of interest or sympathy on the part of the foreign professor, who, though receiving a higher salary than his Japanese colleagues, has no reason and small inclination to imitate their example.

Surely this heroic fact of education sustained by personal sacrifices, in the face of unimaginable difficulties, is enough to redeem much humbug and wrong. In spite of the corruption which has been of late years rife in educational circles, — in spite of official scandals, intrigues, and shams, — all needed reforms can be hoped for while the spirit of generous self-denial continues to rule the world of teachers and students. I can venture also the opinion that most of the official scandals and failures have resulted from the interference of politics with modern education, or from attempting to imitate foreign conventional methods totally at variance with national moral experience. Where Japan has remained true to her old moral ideals she has done nobly and well: where she has needlessly departed from them, sorrow and trouble have been the natural consequences.

There are yet other facts in modern education

suggesting even more forcibly how much of the old
life remains hidden under the new conditions, and
how rigidly race-character has become fixed in the
higher types of mind.   I refer chiefly to the results
of Japanese education abroad, — a higher special
training in German, English, French, or American
Universities.   In some directions these results, to
foreign observation at least, appear to be almost
negative.   Considering the immense psychological
differentiation, — the total oppositeness of mental
structure and habit, — it is astonishing that Japanese
students have been able to do what they actually
have done at foreign Universities.   To graduate at
any European or American University of mark, —
with a mind shaped by Japanese culture, filled with
Chinese learning, crammed with ideographs, — is a
prodigious feat : scarcely less of a feat than it would
be for an American student to graduate at a Chinese
University.   Certainly the men sent abroad to study
are carefully selected for ability ; and one indispensable requisite for the mission is a power of memory
incomparably superior to the average Occidental
memory, and different altogether as to quality, —
a memory for details ; — nevertheless, the feat is
amazing.   But with the return to Japan of these
young scholars, there is commonly an end of effort
in the direction of the speciality studied, — unless it
happens to have been a purely practical subject.
Does this signify incapacity for independent work

upon Occidental lines? incapacity for creative
thought? lack of constructive imagination? disin-
clination or indifference? The history of that terrible mental and moral discipline to which the race
was so long subjected would certainly suggest such
limitations in the modern Japanese mind. Perhaps
these questions cannot yet be answered, — except, I
imagine, as regards the indifference, which is self-
evident and undisguised. But, independently of
any question of capacity or inclination, there is this
fact to be considered, — that proper encouragement
has not yet been given to home-scholarship. The
plain truth is that young men are sent to foreign
seats of learning for other ends than to learn how to
devote the rest of their lives to the study of psychology, philology, literature, or modern philosophy.
They are sent abroad to fit them for higher posts in
Government-service; and their foreign study is but
one obligatory episode in their official career. Each
has to qualify himself for special duty by learning
how Western people study and think and feel in
certain directions, and by ascertaining the range of
educational progress in those directions; but he is
not ordered to think or to feel like Western people
— which would, in any event, be impossible for
him. He has not, and probably could not have,
any deep personal interest in Western learning outside of the domain of applied science. His business
is to learn how to understand such matters from the

Japanese, not from the Occidental, point of view. But he performs his part well, does exactly what he has been told to do, and rarely anything more. His value to his Government is doubled or quadrupled by his allotted experience; but at home — except during a few years of expected duty as professor or lecturer — he will probably use that experience only as a psychological costume of ceremony, — a mental uniform to be donned when official occasion may require.

It is otherwise in the case of men sent abroad for scientific studies requiring, not only intelligence and memory, but natural quickness of hand and eye, — surgery, medicine, military specialities. I doubt whether the average efficiency of Japanese surgeons can be surpassed. The study of war, I need hardly say, is one for which the national mind and character have inherited aptitude. But men sent abroad merely to win a foreign University-degree, and destined, after a term of educational duty, to higher official life, appear to set small value upon their foreign acquirements. However, even if they could win distinction in Europe by further effort at home, that effort would have to be made at a serious pecuniary sacrifice, and its results could not as yet be fairly appreciated by their own countrymen.

Some of us have wondered at times what the old Egyptians or the old Greeks would have done if suddenly brought into dangerous contact with a civilization like our own, — a civilization of applied mathematics, with sciences and branch-sciences of which the mere names would fill a dictionary. I think that the history of modern Japan suggests very clearly what any wise people, with a civilization based upon ancestor-worship, would have done. They would have speedily reconstructed their patriarchal society to meet the sudden peril; they would have adopted, with astonishing success, all the scientific machinery that they could use; they would have created a formidable army and a highly efficient navy; they would have sent their young aristocrats abroad to study alien convention, and to qualify for diplomatic duty; they would have established a new system of education, and obliged all their children to study many new things; — but toward the higher emotional and intellectual life of that alien civilization, they would naturally exhibit indifference: its best literature, its philosophy, its broader forms of tolerant religion could make no profound appeal to their moral and social experience.

Industrial Danger

EVERYWHERE the course of human civilization has been shaped by the same evolutional
law; and as the earlier history of the ancient
European communities can help us to understand
the social conditions of Old Japan, so a later period
of the same history can help us to divine something
of the probable future of the New Japan. It has been
shown by the author of *La Cité Antique* that the
history of all the ancient Greek and Latin communities included four revolutionary periods.[1] The
first revolution had everywhere for its issue the
withdrawal of political power from the priest-king,
who was nevertheless allowed to retain the religious
authority. The second revolutionary period witnessed the breaking up of the *gens* or γένος, the
enfranchisement of the client from the authority
of the patron, and several important changes in

[1] Not excepting Sparta. The Spartan society was evolutionally much in advance of the Ionian societies; the Dorian patriarchal clan having been dissolved at
some very early period. Sparta kept its Kings; but affairs of civil justice were
regulated by the Senate, and affairs of criminal justice by the ephors, who also had
the power to declare war and to make treaties of peace. After the first great revolution of Spartan history the King was deprived of power in civil matters, in criminal
matters, and in military matters: he retained his sacerdotal office. See for details,
La Cité Antique, pp. 285–287.

the legal constitution of the family. The third
revolutionary period saw the weakening of the
religious and military aristocracy, the entrance of
the common people into the rights of citizenship,
and the rise of a democracy of wealth, — presently
to be opposed by a democracy of poverty. The
fourth revolutionary period witnessed the first
bitter struggles between rich and poor, the final
triumph of anarchy, and the consequent establishment of a new and horrible form of despotism, —
the despotism of the popular Tyrant.

To these four revolutionary periods, the social
history of Old Japan presents but two correspond-
ences. The first Japanese revolutionary period
was represented by the Fujiwara usurpation of the
imperial civil and military authority, — after which
event the aristocracy, religious and military, really
governed Japan down to our own time. All the
events of the rise of the military power and the
concentration of authority under the Tokugawa
Shōgunate properly belong to the first revolutionary
period. At the time of the opening of Japan,
society had not evolutionally advanced beyond a
stage corresponding to that of the antique Western
societies in the seventh or eighth century before
Christ. The second revolutionary period really
began only with the reconstruction of society in
1871. But within the space of a single generation
thereafter Japan entered upon her third revolution-

ary period. Already the influence of the elder aristocracy is threatened by the sudden rise of a new
oligarchy of wealth, — a new industrial power
probably destined to become omnipotent in politics.
The disintegration (now proceeding) of the clan,
the changes in the legal constitution of the family,
the entrance of the people into the enjoyment of
political rights, must all tend to hasten the coming
transfer of power. There is every indication that,
in the present order of things, the third revolutionary period will run its course rapidly; and then a
fourth revolutionary period, fraught with serious
danger, would be in immediate prospect.

Consider the bewildering rapidity of recent changes,
— from the reconstruction of society in 1871 to the
opening of the first national parliament in 1891.
Down to the middle of the nineteenth century the
nation had remained in the condition common to
European patriarchal communities twenty-six hundred years ago: society had indeed entered upon a
second period of integration, but had traversed only
one great revolution. And then the country was
suddenly hurried through two more social revolu-
tions of the most extraordinary kind, — signalized
by the abolition of the daimiates, the suppression of
the military class, the substitution of a plebeian for
an aristocratic army, popular enfranchisement, the
rapid formalism of a new commonalty, industrial ex-

pansion, the rise of a new aristocracy of wealth, and popular representation in government! Old Japan had never developed a wealthy and powerful middle class: she had not even approached that stage of industrial development which, in the ancient European societies, naturally brought about the first political struggles between rich and poor. Her social organization made industrial oppression impossible: the commercial classes were kept at the bottom of society, — under the feet even of those who, in more highly evolved communities, are most at the mercy of money-power. But now those commercial classes, set free and highly privileged, are silently and swiftly ousting the aristocratic ruling-class from power, — are becoming supremely important. And under the new order of things, forms of social misery, never before known in the history of the race, are being developed. Some idea of this misery may be obtained from the fact that the number of poor people in Tōkyō unable to pay their annual resident-tax is upwards of 50,000; yet the amount of the tax is only about 20 *sen*, or 5 pence English money. Prior to the accumulation of wealth in the hands of a minority there was never any such want in any part of Japan, — except, of course, as a temporary consequence of war.

The early history of European civilization supplies analogies. In the Greek and Latin communities, up to the time of the dissolution of the *gens*, there was no poverty in the modern meaning of that word. Slavery, with some few exceptions, existed only in the mild domestic form ; there were yet no commercial oligarchies, and no industrial oppressions ; and the various cities and states were ruled, after political power had been taken from the early kings, by military aristocracies which also exercised religious functions. There was yet little trade in the modern signification of the term ; and money, as current coinage, came into circulation only in the seventh century before Christ. Misery did not exist. Under any patriarchal system, based upon ancestor-worship, there is no misery, as a consequence of poverty, except such as may be temporarily created by devastation or famine. If want thus comes, it comes to all alike. In such a state of society everybody is in the service of somebody, and receives in exchange for service all the necessaries of life : there is no need for any one to trouble himself about the question of living. Also, in such a patriarchal community, which is self-sufficing, there is little need of money : barter takes the place of trade. . . . In all these respects, the condition of Old Japan offered a close parallel to the conditions of patriarchal society in ancient Europe. While the *uji* or clan existed, there was no misery except as a result of war, famine, or pestilence. Throughout society — excepting the small commercial class — the need of money was rare ; and such coinage as existed

was little suited to general circulation. Taxes were
paid in rice and other produce. As the lord nourished his retainers, so the samurai cared for his dependants, the farmer for his labourers, the artizan for
his apprentices and journeymen, the merchant for
his clerks. Everybody was fed; and there was no
need, in ordinary times at least, for any one to go
hungry. It was only with the breaking-up of the
clan-system in Japan that the possibilities of starvation for the worker first came into existence. And
as, in antique Europe, the enfranchised client-class
and plebeian-class developed, under like conditions,
into a democracy clamouring for suffrage and all
political rights, so in Japan have the common people
developed the political instinct, in self-protection.

It will be remembered how, in Greek and Roman
society, the aristocracy founded upon religious tradition and military power had to give way to an
oligarchy of wealth, and how there subsequently
came into existence a democratic form of government,—democratic, not in the modern, but in the
old Greek meaning. At a yet later day the results
of popular suffrage were the breaking-up of this
democratic government, and the initiation of an
atrocious struggle between rich and poor. After
that strife had begun there was no more security
for life or property until the Roman conquest enforced order. . . . Now it seems not unlikely
that there will be witnessed in Japan, at no very

distant day, a strong tendency to repeat the history
of the old Greek anarchies. With the constant
increase of poverty and pressure of population,
and the concomitant accumulation of wealth in the
hands of a new industrial class, the peril is obvious.
Thus far the nation has patiently borne all changes,
relying upon the experience of its past, and trusting implicitly to its rulers. But should wretch-
edness be so permitted to augment that the
question of how to keep from starving becomes
imperative for the millions, the long patience and
the long trust may fail. And then, to repeat a
figure effectively used by Professor Huxley, the
Primitive Man, finding that the Moral Man has
landed him in the valley of the shadow of death,
may rise up to take the management of affairs into
his own hands, and fight savagely for the right of
existence. As popular instinct is not too dull to
divine the first cause of this misery in the introduction of Western industrial methods, it is unpleasant
to reflect what such an upheaval might signify. But
nothing of moment has yet been done to ameliorate
the condition of the wretched class of operatives,
now estimated to exceed half a million.

M. de Coulanges has pointed out[1] that the absence of individual liberty was the real cause of the
disorders and the final ruin of the Greek societies.

[1] *La Cité Antique*, pp. 400–401.

Rome suffered less, and survived, and dominated,—
because within her boundaries the rights of the individual had been more respected. . . . Now the
absence of individual freedom in modern Japan
would certainly appear to be nothing less than a
national danger. For those very habits of unquestioning obedience, and loyalty, and respect for
authority, which made feudal society possible, are
likely to render a true democratic régime impossible,
and would tend to bring about a state of anarchy.
Only races long accustomed to personal liberty, —
liberty to think about matters of ethics apart from
matters of government, — liberty to consider questions of right and wrong, justice and injustice, independently of political authority, — are able to face
without risk the peril now menacing Japan. For
should social disintegration take in Japan the same
course which it followed in the old European societies, — unchecked by any precautionary legislation,
— and so bring about another social revolution, the
consequence could scarcely be less than utter ruin.
In the antique world of Europe, the total disintegration of the patriarchal system occupied centuries:
it was slow, and it was normal — not having been
brought about by external forces. In Japan, on
the contrary, this disintegration is taking place
under enormous outside pressure, operating with
the rapidity of electricity and steam. In Greek
societies the changes were effected in about three

hundred years; in Japan it is hardly more than thirty years since the patriarchal system was legally dissolved and the industrial system reshaped; yet already the danger of anarchy is in sight, and the population — astonishingly augmented by more than ten millions — already begins to experience all the forms of misery developed by want under industrial conditions.

It was perhaps inevitable that the greatest freedom accorded under the new order of things should have been given in the direction of greatest danger. Though the Government cannot be said to have done much for any form of competition within the sphere of its own direct control, it has done even more than could have been reasonably expected on behalf of national industrial competition. Loans have been lavishly advanced, subsidies generously allowed; and, in spite of various panics and failures, the results have been prodigious. Within thirty years the value of articles manufactured for export has risen from half a million to five hundred million *yen*. But this immense development has been effected at serious cost in other directions. The old methods of family production — and therefore most of the beautiful industries and arts, for which Japan has been so long famed — now seem doomed beyond hope; and instead of the ancient kindly relations between master and workers, there have been brought into existence — with no legislation to restrain inhuman-

ity — all the horrors of factory-life at its worst. The
new combinations of capital have actually reëstablished servitude, under harsher forms than ever
were imagined under the feudal era; the misery of
the women and children subjected to that servitude
is a public scandal, and proves strange possibilities
of cruelty on the part of a people once renowned for
kindness, — kindness even to animals.

There is now a humane outcry for reform; and
earnest efforts have been made, and will be made,
to secure legislation for the protection of operatives.
But, as might be expected, these efforts have been
hitherto strongly opposed by manufacturing companies and syndicates with the declaration that any
Government interference with factory management
will greatly hamper, if not cripple, enterprise, and
hinder competition with foreign industry. Less
than twenty years ago the very same arguments were
used in England to oppose the efforts then being
made to improve the condition of the industrial
classes; and that opposition was challenged by Professor Huxley in a noble address, which every
Japanese legislator would do well to read to-day.
Speaking of the reforms in progress during 1888,
the professor said: —

"If it is said that the carrying out of such arrangements
as those indicated must enhance the cost of production,
and thus handicap the producer in the race of competition,
I venture, in the first place, to doubt the fact; but, if it be

so, it results that industrial society has to face a dilemma, either alternative of which threatens destruction.

"On the one hand, a population, the labour of which is sufficiently remunerated, may be physically and morally healthy, and socially stable, but may fail in industrial competition by reason of the dearness of its produce. On the other hand, a population, the labour of which is insufficiently remunerated, must become physically and morally unhealthy, and socially unstable; and though it may succeed for a while in competition, by reason of the cheapness of its produce, it must in the end fall, through hideous misery and degradation, to utter ruin.

"Well, if these be the only alternatives, let us for ourselves and our children choose the former, and, if need be, starve like men. But I do not believe that a stable society, made up of healthy, vigorous, instructed, and self-ruling people would ever incur serious risk of that fate. They are not likely to be troubled with many competitors of the same character just yet; and they may be safely trusted to find ways of holding their own." [1]

If the future of Japan could depend upon her army and her navy, upon the high courage of her people and their readiness to die by the hundred thousand for ideals of honour and of duty, there would be small cause for alarm in the present state of affairs. Unfortunately her future must depend upon other qualities than courage, other abilities than those of

[1] *The Struggle for Existence in Human Society*, "Collected Essays," Vol. IX, pp. 218-219.

sacrifice; and her struggle hereafter must be one in
which her social traditions will place her at an
immense disadvantage. The capacity for industrial
competition cannot be made to depend upon the
misery of women and children; it must depend
upon the intelligent freedom of the individual; and
the society which suppresses this freedom, or suffers
it to be suppressed, must remain too rigid for competition with societies in which the liberties of the
individual are strictly maintained. While Japan continues to think and to act by groups, even by groups
of industrial companies, so long she must always
continue incapable of her best. Her ancient social
experience is not sufficient to avail her for the future
international struggle, — rather it must sometimes
impede her as so much dead weight. Dead, in the
ghostliest sense of the word, — the viewless pressure
upon her life of numberless vanished generations.
She will have not only to strive against colossal odds
in her rivalry with more plastic and more forceful
societies; she will have to strive much more against
the power of her phantom past.

Yet it were a grievous error to imagine that she
has nothing further to gain from her ancestral faith.
All her modern successes have been aided by it;
and all her modern failures have been marked by
needless breaking with its ethical custom. She could
compel her people, by a simple fiat, to adopt the

civilization of the West, with all its pain and struggle, only because that people had been trained for ages in submission and loyalty and sacrifice ; and the time has not yet come in which she can afford to cast away the whole of her moral past.   More freedom indeed she requires, — but freedom restrained by wisdom ; freedom to think and act and strive for self as well as for others, — not freedom to oppress the weak, or to exploit the simple.   And the new cruelties of her industrial life can find no justification in the traditions of her ancient faith, which exacted absolute obedience from the dependant, but equally required the duty of kindness from the master.   In so far as she has permitted her people to depart from the way of kindness, she herself has surely departed from the Way of the Gods. . . .

And the domestic future appears dark.   Born of that darkness, an evil dream comes oftentimes to those who love Japan : the fear that all her efforts are being directed, with desperate heroism, only to prepare the land for the sojourn of peoples older by centuries in commercial experience ; that her thousands of miles of railroads and telegraphs, her mines and forges, her arsenals and factories, her docks and fleets, are being put in order for the use of foreign capital ; that her admirable army and her heroic navy may be doomed to make their last sacrifices in hopeless contest against some combination of greedy states, provoked or encouraged to aggression by circumstances beyond the power of Government to control. . . . But the statesmanship that has already guided Japan through so many storms should prove able to cope with this gathering peril.

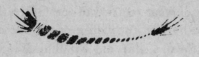

Reflections

IN the preceding pages I have endeavoured to suggest a general idea of the social history of Japan, and a general idea of the nature of those forces which shaped and tempered the character of her people. Certainly this attempt leaves much to be desired: the time is yet far away at which a satisfactory work upon the subject can be prepared. But the fact that Japan can be understood only through the study of her religious and social evolution, has been, I trust, sufficiently indicated. She affords us the amazing spectacle of an Eastern society maintaining all the outward forms of Western civilization; using, with unquestionable efficiency, the applied science of the Occident; accomplishing, by prodigious effort, the work of centuries within the time of three decades, — yet sociologically remaining at a stage corresponding to that which, in ancient Europe, preceded the Christian era by hundreds of years.

But no suggestion of origins and causes should diminish the pleasure of contemplating this curious world, psychologically still so far away from us in the course of human evolution. The wonder and the beauty of what remains of the Old Japan cannot be lessened by any knowledge of the conditions that produced them. The old kindliness and grace of manners need not cease to charm us because we know that such manners were cultivated, for a thousand years, under the edge of the sword. The common politeness which appeared, but a few years ago, to be almost universal, and the rarity of quarrels, should not prove less agreeable because we have learned that, for generations and generations, all quarrels among the people were punished with extraordinary rigour; and that the custom of the vendetta, which rendered necessary such repression, also made everybody cautious of word and deed. The popular smile should not seem less winning because we have been told of a period, in the past of the subject-classes, when not to smile in the teeth of pain might cost life itself. And the Japanese woman, as cultivated by the old home-training, is not less sweet a being because she represents the moral ideal of a vanishing world, and because we can faintly surmise the cost, — the incalculable cost in pain, — of producing her.

No: what remains of this elder civilization is full of charm, — charm unspeakable, — and to witness its gradual destruction must be a grief for whomsoever has felt that charm. However intolerable may seem, to the mind of the artist or poet, those countless restrictions which once ruled all this fairy-world

and shaped the soul of it, he cannot but admire and
love their best results : the simplicity of old custom,
— the amiability of manners, — the daintiness of
habits, — the delicate tact displayed in pleasure-giv-
ing, — the strange power of presenting outwardly,
under any circumstances, only the best and brightest
aspects of character. What emotional poetry, for
even the least believing, in the ancient home-religion, — in the lamplet nightly kindled before the
names of the dead, the tiny offerings of food and
drink, the welcome-fires lighted to guide the visiting
ghosts, the little ships prepared to bear them back
to their rest! And this immemorial doctrine of
filial piety, — exacting all that is noble, not less than
all that is terrible, in duty, in gratitude, in self-
denial, — what strange appeal does it make to our
lingering religious instincts ; and how close to the
divine appear to us the finer natures forged by it!
What queer weird attraction in those parish-temple
festivals, with their happy mingling of merriment
and devotion in the presence of the gods! What
a universe of romance in that Buddhist art which
has left its impress upon almost every product
of industry, from the toy of a child to the heir-
loom of a prince; — which has peopled the soli-
tudes with statues, and chiselled the wayside
rocks with texts of sûtras! Who can forget the
soft enchantment of this Buddhist atmosphere?
— the deep music of the great bells? — the

green peace of gardens haunted by fearless things:
doves that flutter down at call, fishes rising
to be fed? . . . Despite our incapacity to enter
into the soul-life of this ancient East, — despite
the certainty that one might as well hope to re-
mount the River of Time and share the vanished existence of some old Greek city, as to
share the thoughts and the emotions of Old
Japan, — we find ourselves bewitched forever by
the vision, like those wanderers of folk-tale who
rashly visited Elf-land.

We know that there is illusion, — not as to the
reality of the visible, but as to its meanings, — very
much illusion. Yet why should this illusion attract
us, like some glimpse of Paradise? — why should
we feel obliged to confess the ethical glamour of a
civilization as far away from us in thought as the
Egypt of Ramses? Are we really charmed by the
results of a social discipline that refused to recognize
the individual? — enamoured of a cult that exacted
the suppression of personality?

No: the charm is made by the fact that this
vision of the past represents to us much more than
past or present, — that it foreshadows the possibilities of some higher future, in a world of perfect
sympathy. After many a thousand years there may
be developed a humanity able to achieve, with never
a shadow of illusion, those ethical conditions prefig-
ured by the ideals of Old Japan: instinctive unself-

ishness, a common desire to find the joy of life in making happiness for others, a universal sense of moral beauty. And whenever men shall have so far gained upon the present as to need no other code than the teaching of their own hearts, then indeed the ancient ideal of Shintō will find its supreme realization.

Moreover, it should be remembered that the social state, whose results thus attract us, really produced much more than a beautiful mirage. Simple characters of great charm, though necessarily of great fixity, were developed by it in multitude. Old Japan came nearer to the achievement of the highest moral ideal than our far more evolved societies can hope to do for many a hundred years. And but for those ten centuries of war which followed upon the rise of the military power, the ethical end to which all social discipline tended might have been much more closely approached. Yet if the better side of this human nature had been further developed at the cost of darker and sterner qualities, the consequence might have proved unfortunate for the nation. No people so ruled by altruism as to lose its capacities for aggression and cunning, could hold their own, in the present state of the world, against races hardened by the discipline of competition as well as by the discipline of war. The future Japan must rely upon the least amiable qualities of her character for success in the universal struggle; and she will need to develop them strongly.

* *

How strongly she has been able to develop them in one direction, the present war with Russia bears startling witness. But it is certainly to the long discipline of the past that she owes the moral strength behind this unexpected display of aggressive power. No superficial observation could discern the silent energies masked by the resignation of the people to change, — the unconscious heroism informing this mass of forty million souls, — the compressed force ready to expand at Imperial bidding either for construction or destruction. From the leaders of a nation with such a military and political history, one might expect the manifestation of all those abilities of supreme importance in diplomacy and war. But such capacities could prove of little worth were it not for the character of the masses, — the quality of the material that moves to command with the power of winds and tides. The veritable strength of Japan still lies in the moral nature of her common people, — her farmers and fishers, artizans and labourers, — the patient quiet folk one sees toiling in the rice-fields, or occupied with the humblest of crafts and callings in city by-ways. All the unconscious heroism of the race is in these, and all its splendid courage, — a courage that does not mean indifference to life, but the desire to sacrifice life at the bidding of the Imperial Master who raises the rank of the dead. From the thousands of young men now being summoned to the war, one hears no expression of hope to return to their homes with glory; — the common wish uttered is only to win remembrance at the Shōkonsha — that "Spirit-Invoking Temple," where the souls of all who die for Emperor and fatherland are believed to gather. At no time was the ancient faith stronger than in this hour of struggle; and Russian power will have very much more to fear from that faith than from repeating rifles or Whitehead torpedoes.[1] Shintō, as a religion of patriotism, is a force that should suffice, if permitted fair-play, to affect not only the destinies of the whole Far East, but the future of civilization. No more irrational assertion was ever made about the Japanese than the statement of their indifference to religion. Religion is still, as it has

[1] The following reply, made by Vice-Admiral Togo Commander-in-Chief of the Japanese fleet, to an Imperial message of commendation received after the second attempt to block the entrance to Port Arthur, is characteristically Shintō: —

"The warm message which Your Imperial Majesty condescended to grant us with regard to the second attempt to seal Port Arthur, has not only overwhelmed us with gratitude, but may also influence the patriotic *manes* of the departed heroes to hover long over the battle-field and give unseen protection to the Imperial forces." . . . [*Translated in the* JAPAN TIMES *of March 31st, 1904.*]

— Such thoughts and hopes about the brave dead might have been uttered by a Greek admiral after the battle of Salamis. The faith and courage which helped the Greeks to repel the Persian invasion were of precisely the same quality as that religious heroism which now helps the Japanese to challenge the power of Russia.

ever been, the very life of the people, — the motive
and the directing power of their every action : a religion of doing and suffering, a religion without cant
and hypocrisy. And the qualities especially developed by it are just those qualities which have startled
Russia, and may yet cause her many a painful surprise. She has discovered alarming force where she
imagined childish weakness ; she has encountered
heroism where she expected to find timidity and
helplessness.[1]

*
* *

For countless reasons this terrible war (of which
no man can yet see the end) is unspeakably to be
regretted ; and of these reasons not the least are
industrial. War must temporarily check all tendencies towards the development of that healthy
individualism without which no modern nation can
become prosperous and wealthy. Enterprise is
numbed, markets paralyzed, manufactures stopped.
Yet, in the extraordinary case of this extraordinary
people, it is possible that the social effects of the
contest will prove to some degree beneficial. Prior
to hostilities, there had been a visible tendency to

[1] The case of the Japanese officers and men on the transport *Kinshu Maru*,
sunk by the Russian warships on the 26th of last April, should have given the
enemy matter for reflection. Although allowed an hour's time for consideration,
the soldiers refused to surrender, and opened fire with their rifles on the battleships.
Then, before the *Kinshu Maru* was blown in two by a torpedo, a number of the
Japanese officers and men performed *barakiri*. . . . This striking display of the
fierce old feudal spirit suggests how dearly a Russian success would be bought.

the premature dissolution of institutions founded upon centuries of experience, — a serious likelihood of moral disintegration. That great changes must hereafter be made, — that the future well-being of the country requires them, — would seem to admit of no argument. But it is necessary that such changes be effected by degrees, — not with such inopportune haste as to imperil the moral constitution of the nation. A war for independence, — a war that obliges the race to stake its all upon the issue, — must bring about a tightening of the old social bonds, a strong quickening of the ancient sentiments of loyalty and duty, a reinforcement of conservatism. This will signify retrogression in some directions; but it will also mean invigoration in others. Before the Russian menace, the Soul of Yamato revives again. Out of the contest Japan will come, if successful, morally stronger than before; and a new sense of self-confidence, a new spirit of independence, might then reveal itself in the national attitude toward foreign policy and foreign pressure.

— There would be, of course, the danger of over-confidence. A people able to defeat Russian power on land and sea might be tempted to believe themselves equally able to cope with foreign capital upon their own territory; and every means would certainly be tried of persuading or bullying the government into some fatal compromise on the question of the right of foreigners to hold land. Efforts in this direction have been carried on persistently and systematically for years; and these efforts seem to have received some support from a class of Japanese politicians, apparently incapable of understanding what enormous tyranny a single privileged syndicate of foreign capital would be capable of exercising in such a country. It appears to me that any person comprehending, even in the vaguest way, the nature of money-power and the average conditions of life throughout Japan, must recognize the certainty that foreign capital, with right of land-tenure, would find means to control legislation, to control government, and to bring about a state of affairs that would result in the practical domination of the empire by alien interests. I cannot resist the conviction that when Japan yields to foreign industry the right to purchase land, she is lost beyond hope. The self-confidence that might tempt to such yielding, in view of immediate advantages, would be fatal. Japan has incomparably more to fear from English or American capital than from Russian battleships and bayonets. Behind her military capacity is the disciplined experience of a thousand years; behind her industrial and commercial power, the experience of half-a-century. But she has been fully warned; and if she chooses hereafter to invite her own ruin, it will not have been for lack of counsel, — since she had the wisest man in the world to advise her.[1]

To the reader of these pages, at least, the strength and the weakness of the new social organization — its great capacities for offensive or defensive action in military directions, and its comparative feebleness in other directions — should now be evident. All things considered, the marvel is that Japan should have been so well able to hold her own; and it was assuredly no common wisdom that guided her first unsteady efforts in new and perilous ways. Certainly her power to accomplish what she has accomplished was derived from her old religious and social training: she was able to keep strong because, under the new forms of rule and the new conditions of social activity, she could still maintain a great deal of the ancient discipline But even thus it was only by the firmest and shrewdest policy that she could avert disaster, — could prevent the disruption of her whole social structure under the weight of alien pressure. It was imperative that vast changes should be made, but equally imperative that they should not be of a character to endanger the foundations; and it was above all things necessary, while preparing for immediate necessities, to provide against future perils. Never before, perhaps, in the history of human civilization, did any rulers find themselves

[1] Herbert Spencer.

obliged to cope with problems so tremendous, so
complicated, and so inexorable. And of these problems the most inexorable remains to be solved. It
is furnished by the fact that although all the successes of Japan have been so far due to unselfish
collective action, sustained by the old Shintō ideals
of duty and obedience, her industrial future must
depend upon egoistic individual action of a totally
opposite kind!

* *

What then will become of the ancient morality?
— the ancient cult?

— In this moment the conditions are abnormal.
But it seems certain that there will be, under normal
conditions, a further gradual loosening of the old
family-bonds; and this would bring about a further
disintegration. By the testimony of the Japanese
themselves, such disintegration was spreading rapidly
among the upper and middle classes of the great
cities, prior to the present war. Among the people
of the agricultural districts, and even in the country
towns, the old ethical order of things has yet been
little affected. And there are other influences than
legislative change or social necessity which are working for disintegration. Old beliefs have been rudely
shaken by the introduction of larger knowledge: a
new generation is being taught, in twenty-seven
thousand primary schools, the rudiments of science
and the modern conception of the universe. The

Buddhist cosmology, with its fantastic pictures of Mount Meru, has become a nursery-tale; the old Chinese nature-philosophy finds believers only among the little educated, or the survivors of the feudal era; and the youngest schoolboy has learned that the constellations are neither gods nor Buddhas, but far-off groups of suns. No longer can popular fancy picture the Milky Way as the River of Heaven; the legend of the Weaving-Maiden, and her waiting lover, and the Bridge of Birds, is now told only to children; and the young fisherman, though steering, like his fathers, by the light of stars, no longer discerns in the northern sky the form of Mioken Bosatsu.

Yet it were easy to misinterpret the weakening of a certain class of old beliefs, or the visible tendency to social change. Under any circumstances a religion decays slowly; and the most conservative forms of religion are the last to yield to disintegration. It were a grave mistake to suppose that the ancestor-cult has yet been appreciably affected by exterior influences of any kind, or to imagine that it continues to exist merely by force of hallowed custom, and not because the majority still believe. No religion — and least of all the religion of the dead — could thus suddenly lose its hold upon the affections of the race that evolved it. Even in other directions the new scepticism is superficial: it has not spread downwards into the core of things. There is indeed

a growing class of young men with whom scepticism of a certain sort is the fashion, and scorn of the
past an affectation ; but even among these no word
of disrespect concerning the religion of the home is
ever heard.   Protests against the old obligations of
filial piety, complaints of the growing weight of the
family yoke, are sometimes uttered ; but the domestic cult is never spoken of lightly.   As for the communal and other public forms of Shintō, the vigour
of the old religion is sufficiently indicated by the
continually increasing number of temples.   In 1897
there were 191,962 Shintō temples ; in 1901 there
were 195,256.

It seems probable that such changes as must occur
in the near future will be social rather than religious ;
and there is little reason to believe that these changes
— however they may tend to weaken filial piety in
sundry directions — will seriously affect the ancestor-
cult itself.   The weight of the family-bond, aggra-
vated by the increasing difficulty and cost of life,
may be more and more lightened for the individual ; but no legislation can abolish the sentiment of duty to the dead.   When that sentiment
utterly fails, the heart of a nation will have ceased
to beat.   Belief in the old gods, as gods, may slowly
pass ; but Shintō may live on as the Religion of the
Fatherland, a religion of heroes and patriots ; and
the likelihood of such future modification is indicated
by the memorial character of many new temples.

— It has been much asserted of late years (chiefly because of the profound impression made by Mr. Percival Lowell's *Soul of the Far East*) that Japan is desperately in need of a Gospel of Individualism; and many pious persons assume that the conversion of the country to Christianity would suffice to produce the Individualism. This assumption has nothing to rest on except the old superstition that national customs and habits and modes of feeling, slowly shaped in the course of thousands of years, can be suddenly transformed by a mere act of faith. Those further dissolutions of the old order which would render possible, under normal conditions, a higher social energy, can be safely brought about through industrialism only, — through the working of necessities that enforce competitive enterprise and commercial expansion. A long peace will be required for such healthy transformation; and it is not impossible that an independent and progressive Japan would then consider questions of religious change from the standpoint of political expediency. Observation and study abroad may have unduly impressed Japanese statesmen with the half-truth so forcibly uttered by Michelet, — that " money has a religion," — that " capital is Protestant," — that the power and wealth and intellectual energy of the world belong to the races who cast off the yoke of Rome, and freed themselves from the creed of the Middle

Ages.[1] A Japanese statesman is said to have lately
declared that his countrymen were " rapidly drifting
towards Christianity " !   Newspaper reports of emi-
nent utterances are not often trustworthy ; but the
report in this case is probably accurate, and the
utterance intended to suggest possibilities.   Since
the declaration of the Anglo-Japanese alliance, there
has been a remarkable softening in the attitude of
safe conservatism which the government formerly
maintained toward Western religion. . . .   But as
for the question whether the Japanese nation will ever
adopt an alien creed under official encouragement, I
think that the sociological answer is evident.   Any
understanding of the fundamental structure of society
should make equally obvious the imprudence of attempting hasty transformations, and the impossibility
of effecting them.   For the present, at least, the
religious question in Japan is a question of social
integrity ; and any efforts to precipitate the natural
course of change can result only in provoking reaction
and disorder.   I believe that the time is far away at
which Japan can venture to abandon the policy of

[1] No inferences can be safely drawn from the apparent attitude of the government towards religious bodies in Japan.   Of late years the seeming policy has been
to encourage the less tolerant forms of Western religion.   In curious contrast to
this attitude is the non-toleration of Freemasonry.   Strictly speaking, Freemasonry
is not allowed in Japan — although, since the abolition of exterritoriality, the foreign
lodges at the open ports have been permitted (or rather, suffered) to exist upon certain
conditions.   A Japanese in Europe or America is free to become a Mason ; but he
cannot become a Mason in Japan, where the proceedings of all societies must remain
open to official surveillance.

caution that has served her so well. I believe that
the day on which she adopts a Western creed, her
immemorial dynasty is doomed; and I cannot help
fearing that whenever she yields to foreign capital
the right to hold so much as one rood of her soil,
she signs away her birthright beyond hope of re-
covery.

* *

With a few general remarks upon the religion of
the Far East, in its relation to Occidental aggressions, this attempt at interpretation may fitly con-
clude.

— All the societies of the Far East are founded,
like that of Japan, upon ancestor-worship. This
ancient religion, in various forms, represents their
moral experience; and it offers everywhere to the
introduction of Christianity, as now intolerantly
preached, obstacles of the most serious kind. Attacks upon it must seem, to those whose lives are
directed by it, the greatest of outrages and the most
unpardonable of crimes. A religion for which every
member of a community believes it his duty to die
at call, is a religion for which he will fight. His
patience with attacks upon it will depend upon the
degree of his intelligence and the nature of his
training. All the races of the Far East have not
the intelligence of the Japanese, nor have they been
equally well trained, under ages of military discipline, to adapt their conduct to circumstances. For

the Chinese peasant, in especial, attacks upon his
religion are intolerable.   His cult remains the most
precious of his possessions, and his supreme guide
in all matters of social right and wrong.   The East
has been tolerant of all creeds which do not assault
the foundations of its societies ; and if Western missions had been wise enough to leave those foundations alone, — to deal with the ancestor-cult as
Buddhism did, and to show the same spirit of
tolerance in other directions, — the introduction
of Christianity upon a very extensive scale should
have proved a matter of no difficulty.   That the
result would have been a Christianity differing considerably from Western Christianity is obvious, —
the structure of Far-Eastern society not admitting
of sudden transformations ; — but the essentials of
doctrine might have been widely propagated, without exciting social antagonism, much less race-hatred.
To-day it is probably impossible to undo what the
sterile labour of intolerance has already done.   The
hatred of Western religion in China and adjacent
countries is undoubtedly due to the needless and
implacable attacks which have been made upon the
ancestor-cult.   To demand of a Chinese or an
Annamese that he cast away or destroy his ancestral tablets is not less irrational and inhuman than
it would be to demand of an Englishman or a
Frenchman that he destroy his mother's tombstone in proof of his devotion to Christianity.

Nay, it is much more inhuman, — for the European attaches to the funeral monument no such idea of sacredness as that which attaches, in Eastern belief, to the simple tablet inscribed with the name of the dead parent. From old time these attacks upon the domestic faith of docile and peaceful communities have provoked massacres; and, if persisted in, they will continue to provoke massacres while the people have strength left to strike. How foreign religious aggression is answered by native religious aggression; and how Christian military power avenges the foreign victims with tenfold slaughter and strong robbery, need not here be recorded. It has not been in these years only that ancestor-worshipping peoples have been slaughtered, impoverished, or subjugated in revenge for the uprisings that missionary intolerance provokes. But while Western trade and commerce directly gain by these revenges, Western public opinion will suffer no discussion of the right of provocation or the justice of retaliation. The less tolerant religious bodies call it a wickedness even to raise the question of moral right; and against the impartial observer, who dares to lift his voice in protest, fanaticism turns as ferociously as if he were proved an enemy of the human race.

From the sociological point of view the whole missionary system, irrespective of sect and creed, represents the skirmishing-force of Western civilization in its general attack upon all civilizations of the

ancient type, — the first line in the forward movement of the strongest and most highly evolved
societies upon the weaker and less evolved. The
conscious work of these fighters is that of preachers
and teachers; their unconscious work is that of
sappers and destroyers. The subjugation of weak
races has been aided by their work to a degree
little imagined; and by no other conceivable means
could it have been accomplished so quickly and so
surely. For destruction they labour unknowingly,
like a force of nature. Yet Christianity does not
appreciably expand. They perish; and they really
lay down their lives, with more than the courage of
soldiers, not, as they hope, to assist the spread of
that doctrine which the East must still of necessity
refuse, but to help industrial enterprise and Occidental aggrandizement. The real and avowed object
of missions is defeated by persistent indifference to
sociological truths; and the martyrdoms and sacrifices are utilized by Christian nations for ends
essentially opposed to the spirit of Christianity.

Needless to say that the aggressions of race upon
race are fully in accord with the universal law of
struggle, — that perpetual struggle in which only the
more capable survive. Inferior races must become
subservient to higher races, or disappear before them;
and ancient types of civilization, too rigid for progress, must yield to the pressure of more efficient and

more complex civilizations. The law is pitiless and plain : its operations may be mercifully modified, but never prevented, by humane consideration.

Yet for no generous thinker can the ethical questions involved be thus easily settled. We are not justified in holding that the inevitable is morally ordained, — much less that, because the higher races happen to be on the winning side in the world-struggle, might can ever constitute right. Human progress has been achieved by denying the law of the stronger, — by battling against those impulses to crush the weak, to prey upon the helpless, which rule in the world of the brute, and are no less in accord with the natural order than are the courses of the stars. All virtues and restraints making civilization possible have been developed in the teeth of natural law. Those races which lead are the races who first learned that the highest power is acquired by the exercise of forbearance, and that liberty is best maintained by the protection of the weak, and by the strong repression of injustice. Unless we be ready to deny the whole of the moral experience thus gained, — unless we are willing to assert that the religion in which it has been expressed is only the creed of a particular civilization, and not a religion of humanity, — it were difficult to imagine any ethical justification for the aggressions made upon alien peoples in the name of Christianity and enlightenment. Certainly the results in China of such aggression have not been Christianity nor enlightenment, but revolts, massacres, detestable cruelties, — the destruction of cities, the devastation of provinces, the loss of tens of thousands of lives, the extortion of hundreds of millions of money. If all this be right, then might is might indeed; and our professed religion of humanity and justice is proved to be as exclusive as any primitive cult, and intended to regulate conduct only as between members of the same society.

But to the evolutionist, at least, the matter appears in a very different light. The plain teaching of sociology is that the higher races cannot with impunity cast aside their moral experience in dealing with feebler races, and that Western civilization will have to pay, sooner or later, the full penalty of its deeds of oppression. Nations that, while refusing to endure religious intolerance at home, steadily maintain religious intolerance abroad, must eventually lose those rights of intellectual freedom which cost so many centuries of atrocious struggle to win. Perhaps the period of the penalty is not very far away. With the return of all Europe to militant conditions, there has set in a vast ecclesiastical revival of which the menace to human liberty is unmistakable; the spirit of the Middle Ages threatens to prevail again; and anti-semitism has actually become a factor in the politics of three Continental powers. . . .

— It has been well said that no man can estimate the force of a religious conviction until he has tried to oppose it.   Probably no man can imagine the wicked side of convention upon the subject of missions until the masked batteries of its malevolence have been trained against him.   Yet the question of mission-policy cannot be answered either by secret slander or by public abuse of the person raising it. To-day it has become a question that concerns the peace of the world, the future of commerce, and the interests of civilization.   The integrity of China depends upon it; and the present war is not foreign to it.   Perhaps this book, in spite of many short-comings, will not fail to convince some thoughtful persons that the constitution of Far-Eastern society presents insuperable obstacles to the propaganda of Western religion, as hitherto conducted; that these obstacles now demand, more than at any previous epoch, the most careful and humane consideration; and that the further needless maintenance of an uncompromising attitude towards them can result in nothing but evil.   Whatever the religion of ancestors may have been thousands of years ago, to-day throughout the Far East it is the religion of family affection and duty; and by inhumanly ignoring this fact, Western zealots can scarcely fail to provoke a few more " Boxer " uprisings.   The real power to force upon the world a peril from China (now that the chance seems lost for Russia) should not be suffered to rest with those who demand religious tolerance for the purpose of preaching intolerance. Never will the East turn Christian while dogmatism requires the convert to deny his ancient obligation to the family, the community, and the government, — and further insists that he prove his zeal for an alien creed by destroying the tablets of his ancestors, and outraging the memory of those who gave him life.

Appendix

HERBERT SPENCER'S ADVICE TO JAPAN

SOME five years ago I was told by an American professor, then residing in Tōkyō, that after Herbert Spencer's death there would be published a letter of advice, which the philosopher had addressed to a Japanese statesman, concerning the policy by which the Empire might be able to preserve its independence. I was not able to obtain any further information; but I felt tolerably sure, remembering the statement regarding Japanese social disintegration in " First Principles " (§ 178), that the advice would prove to have been of the most conservative kind. As a matter of fact it was even more conservative than I had imagined.

Herbert Spencer died on the morning of December 8th, 1903 (while this book was in course of preparation); and the letter, addressed to Baron Kanéko Kentarō, under circumstances with which the public have already been made familiar, was published in the London *Times* of January 18th, 1904.

FAIRFIELD, PEWSEY, WILTS,
Aug. 26, 1892.

MY DEAR SIR, — Your proposal to send translations of my two letters [1] to Count Ito, the newly-appointed Prime Minister, is quite satisfactory. I very willingly give my assent.

Respecting the further questions you ask, let me, in the first place, answer generally that the Japanese policy should, I think, be that of *keeping Americans and Europeans as much as possible at arm's length.* In presence of the more powerful races your position is one of chronic danger, and you should take every precaution to give as little foothold as possible to foreigners.

[1] These letters have not as yet been made public.

481

It seems to me that the only forms of intercourse which you may with advantage permit are those which are indispensable for the exchange of commodities — importation and exportation of physical and mental products. No further privileges should be allowed to people of other races, and especially to people of the more powerful races, than is absolutely needful for the achievement of these ends. Apparently you are proposing by revision of the treaty with the Powers of Europe and America "to open the whole Empire to foreigners and foreign capital." I regret this as a fatal policy. If you wish to see what is likely to happen, study the history of India. Once let one of the more powerful races gain a *point d' appui* and there will inevitably in course of time grow up an aggressive policy which will lead to collisions with the Japanese ; these collisions will be represented as attacks by the Japanese which must be avenged, as the case may be ; a portion of territory will be seized and required to be made over as a foreign settlement ; and from this there will grow eventually subjugation of the entire Japanese Empire. I believe that you will have great difficulty in avoiding this fate in any case, but you will make the process easy if you allow of any privileges to foreigners beyond those which I have indicated.

In pursuance of the advice thus generally indicated, I should say, in answer to your first question, that there should be, not only a prohibition of foreign persons to hold property in land, but also a refusal to give them leases, and a permission only to reside as annual tenants.

To the second question I should say decidedly prohibit to foreigners the working of the mines owned or worked by Government. Here there would be obviously liable to arise grounds of difference between the Europeans or Americans who worked them and the Government, and these grounds of quarrel would be followed by invocations to the English or American Governments or other Powers to send forces to insist on whatever the European workers claimed, *for always the habit here and elsewhere among the civilized peoples is to believe what their agents or sellers abroad represent to them.*

In the third place, in pursuance of the policy I have indicated, you ought also to keep the coasting trade in your own hands and forbid foreigners to engage in it. This coasting trade is clearly not included in the requirement I have indicated as the sole one to be recognized — a requirement to facilitate exportation and importation of commodities. The distribution of commodities brought to Japan from other places may be properly left to the Japanese themselves, and should be denied to foreigners, for the reason that again the various transactions involved would become so many doors open to quarrels and resulting aggressions.

To your remaining question respecting the intermarriage of foreigners and Japanese, which you say is " now very much agitated among our scholars and politicians " and which you say is " one of the most difficult problems," my reply is that, as rationally answered, there is no difficulty at all. It should be positively forbidden. It is not at root a question of social philosophy. It is at root a question of biology. There is abundant proof, alike furnished by the intermarriages of human races and by the interbreeding of animals, that when the varieties mingled diverge beyond a certain slight degree *the result is inevitably a bad one* in the long run. I have myself been in the habit of looking at the evidence bearing on this matter for many years past, and my conviction is based on numerous facts derived from numerous sources. This conviction I have within the last half-hour verified, for I happen to be staying in the country with a gentleman who is well known and has had much experience respecting the interbreeding of cattle ; and he has just, on inquiry, fully confirmed my belief that when, say of the different varieties of sheep, there is an interbreeding of those which are widely unlike, the result, especially in the second generation, is a bad one — there arise an incalculable mixture of traits, and what may be called a chaotic constitution. And the same thing happens among human beings — the Eurasians in India, the half-breeds in America, show this. The physiological basis of this experience appears to be that any one variety of creature in course of many generations acquires a certain constitutional adaptation to its particular form of life, and every other variety similarly acquires its own special adaptation. The consequence is that, if you mix the constitution of two widely divergent varieties which have severally become adapted to widely divergent modes of life, you get a constitution which is adapted to the mode of life of neither — a constitution which will not work properly, because it is not fitted for any set of conditions whatever. By all means, therefore, peremptorily interdict marriages of Japanese with foreigners.

I have for the reasons indicated entirely approved of the regulations which have been established in America for restraining the Chinese immigration, and had I the power I would restrict them to the smallest possible amount, my reasons for this decision being that one of two things must happen. If the Chinese are allowed to settle extensively in America, they must either, if they remain unmixed, form a subject race standing in the position, if not of slaves, yet of a class approaching to slaves ; or if they mix they must form a bad hybrid. In either case, supposing the immigration to be large, immense social mischief must arise, and eventually social disorganization. The same thing will happen if there should be any considerable mixture of European or American races with the Japanese.

You see, therefore, that my advice is strongly conservative in all directions, and I end by saying as I began — *keep other races at arm's length as much as possible.*

I give this advice in confidence. I wish that it should not transpire publicly, at any rate during my life, for I do not desire to rouse the animosity of my fellow-countrymen.

      I am sincerely yours,   HERBERT SPENCER.

P.S. — Of course, when I say I wish this advice to be in confidence, I do not interdict the communication of it to Count Ito, but rather wish that he should have the opportunity of taking it into consideration.

How fairly Herbert Spencer understood the prejudices of his countrymen has been shown by the comments of the *Times* upon this letter, — comments chiefly characterized by that unreasoning quality of abuse with which the English conventional mind commonly resents the pain of a new idea opposed to immediate interests. Yet some knowledge of the real facts in the case should serve to convince even the *Times* that if Japan is able in this moment to fight for the cause of civilization in general, and for English interests in particular, it is precisely because the Japanese statesmen of a wiser generation maintained a sound conservative policy upon the very lines indicated in that letter — so unjustly called a proof of " colossal egotism."

Whether the advice itself directly served at any time to influence government policy, I do not know. But that it fully accorded with the national instinct of self-preservation, is shown by the history of that fierce opposition which the advocates of the abolition of extra-territoriality had to encounter, and by the nature of the precautionary legislation enacted in regard to those very matters dwelt upon in Herbert Spencer's letter. Though extra-territoriality has been (unavoidably, perhaps) abolished, foreign capital has not been left free to exploit the resources of the country ; and foreigners are not allowed to own land. Though marriages between Japanese and foreigners have never been forbidden,[1] they have never been encouraged, and can take place only under special legal restrictions. If foreigners could have acquired, through marriage, the right to hold Japanese real estate, a considerable amount of such estate would soon have passed into alien hands. But the law has wisely provided that the Japanese woman marrying a foreigner thereby becomes a foreigner, and that the children by such a marriage remain foreigners. On the other hand, any foreigner adopted by marriage into a Japanese family becomes a Japanese ; and the children in such event remain Japanese. But they also remain under certain disabilities : they are precluded from holding high offices of state ; and they cannot even become officers of the army or navy except by special permission. (This permission appears to have been accorded in one or two cases.) Finally, it is to be observed that Japan has kept her coasting-trade in her own hands.

On the whole, then, it may be said that Japanese policy followed, to a considerable extent, the course suggested in Herbert Spencer's letter of advice ; and it is much to be regretted, in my humble opinion, that the advice could not have been followed more closely. Could the philosopher have lived to hear of the recent Japanese victories, — the defeat of a powerful Russian fleet without the loss of a single Japanese vessel, and the rout of thirty thousand Russian troops on the Yalu, — I do not think that he would have changed his counsel by a hair's-breadth. Perhaps he would have commended,

[1] The number of families in Tōkyō representing such unions is said to be over one hundred.

so far as his humanitarian conscience permitted, the thoroughness
of the Japanese study of the new science of war : he might have
praised the high courage displayed, and the triumph of the ancient
discipline ; — his sympathies would have been on the side of the
country compelled to choose between the necessities of inviting a
protectorate or fighting Russia. But had he been questioned again
as to the policy of the future, in case of victory, he would probably
have reminded the questioner that military efficiency is a very different
thing from industrial power, and have vigorously repeated his warning.
Understanding the structure and the history of Japanese society, he
could clearly perceive the dangers of foreign contact, and the directions from which attempts to take advantage of the industrial weakness
of the country were likely to be made. . . . In another generation
Japan will be able, without peril, to abandon much of her conservatism ; but, for the time being, her conservatism is her salvation.

Bibliographical Notes

— In the preparation of this essay, I have been much indebted to the *Transactions of the Asiatic Society of Japan*, and especially to the following contributions : —

(On the Subject of Shintō)

"The Revival of Pure Shintō," by Sir Ernest Satow, — Appendix to Vol. III.

"The Shintō Temples of Isé," by Satow, — Vol. II.

"Ancient Japanese Rituals," by Satow, — Vols. VII and IX.

"Japanese Funeral Rites," by A. H. Lay, — Vol. XIX.

(On the Subject of Law and Custom)

"Notes on Land Tenure and Local Institutions in Old Japan," by Dr. D. B. Simmons. Edited by Professor J. H. Wigmore, — Vol. XIX.

"Materials for the Study of Private Law in Old Japan," by Professor J. H. Wigmore, — Vol. XX, Supplements 1, 2, 3, 5.

(On the Christian Episode of the Sixteenth and Seventeenth Centuries)

"The Church at Yamaguchi from 1550 to 1586," by Satow, — Vol. VII.

"Review of the Introduction of Christianity into China and Japan," by J. H. Gubbins, — Vol. VI.

"Historical Notes on Nagasaki," by W. A. Wooley, — Vol. IX.

"The Arima Rebellion," by Dr. Geertz, — Vol. IX.

(ON JAPANESE HISTORY AND SOCIOLOGY)

" Early Japanese History," by W. G. Aston, — Vol. XVI.
" The Feudal System of Japan under the Tokugawa Shōguns,"
by J. H. Gubbins, — Vol. XV.

— The extracts quoted from " The Legacy of Iyéyasu " have
been taken from the translation made by J. F. Lowder.

— I regret not having been able, in preparing this essay, to avail
myself of the very remarkable " History of Japan during the Century
of Early Foreign Intercourse (1542–1651)," — by James Murdoch
and Isoh Yamagata, — which was published at Kobé last winter.
This important work contains much documentary material never
before printed, and throws new light upon the religious history of
the period. The authors are inclined to believe that, allowing for
numerous apostasies, the total number of Christians in Japan at no
time much exceeded 300,000 ; and the reasons given for this opinion,
if not conclusive, are at least very strong. Perhaps the most interesting chapters are those dealing with the Machiavellian policy of
Hideyoshi in his attitude to the foreign religion and its preachers, but
there are few dull pages in the book. Help to a correct understanding of the history of the time is furnished by an excellent set of maps,
showing the distribution of the great fiefs and the political partition
of the country before and after the establishment of the Tokugawa
Shōgunate. Not the least merit of the work is its absolute freedom
from religious bias of any sort.

INDEX

Ability, slight opportunity for, to rise, 410-411.

Adams, Will, 254, 313; interviewed by Ieyasu, 314-316, favoured by the Emperor, 316-317; quoted concerning Hidéyori's intrigues and fate, 322-323.

Adoption, custom of, in patriarchal family, 59, 64-65; marriage signified merely, 64; modern practices regarding, 386.

Adultery, enactments of Ieyasu regarding, 345-346.

Affection, limitations placed on, 69 ff.

Age of the Gods, period called the, 259.

Agnosticism, Buddhism is not. 213, 220.

Agriculture, gods of, 126, 153-154; no degradation attached to pursuit of, 245.

Akindo, the commercial class, 246-247. *See* Commerce.

Alcestis, the Japanese woman might be compared to, 366.

Ancestors, imperial, worship of the, 108-123, 279-280.

Ancestor-worship, introduction to religion of, 21-32; the real religion of Japan, 21; summary of the three forms of, 21-22; the family-cult of, 21-22, 25-26; characteristics of earliest, 24 ff.; stability of, in Japan for two thousand years, 32; summary of beliefs surviving from, 31; three stages of, 33-34; evolution of permanent form from funeral-rites, 34-51; characteristics of religion of, to-day, 51-53; bearing of, on family-organization, 55 ff.; marriage under the religion of, 107 ff.; four classes of, to-day, 123-124; accommodation of Buddhism to, 183-184; toleration of ancient European, by Roman Catholicism, 191; Buddhist theory of rebirths reconciled to, 195 n.; Confucian system founded on, 177-178, 292; needless attacks on, account for

smallness of results of modern missions, 339, 473-475; protection of, by modern laws, 386-387; obstacles presented to Christianity by, 473-475.

Ancient Japanese Rituals, 43 n. *See* Satow.

Animals, absence of cruelty to, 12-13; kindness to, taught by Buddhism, 196-197.

Animism, development of, 131-132.

Antigoné, comparison of the Japanese woman to, 366.

Apes, images of Kōshin's symbolic, 200.

Apprentices, obligation of, to avenge masters, 293; past and present position of, 406.

Architecture, displayed in Buddhist temples, 199-200.

Arima, lord of Shimabara, 324, 325.

Army, birth of modern, 376; pay of officers in, 412.

Art, knowledge of Japanese religion necessary to understanding of, 2-3; introduction by Buddhism, 197-198, 204, 459; forms of, in Buddhist temples, 198-199; expulsion of Jesuits, a fortunate thing for, 341-342; causes which tended to production of a multitude of objects of, 356; effect of modern industrial conditions on, 451.

Artizans, gods of, 124-125; clans of, 235; position of, under quasi-feudal system, 245-246; organizations of, *see* Guilds.

Arts, developed in Japan under Buddhist teaching, 188; progress of the, under Ieyasu, 279.

Asada, Lieutenant, suicide of widow of, 289.

Asceticism, Shintō, 149-150.

Ashikaga shōgunate, 271-273. *See under* Ieyasu.

Aston, W.G., translation of the *Nihongi* by, cited, 38, 39, 112 n., 151 n., 164 n., 232 n., 234 n.; *Early Japanese*

History by, cited, 259 n.

Bambêtsu, " Foreign Branch," the mass of people, 235-236.
Banishment, punishment by, 96-99.
Banner-supporters (*hatamoto*), 243.
Bateren, Roman Catholic priests, 311 n.
Batō-Kwannon, images of, 200.
Behaviour, sumptuary regulations as to, 173-174 ; proclamation of Shōtoku Taishi regarding, 359-360.
Births, regulations as to presents on occasions of, 165 ; registration of, by Buddhist priests, 203-204.
Black, an Englishman, as a Japanese story-teller, 10-11.
Bon-odori, dances of the festival of the dead, 202.
Boundaries, gods of, 130.
Bow, etiquette of the, 174.
Boys, conduct of, regulated by the community, 89-90 ; proverb regarding mischievousness of, 421.
Buddhism, Japanese name for (Butsudō), 21 ; mortuary tablets of, 42-43, 201 ; the dead according to, and Shintō, 47-48 ; entry of, into Japan, 183-184 ; disestablishment of (1871), 107-109 ; charm of, to Western thinkers, 209-210 ; summary of teachings of, under Emperor Temmu, 239 ; obstacles to establishment of religious hierarchy by, 251 ; military development of, 269-270 ; violent end to militant, 275-276 ; Jesuitism mistaken for a new kind of, 332-334 ; no essential of Shintō weakened by, 379-380.
Bukê, the military class, 241.
Butsudan, household-shrine, 42.
Butsudō, " The Way of the Buddha," 21.

Capital, danger to Japan from foreign, 465-466, 473.
Carpenters, religious rites preformed by, 125 ; organizations of, 403-404.
Castes, division of society into, 236.
Cauldron and saucepan, god of the, 129.
Celibacy, forbidden by early religion, 58 ; condemned by code of Ieyasu, 349.

Charms, to protect houses, 147 n.
Chastisement, punishment by, 95-96, 421.
Chiara, Giuseppe, 327 n.
Chieftainship, hereditary, 235.
China, date of introduction of spirit-tablet from, 24 ; religion of filial piety in, 49-50 ; belief as to the Demon-Gate imported from, 130 ; penal codes imported from, 176 ; arts and learning of, taught by Buddhism, 201 ; civilization of, brought to Japan by Buddhism, 203 ; *harakiri* perhaps introduced from, 286 ; Jesuit policy in, 331 ; cause for hatred of Western religion in, 474 ; integrity of, depends on mission-policy, 479-480.
Chōri. pariahs, 247-250.
Chōskŭ, clan of, 367, 368, 372, 374.
" Chronicles of Nihon," see *Nihongi*.
Christianity, assumption that individualism would be produced by, 471 ; obstacles to, presented by religion of ancestor-worship, 479-481. *See* Jesuits *and* Missions.
Chŭ-U, the condition of, 191 n.
Circle of Perpetual Hunger for wicked ghosts, 191.
Clan, cult of the, 81-83.
Clans, number of; in ancient Japan, 83 ; three great classes of, 235-236 ; early society an aggregation of, 236-237, 252-253 ; wars between the military, for supremacy, 267 ff. ; misery one result of break-up of, 447-449.
Cleanliness exacted by Shintō, 145-146.
Coffins, size regulated by law, 179.
Colour-prints, production of, 357.
Commerce, contempt for, 246 ; Portuguese, a help to Jesuit missionary work, 334-335 ; rise to power, 446 ; dangers resulting from the rise of, 447-452.
Communism not a modern growth, 255.
Competition, undesirability of, 414-416 ; Government aid to national industrial, 451-452.
Concubines, under patriarchal system, 58, 68-69, 74 ; remarks of Ieyasu regarding, 68, 348.
Confucianism, influence of, in Japan, 187-188, 292 ff.

Conscience, doctrine of, admitted by Buddhism, 196.

Coulanges, Fustel de, 52, 264, 449; quoted, 27, 67.

Courtesy, legal regulation of, 173-176.

Craft-gods, 124, 153-154.

Crafts, effect of Buddhism on, 188; guilds connected with, 246, 252, 402-405.

Crucifixion of Christians at Nagasaki, 307.

Cruelty to animals, apparent absence of, 12-13; punishment of, after death, 197.

Daimyō, lords of provinces, 242; conversion of, to Jesuitism, 304; Jesuits work with aid of, 304, 306, 308, 339; protection of peasantry against, 396.

Dai Nihon-Shi, compilation of, 370.

Dances, sacred, 142-143; of the festival of the dead, 202.

Dancing, Japanese, 202 n. 2.

Dan-no-ura, sea-fight of, 267.

Daughter, gradation of terms signifying, 171.

Daughters, sale of, 72, 75 n.

Daughters-in-law, custom as to, 64-65.

Dead, early conceptions of fate of, 25-28; rites in honour of, 34-46; poems in praise of, 35; Buddhist doctrine of, 47; effects of Buddhism on worship of, 191-192.

Death, penalty of, inflicted for slight offences, 178-179; matters relating to, regulated by law, 179.

Debtors, reduction of, to slavery, 234.

Deities, punishments by tutelar, 102-105; lesser Shintō, 108. See Gods *and* Ujigami.

Demeanour, regulation of, 173-176; cultivation of, as an art, 359-361.

Demon-Gate, the, 130.

Dependants, under the patriarchal system, 76-78, 231-234; conservative attitude of, 400; position of employés in commercial houses, 406; position of maid-servants, 407-409.

Deportment, code of, 173.

Discipline, strength of, in Old Japan, 159-182.

Divination, systems of, 150-152; not used in warfare, 152.

Divorce, in ancient family system, 58, 69-70, 73, 75; the new laws about, 386.

Dominicans in Japan, 307; reckless zeal of, 338.

Drama, introduction by Buddhism, 204; the age of popular, 357; incidents of real tragedy reproduced in, 290-291.

Dress, restrictions as to, 166-168.

Dutch, assistance of, in putting down Shimabara Revolt, 326-327; effect on status of, of Shimabara Revolt, 329-330.

Ear-Monument, the, 277.

Education, effect of Buddhism on, 202-203; introduction of modern system of, 376; of the State, 419-441; the sustaining of, by personal sacrifices, 435-436; of students abroad, 439-441.

Emma (Yama), judge of the dead, 199.

Emperor, application of term, to early rulers, incorrect, 237.

Enactments of the *Kami*, 91-94.

Éta, people, the, 98, 247-250.

Etiquette, cultivation of, in Tokugawa period, 359-361.

Evolution, Buddhism a theory of, 210.

Execution, account of an early, 177-178.

Exports, rise in value of, 451.

Expression, etiquette of, 173.

Factory-life, horrors of modern, 452.

Families of the nobility, number of, 241.

Family, definition of Japanese term, 22; basis of the ancient, 55-57; obligation to perpetuate the, 58-59; constitution of the patriarchal, 60-79.

Farmers, the rank of, 244-245; secured against undue oppression, 396-397. See Agriculture.

Father, gradation of terms signifying, 171.

Feast-days, Shintō, 103, 137.

Fencing, Japanese, an example of antipodal action, 7-8.

Festival of the dead, dances of the, 202.

Festival-processions, Shintō, 103.
Festivals of the Ujigami, 84, 137, 140-142; laws as to presents at boys', 165; *Shin-Shō-Sai*, 245; temple, 84, 459.
Feudalism, Japanese so-called, 230-238, 253.
Flower-arrangement, art of, 358-359.
Flower-daughter, the, 64.
Food, the use by ghosts of, 29-30; offerings of, to the dead, 29-30, 45; offerings of, to the gods, 53 n., 138, 140, 141; for the dead might not be eaten by children, 51 n.; laws as to, at weddings and funerals, 165; offerings of, to Pretas, 191; decree forbidding use of flesh for, 196; Buddhist offerings of, 201; recent increase in price of, 412 n.
"Forty-seven Rōnin," story of the, 295-296; tombs of the, 297 n.
Four Deva Kings, the, 260; temple of, 200.
Franciscans in Japan, 307 ff.
Freedmen, class of, 233, 234-235.
Freemasonry in Japan, 472 n.
Fujiwara clan, rise of the, 260-261; duration of rule of, 260, 266, 281; final degeneration of, 266-267.
Funeral-rites, ancient, 34-46.
Funerals, laws as to food at, 165; laws governing, 179.

Gardening, first development of, under Buddhism, 188; modern, 404.
Gardens, holiness of, 154.
Ghost-house, 36, 56; transformation of, into Shintō temples, 62.
Ghosts, ancestor-worship coëval with belief in, 24; identified in early beliefs with gods, 25, 46-48, 55.
Ghost-ships, Buddhist, 202.
Girl-priestesses in Shintō temples, 142-143.
Girls in service, position of, 407-409.
Gō, definition of, 64 n.
Goblins, admitted to exist by Buddhism, 190-191.
Go-Daigo, Mikado, revolt of, against Hojō, 270; later vicissitudes of, 270-271.
Gods, no early difference between ghosts and, 25, 55; development of

distinctions between greater and lesser, 25-26; early conceptions of, compared with Greek and Roman, 27-28; the dead and, 46-48; the minor, 108; all Japanese considered as, in one sense, 118; of crookedness, 118-119; of crafts and callings, 118-119; number of Shintō, worshipped, 127-128; of the house, 130-131; the great number of, 133-134; of industry, 153-154; identity of Shintō and Buddhist evil, 190-191.
God-shelves, 124; daily prayers before, 134-136; religious charms on, 147 n.
Go-Kaméyama, Emperor, 272.
Go-Komatsu, Emperor, 272.
Gōshi, yeomanry, 243.
Go-Toba, Emperor, works at sword-making, 245.
Go-Tsuchi-mikado, Emperor, 273.
Government, identity of, with religion, 90-91.
Graves, legal dimensions of, 179; white lanterns at, 202.
Greeks, parallels drawn between Japanese and, 15-16, 27-28, 34, 36, 57, 59, 65, 67, 70, 78, 89, 99, 148, 169, 202 n., 229, 264, 443-444, 446.
Guilds, 246, 252; religious organization of, 124-125; modern workings of, 402-403.

Hachiman, the war god, 83; acknowledgment of, in Buddhism, 190.
Hades, development of belief in, 25.
Hair, class indicated by method of wearing, 233.
Harakiri, custom of, 285-286; instance of, in Russian war, 464.
Harmony, Japanese sense of, in tints and colors, 8.
Heavenly sovereigns, worship of the, 108-109; maintained through years of revolt, 279-280.
Heimin, "common folk," 247.
Hell, according to Buddhism, 195.
Hidétada, son of Ieyasu, 321-322.
Hidéyoshi, career of, 276-277; attitude of, toward Jesuits, 306-307.
Hinin, a wandering pariah, 98; "not-human-beings," 250.
Hirata, great Shintō commentator, 27, 369; quoted, 47, 49, 56, 111, 116, 117,

119, 120-121, 122, 134-135, 145, 161;
banishment and death of, 372.
History, scientific knowledge of Japa-
nese, impossible, 1; legendary,
259-260; beginning of authentic, 260.
Hitogaki, the " human hedge," 34.
Hitogata, " mankind-shapes," 147-148.
Hitotsubashi, Shōgun, 374.
Hiyei-san, monastery buildings burnt
at, 275.
Hizen, clan of, 372.
Hōjō, supremacy of the, 268; defeat of
and extinction, 270.
Home, gods of the, 129-130.
Honesty, Japanese, 13.
Hongwanji, Shin sect of, 275.
Hōryūji, the temple called, 200.
House, building of, a religious act, 125,
130-131; gods of the, 129.
Houses, size of, prescribed by law,
164, 165, 166; of prostitution, enact-
ment of Ieyasu regarding, 347;
operation of labour-unions when
building, 403-404.
Husband, seven terms for, 171.
Husbands, position of adopted, 64-65.
Huxley, T.H., quoted concerning in-
dustrial reform, 452-453.

" I," gradations of the pronoun, 171.
Ibuku Mogusa, extract from, 305.
Ihai, " soul-commemoration," Buddhist
mortuary tablets, 42, 201.
Images, Buddhist, 459; setting up of,
200-201.
Imperial ancestors, worship of the,
108-109; duration of, 279-280.
Individual, obligations of the, under
patriarchal system, 88-99; relation
of, to the Ujigami, 120-121; freedom
of, did not exist, 158, 253-254; modern recognition of, 376; now free
in theory, in practice like his forefathers, 384-387, 391-392; Government official authority over the,
409-416.
Individualism, assumption that Christianity would produce, 471.
Industry, developed in Japan under
Buddhist teachings, 188; development of, under Ieyasu, 279.
Industry, gods of, 124-125, 153-154.
Irregularity, the aesthetic value of, 8.

Isé, shrines of, 122,123-124; every Japanese expected to visit, 123-124;
worship at shrines of, 138-139.
Ishijima, suicide of wife of, 290.
Isolation, causes for policy of, 329.
Ito, Marquis, policy of, 390.
Iyémochi, Shōgun, 374.
Ieyasu, Tokugawa, apotheosis of, 127;
enactment of, concerning rudeness,
175; powers of daimyō restricted
by, 242 ; Will Adams created a samurai by, 254; sketch of career of,
277-278; decree of, concerning suicide, 285; decree concerning code
of vengeance, 293; persecution of
Christians by, 307, 308, 320-321; in-
terviews with Will Adams,314-315;
castle of Ōsaka stormed and burnt
by, 322; Legacy of, 68, 319, 345-351,
360.
Izanagi, the legend concerning, 40, 112-
117.
Izumo, farming forbidden to samurai
in, 244-245.
Izumo temple, the, 122; worship at,
138, 139, 142-143.

Jesuitism, effect of, on Japan, 328;
causes of early success of, 330-337;
policy of, in China, 331, 337; inabil-
ity of, to adapt itself to Japanese
social conditions, 341.
Jesuits, arrival of, in Japan, 304;
favoured by Nobunaga, 304-305;
persecutions of, 304-305, 307-308;
partial expulsion of, 321; revolt of
peasantry managed by, 324-325;
final crushing of, 327.
Jigai, method of suicide for women, 287.
Jimmu, Emperor, 259; offerings at
tomb of, 37.
Jingō, Emperor, legend of Korean
conquest by, 259.
Jinrikisha-men, code of, 401-402.
Jitō, Empress, edict of, concerning
slavery, 234 n.
Jizō, playmate of infant ghosts, 199;
first production of icons of, 200.
Joyousness of existence, Japanese, 12-
13.
Junshi, voluntary self-sacrifice, 39-40;
decree of Ieyasu puts stop to,
285-286.

Kami, "gods," 27; significance of, 46-47; devot' ᠇ to, the first of duties according to Ieyasu, 350.

Kannushi, office of, 138-140.

Karma, metaphysics of, 220, 221, 222, 224.

Kasuga, the deity of, 83.

Kataki-uchi, custom of, 294-295.

Kiyomasa, Kato, apotheosis of, 127.

Kōbêtsu, imperial families, 235.

Kōbōdaishi, 185.

Ko-ji-ki, "Record of Ancient Matters," 110-111, 126, 131; extracts from, 112-114.

Korea, Buddhism brought into Japan from (552 A.D.), 184; Hidêyoshi's war against, 277.

Kôshin, protector of highways, 200.

Kôtoku, Emperor, 39, 265; edict of, concerning slaves, 232 n.

Ko-uji, "lesser families," 60, 230.

Kublai Khan, invasion by, 269.

Kugê, noble families, 241.

Kūkai, founder of Shingon sect, 185.

Kumi-enactments of, 91-92.

Kumi-system, the, 91-94, 168-169.

Kwambaku, "regent," office of the, established, 262.

Kwannon, Goddess of Mercy, 199.

La Cité Antique, de Coulanges', cited, 27, 34, 67, 443, 449.

Landscape-gardeners, union of the, 404-405.

Language, impossibility of mastering, by adult Occidental, 9; conventional organization of, 170-172; rules governing use of, 171-172.

Law, method and manner of administration, 351-353.

Laws, sumptuary, 164-180.

Laws of Ieyasu, the, 278.

Laws of Shôtoku Taishi, 344-345.

Legacy of Ieyasu, 68, 319, 345-351, 360.

Libraries under thê Tokugawa rêgime, 357, 370.

Literature, qualifications essential for an understanding of Japanese, 2-3; introduction of Chinese, 187-188; introduction or development by Buddhism, 204; under the patronage of Ieyasu, 279; development of, in Tokugawa period, 357; the party of, 370-372, 375-376.

Mabuchi, Shintō commentator, 159-160, 260, 369.

Maid-servants, position of, 407-409.

Manners, laws as to, 173-176.

Marriage, obligatory in ancient Japan, 58; in patriarchal family, 58-60, 64-67; signified adoption only, 64; a chief duty of filial piety, 65; ceremony of, 65-67; of servants, 77-78; modern innovations in, 385-386; service by girls merely a preparation for, 407-408.

Masashigê, Kusunoki, 50.

Massacre of Shimabara, 325-327.

Massacres, of priests by Nobunaga, 251; caused by Christian attacks on domestic faiths, 475, 479.

Matsuri-goto, "matters of worship," 32.

Matsuri, temple-festivals, 84.

Meat, forbidden for food, 196-197; forbidden as offerings by Buddhism, 201.

Merchants, place of, in social ranking, 246; modern rise of, to power, 446.

Metempsychosis, no doctrine of, in Shintō, 55 ff., 189-190.

Mikado, God of the Living, 122-125; usurpation of powers of, 260-266.

Miko, girl-priestesses, 142-143.

Mimidzuka, "Ear-monument," 277.

Minamoto, regency of the, 267-268.

Mionoseki, Éta settlement at, 249.

Miracle-plays performed by Jesuits, 334.

Missions, Christian, causes of small results of modern, 339, 473-476; consideration of work of foreign 476-478; importance of policy of, in Far East, 479-480. *See* Jesuits.

Mitama-San-no-tana, "shelf of the august spirits," 42.

Mitama-shiro, "spirit-substitutes," 42.

Mitamaya, "august-spirit-dwelling," 42.

Mitsukuni, Prince of Mito, 370.

Miya, "august house," 36, 42.

Money, first appearance of, 447.

Monism, higher Buddhism a species of, 210, 220-222.

Mother, nine terms signifying, 171.

Motowori, Shintō commentator, 368.

Mourning-houses, 36; Shintō temples evolve from, 41-42.

Mythology, of the reigning house, 119; summary of the Japanese, 115-116.

Nakatomi, noble family of, 241.
Nature, controlled by ghosts of ancestors, according to Shintō, 106; Buddhist interpretation of, 192-194.
Nihongi, "Chronicles of Nihon," 110, 111, 115-116, 126; cited, 38-39, 112 n., 164 n., 196 n., 232 n., 234 n., 360 n.
Nirvâna, not preached to common Japanese people, 189, 194-195.
Nobility, origin of the, 241-242. *See* Daimyō.
Nobunaga, Oda, massacres of priests by, 251; career of, 274-276; Jesuits favored by, 304-305.

Obedience, rules of, 48-49, 63, 157, (*see* Filial Piety); modern reversion to law of, 63, 377-378; of individual to the community, 89-99.
Offerings, to the dead, 37; meat forbidden as, 201.
Officers, army pay of, 412.
O-harai, ceremony of purification, 144-147.
Oho - kuni - nushi - no - Kami, 120, .122; Rough and Gentle Spirits of, 126.
Ōjin, Emperor, 83; Korean immigration in reign of, 260.
Ōsaka, Temple of the Four Deva Kings at, 200; military headquarters of the Shin sect at, 275; Ieyasu storms castle of, 322.
Ostracism, the punishment by, 95-96; student, 423-424.
Ō-uji, "great families," 60-62, 252.
Outcasts, the class of, 98, 247, 250.
Outlines of the Mahayana Philosophy, Kuroda's, 214-215, 222.

Painting, effect of Buddhism on, 188; examples of, in temples, 198-199.
Panama railroad, debt of, to religion of filial piety, 50.
Papacy, interference of, in Jesuit missionary system, 337-338.
Parents, rights of, in patriarchal system, 70-72.
Pariahs, class of, 98, 247-250.

Parliament, convocation of first, 377.
Peasants, revolt of, 324-325; security of, against oppression, 395-396; in the quasi-feudal system, 244-245. *See* Farmers.
Perry, Commodore, advent of, 374.
Poems in praise of the dead, 35.
Poetry, contests in, during Tokugawa period, 358.
Politeness as an art, 359-361.
Politics, modern Japanese, 389.
Pollution, death regarded as, 40-41.
Polygyny, in ancient society, 67-69.
Population, alien elements in, 16-17.
Porcelains, Japanese, 9, 356-357.
Poverty, resulting from modern industrial revolution, 446-451.
Prayer, prescribed by Hirata, 134; daily, 134-137.
Presents, sumptuary laws concerning, 165, 168.
Pretas, wicked ghosts, 191.
Priests, Shintō, office and powers of, 86-87, 101-105, 139-140; Buddhist, as teachers, 203-204; ranked with the samurai, 247; massacres of, in the sixteenth century, 251; Buddhist, as warriors, 269, 275-276. *See* Jesuits.
Privacy, lack of, in Japan ancient and modern, 100.
Professions, under divine patronage, 153-154.
Pronouns, rules as to use of, 171.
Property, laws of succession to, in Old Japan, 72-73.
Psychology, difference between Eastern and Western, 9.
Punishment of school-children, 421-422.
Punishment, severity of, under ancient system, 94-95, 176-177; by communities, 94-99; by tutelar deities, 102-105; laws as to, 175-177.
Purification, ceremonies of, 144-145; by ascetic practices, 148-150.

Rebirth, doctrine of, inconsistent with early Japanese beliefs, 55; the Buddhist idea of, and ancestor-worship, 193 n.
Reform, agitation for industrial, 452-454.
Regency, growth of the, 262-264; usurpation of power by the, 264-267.

Registrars, Buddhist priests become public, 203-204.

Relationship, gradation of nouns indicating, 171.

Religion, summary of three forms of Shintō, 21-22; of final piety, 48-51, 57, 65, 188, 459; the basis of organization of patriarchal family, 57, 64; marriage a rite of, 65-67; identity of government with, 100, 101; metaphysics of Buddhist, 207-228; origin in, of customs of the vendetta, 295; tolerance of, by Ieyasu (except Roman Catholicism), 349-350; the life of the Japanese people, 463-464; obstacles to propagation of the Western, in the Far East, 479. *See* Ancestor-worship *and* Missions.

Responsibility from above downward, 395-400.

" Review of the Introduction of Christianty into China and Japan," quoted from, 305.

Revolution, modern industrial, 445-449; dangers of a social, 448-451.

Rice-pot, goddess of the, 130.

Riddle of the Universe, Haeckel's cited, 221.

Roads, under the protection of Buddhist deities, 130.

Romans, ancient, parallels between Japanese and, 27, 29, 34, 57, 65, 67, 70, 78, 99, 148, 169, 229, 234, 264, 443, 444, 446.

Rudeness, Japanese definition of, 175.

Russia, the war with, 462-463.

Ryōbu-Shintō, establishment of; 185-186.

Sacrifices, history of all religious, traceable to offerings to ghosts, 30; ancient funeral, 37-38; origin of human, 284; of one's family, 290-291. *See* Junshi.

Samurai, class of the, 243, 251; obligation of, to perform *harakiri*, 287; suppression of, 376.

Saris, Captain, account by, of an execution, 177-178; quoted, 318.

Satow, Sir Earnest, quoted, 43 n., 49, 68, 126 n., 141, 142, 160-161, 312 n., 333.

Satsuma, clan of the, 367, 372.

Scarecrows, god of, 130, 135, 153.

Scholarship, advance of, in Tokugawa period, 369-370.

School, training of children in, 421-425.

Schools, connected with Buddhist temples, 203; Government, 424-425.

Sculpture, developed in Japan under Buddhist teachings, 188; displayed in roadside images, 200, 459.

Sekigahara, battle of, 278.

Self-control, legal enforcement of, 173-174.

Seppuku, Chinese term for *harakiri*, 287.

Servants, in Old Japan, 76-78; conservative attitude of, 400; position of maid, 407-408. *See* Apprentices *and* Dependants.

"Shadow-Shōgun," the, 268; deposition of, 267.

Shelf of the august spirits, 42.

Shimabara Revolt, the, 324-325.

Shimonoséki, Bombardment of, 374.

Shin, sect of, defeated by Nobunaga, 275-276.

Shinbétsu, "divine branch" of families, 235.

Shin-Shō-Sai, the Ninth Festival, 245.

Shintō, signification, 21; forms of worship, 21-22; the morals of, 100-101; relation to Japanese mythology to, summarized, 115-134; origin of gods of the house in, 129-130; greater gods of, acknowledged by Buddhism, 190; restoration of, 374; no essential of Buddhism weakened by, 379-380. *See* Ancestor-worship.

Shōgun, authority of the, 241, 251-252; significance of term, 267; extention of power of the, 267-268.

Shōgunate, beginning of the history of, 267; abolition of the, 374.

Shōrei-Hikki, "Record of Ceremonies," 66.

Shōryōbuné, "ghost-ships," 202.

Shrines, worship at, 121, 123, 138-139.

Sickness, charms against, 147-148.

Sisters of Charity, comparison of Japanese women to, 366.

Smile, rules and regulations about the, 173-174.

Socialism, not a modern growth, 255.

Societies, secret, 472 n.

Society, organization of Old Japanese, 229-258.

Sociology, difficulties in studing Japanese, 1-2.

INDEX

Soga brothers, the, apotheosis of, 127.

Sohodo-no-kami, god of scarecrows, 130, 135, 153.

Son, eleven graded terms signifying, 171.

Sons-in-law, significant motto concerning, 64 ; customs as to, 64-65.

Speech, non-existence of freedom of, 170 ; regulations of forms of, 171-173.

Spirits, Rough and Gentle, 126.

Story-teller, an Englishman who is a professional Japanese, 10-11.

Strangulation, suicide by, 286.

Student-revolts, significance and results of, 398-399.

Students, private means furnished for education of, 435-436 ; education of abroad, 437-438. *See* Education.

Subsidies, Government, to industries, 451.

Succession laws, in Old Japan, 72-73.

Sugiwara-no-Michizane, spirit of, 127.

Suicide, by the sword, 39-40 ; customs as to, 286-290 ; modern instances of female, 289 ; instances of, in Russian war, 464 n. *See* Harakiri *and* Junshi.

Suikō, Empress, 260, 261.

Suinin, Emperor, abolishes the "human hedge," 38.

Sun, daily greeting to the, 135-136.

Sun-goddess, worship of, 109-110, 116-117; acknowledged by Buddhism; 190 ; offerings of first fruits to, by Emperor, 245 n.

Surgeons, efficiency of Japanese, 441.

Sword-making, most sacred of crafts, 125, 154, 245-246.

Swords, wearing of, prohibited, 376.

Tables, mortuary, 42-43 ; Buddhist mortuary (*ihai*), 201.

Taira, rise and fall of the, 266-267.

Taishi, Shōtoku, proclamation of, regarding politeness, 359-360.

Takatoki, sacrifical suicide by the sword originated by, 39.

Takayama, a Japanese Jesuit, 321.

Take-no-uji-no-Sukuné, apotheosis of, 127.

Tales of Old Japan, Mitford's, 247, 295.

Tattooing of slaves, 232.

Tea-ceremony, in Tokugawa period, 358-359.

Teachers, Buddhist priests as, 202-203 ; duties to, same as to fathers, 294 ; salaries of, 412 ; relation of, to pupils, 422 ; transformation stages in attitude of, pupils toward, 431-433.

Temmu, Emperor, decree of, forbidding use of meat, 196 ; reorganization of castes by, 236 ; reign of, 237.

Temple of the Four Deva Kings at Ōsaka, 200.

Temples, Shintō, evolved from mourning-houses, 41 ; Shintō parish dedicated to Uji-gods (Ujigami), 82-84 ; Shintō, of the first grade, 121 ; Shintō, classification of, 123 ; forms of art in Buddhist, 198-199 ; notable examples of, 200 ; schools connected with, 203 ; Buddhist, burned by Jesuits, 306, 308; Shintō; in Formosa, 388 ; number of Shintō, at present, 470 ; memorial character of new, 470.

Terakoya, drama of, 291.

Thieves sentenced to slavery, 234.

Togo, Vice-Admiral, reply of, to Imperial message, 463.

Tokugawa, shōgunate of, Japanese civilization reaches limit of development under, 343. *See* Ieyasu.

Tōkyō, widespread poverty in, resulting from industrial revolution, 446.

Tools, surprising shapes of, 7 ; sacredness of, 153.

Tōshogū, Ieyasu worshipped under name of, 127.

Trade, mean rank of those engaged in, 246. *See* Commerce.

Tragedy, Japanese, founded on fact, 290-291.

Ujigami, original relation of community to, 81-82 ; as clan-deities, 82-84 ; offences against, 88 ; relation of the individual to, 120-121 ; cults of, maintained, and not supplanted, by Buddhism, 379.

Uneme-no-kami, Takenaka, 324.

University, students at the, 425-426.

Utensils, domestic, sacredness of, 153 ; art displayed in, 357.

Uyemon no Hyoge, decree concerning *junshi* disobeyed by, 285.

Variety to be found in Japanese form of civilization, 256-257.

Vendetta, religious origin for customs of, 295.

Vengeance, the duty of, 292-293; Ieyasu's decree concerning code of, 293.

Verb, etiquette governing uses of the, 171-172.

Vice, Ieyasu on suppression of, 346-347.

Village-laws, peasants' 395-396.

Wages of maid-servants, 408.

"Wanderings of Cain," Coleridge's, 122.

War, ten centuries of, following rise of military power, 259-267; against Korea, 277; with peasantry, 324-325; with Russia, 462-463.

Warfare, divination in, 152.

Way of the Buddha, the (Butsudō), 21.

Way of the Gods, the (Shintō), 21, 41.

Weddings, customs as to, 65-67; laws as to food at, 73; presents at, 165-166.

Whipping, infrequency of now, as punishment, 421. See Punishments.

Wife, gradation of terms signifying, 171.

Wine, Buddhist forbids offerings of, 201.

Woman, tribute paid to the Japanese, 361-362.

Women, mourning rites intrusted to, 43; position of, in old Japanese family, 73-74; as priestesses, 143; forms of speech for use of, 172; methods of suicide for, 287; modern instances of suicide by, 289, 290; duty of vengeance performed by, 293.

Worship, three forms of Shintō, 21-22 (See Ancestor-worship); of Imperial ancestors, 108-109; of Sun-goddess, 109-110; at shrines, 119; phallic, 132.

Yama, judge of the dead, 198-199.

Yamaguchi, land granted to Jesuits at, 332-333.

Yamato-damashi, "The Soul of Yamato," 159.

Yedo, obligatory residence of daimyō in, 278; Ieyasu, the founder of, 279.

Yeizan, Buddhist high priest, 351.

Yūriaku, Emperor, deaths inflicted by, for rudeness, 176.